JOURNAL FOR THE STUDY OF THE PSEUDEPIGRAPHA
SUPPLEMENT SERIES
28

Editors
Lester L. Grabbe
James H. Charlesworth

Sheffield Academic Press

Four Powers in Heaven

The Interpretation of Daniel 7
in the Testament of Abraham

Phillip B. Munoa, III

Journal for the Study of the Pseudepigrapha
Supplement Series 28

To Kathy,
Phillip, Anna and Elle

You fill my life with love

Published by
Sheffield Academic Press Ltd
Mansion House
19 Kingfield Road
Sheffield S11 9AS
England

Typeset by Sheffield Academic Press
and
Printed on acid-free paper in Great Britain
by Bookcraft Ltd
Midsomer Norton, Bath

British Library Cataloguing in Publication Data

A catalogue record for this book is available
from the British Library

ISBN 1-85075-885-9

CONTENTS

PREFACE

Dan. 7.9-27 has exercised considerable influence on apocalyptic texts. Its descriptions of the 'Ancient of Days', 'one like a son of man', and the 'holy ones of the Most High' influenced many Middle Jewish documents[1] and resurface in later rabbinic and Christian literature. The *Testament of Abraham* should be counted among such writings. There is a strong probability that Dan. 7.9-27, with its portrayal of exalted figures, influenced the depiction of Adam, Abel and the tribes of Israel in the judgment scene of the *Testament of Abraham*.

A close examination of the context of the *T. Abr.* 11.1–13.7 reveals something more than an allusion to Dan. 7.13-27. From 11.1 to 13.7 there is a lengthy description of Abraham's visit to heaven during which he gains insight about the judgment of all mankind. He learns that several figures are part of the process of judgment: Adam, before whom all souls must pass; Abel, the son of Adam, who judges the entire creation; the 12 tribes of Israel, who are granted a part in the judgment of mankind at the parousia; and lastly, the 'Master God of all', who will render the final judgment. The way these characters parallel those described in Dan. 7.9-27 is striking. There is a strong probability that the entire pericope of Dan. 7.9-27 influenced the depiction of the judgment scene in the *Testament of Abraham*.

The *Testament of Abraham* bears witness to an ongoing exegetical interest in apocalyptic materials. Just as first-century Jesus communities studied apocalyptic passages, so too other Jewish communities worked to interpret the same enigmatic passages, like Dan. 7.9-27. This was an intra-Jewish development, rooted in pre-Christian speculations about exalted biblical figures, and fueled by dependence on the same scriptures. The diverse interpretations reflect the traditions held dear by each community and illustrate how they associated their revered

---

1. G. Boccaccini has proposed that Judaism between the third century BCE and the second century CE be known by the term 'Middle Judaism' (*Middle Judaism: Jewish Thought 300 BCE to 200 CE* [Minneapolis: Fortress Press, 1991], pp. 21-25).

figures—whether they be Jesus, Adam, Abel, or some other exalted person—with ambiguous biblical texts.

ACKNOWLEDGMENTS

Space does not permit me to thank all those who have helped me write this book. Family and friends have been a constant source of support and encouragement. My wife Kathy, and my children, Phillip, Anna and Elle, were fully supportive of me, even when it infringed upon the time we would spend together. They kept me grounded. The University of Michigan, with its generous fellowship support, made it possible for me to return to school and devote five years to the study of biblical literature. Fellow students have given of their time, insights and careful thinking. I have learned from all my teachers and deeply appreciate their scholarship.

I want to thank personally the members of my dissertation committee: Dr Gabriele Boccaccini, Dr Brian Schmidt and Dr Ralph Williams. Your willingness to read and critique my research will make my work better.

Lastly, I want to thank Dr Jarl Fossum. We met during your first year at Michigan. When you accepted me as your student you made my doctoral studies possible. What merit there is in my work is only because you guided and directed me. You are a model scholar and teacher.

Phillip B. Munoa, III
June, 1997

ABBREVIATIONS

ABD	David Noel Freedman (ed.), *The Anchor Bible Dictionary* (New York: Doubleday, 1992)
AGJU	Arbeiten zur Geschichte des antiken Judentums und des Urchristentums
ANRW	Hildegard Temporini and Wolfgang Haase (eds.), *Aufstieg und Niedergang der römischen Welt: Geschichte und Kultur Roms im Spiegel der neueren Forschung* (Berlin: W. de Gruyter, 1972–)
ATS	Armenian Texts and Studies
BASOR	*Bulletin of the American Schools of Oriental Research*
BEATAJ	Beiträge zur Erforschung des Alten Testaments und des Antiken Judentums
BHS	*Biblia hebraica stuttgartensia*
Bib	*Biblica*
BNTC	Black's New Testament Commentaries
BZAW	Beihefte zur *ZAW*
CahArch	*Cahiers Archéologiques*
CBQ	*Catholic Biblical Quarterly*
CBQMS	*Catholic Biblical Quarterly*, Monograph Series
ConBNT	Coniectanea biblica, New Testament
ConBOT	Coniectanea biblica, Old Testament
CRINT	Compendia rerum iudaicarum ad Novum Testamentum
CTA	A. Herdner (ed.), *Corpus des tablettes en cunéiformes alphabétiques découvertes à Ras Shamra–Ugarit de 1929 à 1939* (Paris: Imprimerie nationale Geuthner, 1963)
EncJud	*Encyclopedia Judaica*
EPRO	Etudes préliminaires aux Religions Orientales dans l'Empire Romain
ErJb	*Eranos-Jahrbuch*
ETL	*Ephemerides theologicae lovanienses*
FRLANT	Forschungen zur Religion und Literatur des Alten und Neuen Testaments
HAT	Handbuch zum Alten Testament
Hen	*Henoch*
HNTC	Harper's NT Commentaries
HSM	Harvard Semitic Monographs

HTR	*Harvard Theological Review*
IDBSup	*IDB*, Supplementary Volume
JA	*Journal asiatique*
JBL	*Journal of Biblical Literature*
JewEnc	*The Jewish Encyclopedia*
JETS	*Journal of the Evangelical Theological Society*
JJS	*Journal of Jewish Studies*
JQR	*Jewish Quarterly Review*
JSHRZ	*Jüdische Schriften aus hellenistisch-römischer Zeit*
JSJ	*Journal for the Study of Judaism in the Persian, Hellenistic and Roman Period*
JSNT	*Journal for the Study of the New Testament*
JSNTSup	*Journal for the Study of the New Testament*, Supplement Series
JSPSup	*Journal for the Study of the Pseudepigrapha*, Supplement Series
JTSA	Jewish Theological Seminary of America
JU	Judentum und Umwelt
Jud	*Judaism*
NHS	Nag Hammadi Studies
NICNT	New International Commentary on the New Testament
NovTSup	*Novum Testamentum*, Supplements
NTL	New Testament Library
NTOA	Novum Testamentum et orbis antiquus
OTP	James Charlesworth (ed.), *Old Testament Pseudepigrapha*
OTS	*Oudtestamentische Studiën*
PTS	Patristische Texte und Studien
RB	*Revue biblique*
RSPT	*Revue des sciences philosophiques et théologiques*
SBLDS	SBL Dissertation Series
SBLEJ	SBL Early Judaism and its Literature
SBLSCS	SBL Septuagint and Cognate Studies
SBLSP	SBL Seminar Papers
SCS	Septuagint and Cognate Studies
SecCent	*Second Century*
SHR	Studies in the History of Religion
SJLA	Studies in Judaism in Late Antiquity
ST	*Studia theologica*
STDJ	Studies on the Texts of the Desert of Judah
StudPhilo	*Studia Philonica*
SUNT	Studien zur Umwelt des Neuen Testaments
SVTP	Studia in Veteris Testamenti pseudepigrapha
TDNT	Gerhard Kittel and Gerhard Friedrich (eds.), *Theological Dictionary of the New Testament* (trans. Geoffrey W. Bromiley; 10 vols.; Grand Rapids: Eerdmans, 1964–)

Theo	*Theologica*
TOTL	The Old Testament Library
T & S	Text and Studies
T & T	Texts and Translations
UUÅ	Uppsala universitetsårsskrift
VC	*Vigiliae christianae*
VTSup	*Vetus Testamentum*, Supplements
WBC	Word Biblical Commentary
WUNT	Wissenschaftliche Untersuchungen zum Neuen Testament

Chapter 1

THE *TESTAMENT OF ABRAHAM*: INTRODUCTORY ISSUES

The modern study of the *Testament of Abraham* was inaugurated by M. James's publication of the Greek text in 1892.[1] This was soon followed by the first English translation by W. Craigie,[2] and since then a number of studies have appeared in different languages.

---

1. M. James (ed.), *The Testament of Abraham: The Greek Text Now First Edited with an Introduction and Notes* (T & S, 2.2; Cambridge: Cambridge University Press, 1892). The latest examination of introductory issues for the *Testament of Abraham* is by G. Vermes, M. Goodman and F. Millar in their revision of Emil Schürer's *The History of the Jewish People in the Age of Jesus Christ* (3 vols.; eds. G. Vermes, F. Millar and M. Goodman; Edinburgh: T. & T. Clark, 1987), III, pp. 761-67. See also G.W.E. Nickelsburg's treatments in '*Testament of Abraham*', in M. Stone (ed.), *Jewish Writings of the Second Temple Period* (CRINT, 2; Philadelphia: Fortress Press, 1984), pp. 60-64, and in *Jewish Literature between the Bible and the Mishnah* (Philadelphia: Fortress Press, 1981), pp. 248-53; and his edited work, *Studies in the Testament of Abraham* (SBLSCS, 6; Missoula, MT: Scholars Press, 1976); E. Sanders's excellent summary in *OTP*, I, pp. 871-91; M. Delcor, *Le Testament d'Abraham* (SVTP, 2; Leiden: E.J. Brill, 1973), pp. 1-77; N. Turner, 'The Testament of Abraham: A Study of the Original Language, Place of Origin, Authorship, and Relevance' (PhD Dissertation, University of London, 1953), pp. 13-143, and his updated summary and English translation in *The Apocryphal Old Testament* (ed. H. Sparks; Oxford: Clarendon Press, 1984), pp. 393-421; A.-M. Denis, *Introduction aux pseudépigraphes grecs d'Ancien Testament* (SVTP, 1; Leiden: E.J. Brill, 1970), pp. 31-39; and G.H. Box (ed. and trans.), *The Testament of Abraham: Translated from the Greek Text with Introduction and Notes* (London: SPCK, 1927), pp. vii-xxix. For a bibliography on the *Testament of Abraham* see J. Charlesworth, *The Pseudepigrapha and Modern Research* (SCS, 7; Missoula, MT: Scholars Press, 1976), pp. 70-72.

2. A. Roberts and J. Donaldson (eds.), *The Ante-Nicene Fathers* (repr.; 12 vols.; Grand Rapids: Eerdmans, 1989), IX, pp. 182-201.

Contents

The book tells the story of Abraham's death and the events immediately preceding it. Abraham, who is depicted as a righteous man, is visited by God's representative, the angel Michael, and told that he must soon die. Abraham, however, resists and argues that he will accept death only if allowed to see all the inhabited world. God agrees and Michael takes Abraham on a tour during which Abraham condemns the evildoers he sees. Immediately he is taken to see the judgment of souls lest he should call down condemnation on the whole world. At this point Abraham sees an enthroned Adam, before whom souls are being driven to a judgment that will be carried out first by an enthroned Abel, then by the 12 tribes of Israel, and lastly by the Master God of all. After learning about the process of judgment Abraham realizes how harsh he has been on human beings and asks God to show mercy to a person about to face judgment. God responds to Abraham's request and Abraham is taken home. After all this Abraham still will not accept death. Ultimately, God sends the angel named Death who tricks Abraham into dying and the patriarch is taken to Paradise by angels.

Text and Recensions

The text of the *Testament of Abraham* survives in two forms: a long form known as recension A and a short form known as recension B.[3] Both forms are attested by several Greek manuscripts which are considered the best witnesses and they are thought to have a common textual ancestor. E. Sanders notes how the relationship between the two forms has often been debated and opts for an 'indirect and complicated relationship between the two recs. and for a common ancestor at some remove from the extant witnesses'.[4] There are also a greater number of

3. F. Schmidt has given the most complete discussion of the text in his unpublished doctoral dissertation, 'Le Testament d'Abraham: Introduction, edition de la recension courte, traduction et notes' (2 vols.; PhD Dissertation, University of Strasbourg, 1971), I, pp. 1-20, and in his updated work *Le Testament grec d'Abraham* (TSAJ, 11; Tübingen: J.C.B. Mohr, 1986), pp. 1-32. Two other helpful studies of the text are Delcor, *Le Testament*, pp. 5-24, and Denis, *Introduction aux pseudépigraphes*, pp. 32-34.

4. *OTP*, I, p. 872 n. 4. For a discussion of this issue see R. Kraft, 'Reassessing the "Recessional Problem" in the *Testament of Abraham*', in Nickelsburg (ed.),

versions of varying importance in other languages.[5] James produced the first critical text of the two recensions, but it has since been superseded by the careful study of F. Schmidt, and his edition will be used in this study.[6]

The differences between recensions A and B are twofold. First, in comparison to recension B, the style of recension A is more complex, its vocabulary is later and more verbose, and it shows more evidence of Christian influence.[7] Secondly, besides a number of small additions to the story, recension A also has two significant changes in its narrative: Abraham's tour of the judgment is *after* his tour of the world, not before as in recension B; and the judgment scene is more fully described and involves what has come to be known as a 'triple judgment' scene.[8] The triple judgment scene deals specifically with Adam, Abel, Israel and God. This episode will be the focus of the present study.

Scholarly opinion favors the position that recension A most accurately preserves the contents and order of the original work, while recension B preserves more original wording. James was the first to argue for this position and he has been followed by G. Box, M. Delcor, G. Nickelsburg and Sanders.[9] E. Turdeanu and Schmidt have taken the

Studies in the Testament of Abraham, pp. 121-37. For a list of the extant Greek manuscripts and further discussion about their importance, see Schmidt (ed.), *Le Testament grec d'Abraham*, pp. 6-29.

5. *T. Abr.* A is supported by a Rumanian version, and *T. Abr.* B is supported by Slavonic, Rumanian, Coptic, Bohairic, Arabic and Ethiopic versions. For their value see Schmidt (ed.), *Le Testament grec d'Abraham*, pp. 33-44, and Delcor, *Le Testament*, pp. 15-22. The Rumanian version was translated by M. Gaster under the title, 'The Apocalypse of Abraham', in *Transactions of the Society of Biblical Archaeology* 9 (1887), pp. 1-32.

6. Schmidt (ed.), *Le Testament grec d'Abraham*, pp. 46-173. For James's text see *The Testament of Abraham*, pp. 77-130. Translations of the *Testament of Abraham* are mine unless indicated otherwise.

7. The most complete study of the styles and vocabularies of *T. Abr.* A and *T. Abr.* B is that of Turner ('The Testament of Abraham: A Study', pp. 13-143, 194-256).

8. As identified by Delcor (*Le Testament*, pp. 59-61). In *T. Abr.* B there is a description of Adam and Abel but there is no reference to the 12 tribes or God when the judgment is described (8.1–11.10).

9. James (ed.), *The Testament of Abraham*, p. 49; Box (ed. and trans.), *The Testament of Abraham*, p. xiii; Delcor, *Le Testament*, p. 33; Nickelsburg (ed.), *Studies in the Testament of Abraham*, pp. 47-64, 85-93; Sanders, *OTP*, I, pp. 872-73.

opposite view and argue for the priority of recension B with regard to
contents and order.[10] Ultimately, the two recensions suggest that an
original book about Abraham, containing approximately the contents of
recension A, was rewritten into the two forms from which recension A
and recension B, and their various versions, were produced.[11] As N.
Turner observes,

> these recensions are distinct in the sense that they represent different
> arrangements of what is frequently different material, and there is no
> reason for thinking either that B is an abridgement of A or that A is an
> expansion of B.[12]

Language

The original language of the *Testament of Abraham* appears to have
been Greek. Turner, in his unpublished dissertation, at first championed
the earlier view of K. Kohler and L. Ginzberg that there was a Hebrew
original.[13] Since then he has modified his view and now believes that
the Semitic Greek style, which suggested that the *Testament of Abraham* was originally composed in Hebrew, was current at the time of
composition.[14] Interestingly, Box, who held to the probability of there

10. E. Turdeanu, 'Notes sur la tradition littéraire du Testament d'Abraham', in
Silloge bizantina in onore di Silvio Giuseppe Mercati (Studi bizantini e neo
ellenici, IX; Rome: Pontifical Institute, 1957), pp. 405-10; F. Schmidt, 'The Two
Recensions of the *Testament of Abraham*: In Which Way did the Transformation
Take Place?', in Nickelsburg (ed.), *Studies in the Testament of Abraham*, pp. 65-83.

11. Sanders succinctly summarizes this position (*OTP*, I, pp. 872-73). Kraft
describes the variety of possible relations in his study 'Reassessing the
"Recensional Problem" ', pp. 121-31.

12. Turner points out how the Coptic version does not follow either recension
exactly (*The Apocryphal Old Testament*, p. 393).

13. Turner, 'The Testament of Abraham: A Study', pp. 13-143. See K. Kohler,
'The Pre-Talmudic Haggada II: The Apocalypse of Abraham and its Kindred', *JQR*
7 (1895), pp. 581-606; L. Ginzberg, 'Abraham, (Testament of)', *JewEnc*, I, pp. 93-
96; Kohler may have indicated a change in his view when he wrote that the book
was an Alexandrian product of the first century CE (*Heaven and Hell in Comparative Religion* [New York: Scribners, 1923], p. 77). Box argued for a Palestinian
identity and a possible Semitic original (*The Testament of Abraham*, pp. xxvii-
xxix).

14. See Turner's article, 'The *Testament of Abraham*: Problems in Biblical
Greek', *NTS* 1 (1954–55), pp. 219-23, where he softened his insistence on the *Testament of Abraham*'s Hebrew original, and Sanders's comments about Turner's

being a Semitic original, confessed that the Greek does not read like a translation.[15] Schmidt continues to argue, though tentatively, for a Semitic original, as does R. Martin on the basis of syntax criticism.[16]

While recensions A and B of the *Testament of Abraham* present differ-ent styles of Greek, they are now seen to be variations of the Semitic style of its period. Delcor first argued for a Greek original on the basis of the view that the Greek of the *Testament of Abraham* is similar to the Greek of the Septuagint, but his primary reference was to recension A.[17] Turner's later research, which focused on recension B because he believed it was more representative of the original text, has led him to disavow his earlier view that it was written in 'translation' Greek.[18] Sanders has clearly identified how the 'Semitizing' style of Greek was common when the *Testament of Abraham* and its recensions were written.[19]

Date

Dates for the *Testament of Abraham* in its original form[20] vary from the third century BCE to the third century CE. James dated it to the second or early third century CE on the basis of its supposed dependence on the *Apocalypse of Peter*, which is at the earliest a late second-century

present position (*OTP*, I, pp. 873-74). Both Sanders and Vermes and Goodman (*The History of the Jewish People*, III, p. 763) agree with Turner.

15. Box (ed. and trans.), *The Testament of Abraham*, p. xxviii.

16. See Schmidt, 'The Two Recensions', pp. 65-83, and R.A. Martin, 'Syntax Criticism of the *Testament of Abraham*', in Nickelsburg (ed.) *Studies in the Testa-ment of Abraham*, pp. 95-102. Attention should also be paid to Kraft's criticism of Martin's syntactical analysis in his article, 'Reassessing the "Recensional Prob-lem"', pp. 134-35.

17. Delcor, *Le Testament*, pp. 32-33. See also E. Janssen, 'Testament Abra-hams', *JSHRZ* 3 (1975), pp. 193-256.

18. Turner's comments are contained in a letter written to Sanders (*OTP*, I, p. 873, esp. n. 14).

19. Sanders has summarized the issues involved. For the subject of 'Jewish Greek' see N. Turner, *A Grammar of New Testament Greek*. IV. *Style* (Edinburgh: T. & T. Clark, 1976), pp. 7-8, and especially E. Sanders, *The Tendencies of the Synoptic Tradition* (Cambridge: Cambridge University Press, 1969), pp. 200-202, 226, 228.

20. The date for the final form of the long recension may be as late as the fifth or sixth century CE according to Schmidt ('Le Testament d'Abraham', I, pp. 115-17) and Delcor (*Le Testament*, pp. 73-77).

text.[21] Turner, when working with the assumption of a Hebrew original, argued for an early third-century BCE date.[22] Schmidt supports an early first-century CE date because of the document's supposed Essene-like interests.[23] Sanders works with the theory of the *Testament of Abraham*'s Egyptian background and the text's combination of genres and motifs to suggest a date no later than 125 CE and no earlier than 75 CE.[24] G. Vermes and M. Goodman think the *Testament of Abraham*'s adoption by Christians, as evidenced by several later interpolations from documents in the New Testament in recension A, signals a date no later than 150 CE, but perhaps as early as the late second century BCE.[25] Given the *Testament of Abraham*'s non-Hebrew composition, distinctly Jewish interests,[26] combination of genres, and its Egyptian provenance[27] (both its combination of genres and its Egyptian provenance will be illustrated later in this chapter), it seems most reasonable to place it no later than the early second century CE.

21. James (ed.), *The Testament of Abraham*, pp. 23-29.

22. Turner, 'The Testament of Abraham: A Study', pp. 242-48. Box also assumes a Hebrew original but supports a date in the first half of the first century CE by paralleling the text's devotion to Abraham with an early first-century interest in the patriarch (*The Testament of Abraham*, p. xxviii).

23. Schmidt, 'Le Testament d'Abraham', I, p. 120.

24. Sanders, *OTP*, I, pp. 874-75.

25. Vermes and Goodman, *The History of the Jewish People*, III, pp. 763-64. The interpolations will be discussed later in this chapter. C.C. Caragounis believes a second-century CE dating of the *Testament of Abraham* is decisive due to its use of New Testament terminology (both by the author and by later copyists), but he admits that it is not a Christian composition (*The Son of Man: Vision and Interpretation* [WUNT, 38; Tübingen: J.C.B. Mohr, 1986], pp. 91-92).

26. Sanders points out the judgment scene is strictly Jewish and warrants an early first-century CE date (*OTP*, I, p. 875 n. 27). The motif of an enthroned judge can be traced to the Parables of *Enoch* (*1 En.* 37–71) and Matthew, both first-century CE works. Kohler, when discussing the *Testament of Abraham*, says that 'the Jewish view of later times placed Abraham, the progenitor of Israel, in Adam's place' (Lk. 16.19-31) and thus implies a date no later than the first century CE for the *Testament of Abraham* ('Abraham, [Apocalypse of]', *JewEnc*, I, pp. 91-93).

27. V. Tcherikover is convinced that after 117 CE Alexandrian Judaism was not sufficiently intact to allow the production of a document like the *Testament of Abraham* (*Hellenistic Civilization and the Jews* [Philadelphia: Fortress Press, 1959], p. 356).

Origin

An Egyptian provenance appears to be the most likely origin of the text. This view is supported by the assumption of a Greek original, and by the belief that recension A is nearer to the original form. As Sanders writes, the vocabulary of both recensions shows a similarity to the late books of the Septuagint (which are traditionally understood as Alexandrian) and other Jewish books written during that period in Egypt.[28] And in contrast to recension B,[29] recension A's additional material regarding the triple judgment scene is taken to be quite similar to Egyptian court practices and is used by Delcor, along with its Septuagint-like Greek, to support an Egyptian origin.[30] James listed eight reasons in support of an Egyptian provenance.[31] Vermes and Goodman also recognize how the language and motifs may indicate an Egyptian provenance, but do not think a non-Egyptian origin is impossible.[32] An Egyptian provenance naturally suggests Alexandria, a home to many Jews in Egypt. This study will raise the issue of Daniel 7's influence on the judgment scene. Egyptian judicial procedures, as identified by Delcor, may not be the chief influence on this episode.

There has been a persistent effort to trace certain attributes of the *Testament of Abraham* to the Essenes. Kohler, Ginzberg, Schmidt and,

---

28. Sanders also notes how Turner, who rejected a Greek original, identified Egypt as the origin of the *Testament of Abraham* on the basis of the Greek recensions, and how Schmidt, who supported a Palestinian origin, believed *T. Abr.* A was an Egyptian redaction (*OTP*, I, p. 875 esp. n. 28). Janssen, who supports a Greek original, wrongly places the *Testament of Abraham* in Palestine when he attributes an interest in Mamre to Palestine instead of to Septuagint influence ('Testament Abrahams', pp. 198-99). Box, who holds to a Semitic original and Palestinian provenance (on the basis of Palestinian as opposed to Alexandrian eschatology), accepts the probability of a Greek version redone with Alexandrian features (*The Testament of Abraham*, pp. xxviii-xxix).

29. Sanders describes *T. Abr.* B as 'lacking in definite signs of its place of origin' (*OTP*, I, p. 875).

30. Delcor, *Le Testament*, pp. 34, 59-62. See also Nickelsburg's article, 'Eschatology in the *Testament of Abraham*: A Study of the Judgment Scene in the Two Recensions', in his *Studies in the Testament of Abraham*, pp. 23-64.

31. The majority of James's reasons touched upon motifs current in Egypt (*The Testament of Abraham*, p. 76).

32. Vermes and Goodman argue that such characteristics were not limited to Egypt (*The History of the Jewish People*, III, p. 763).

most recently, Delcor are representatives of this view and have linked
elements like exorcisms, celestial references, evening prayers, the
magical use of the divine name, an interest in the divine chariot and
angelology to Essenism.[33] Sanders has dismissed this effort on the
ground that the *Testament of Abraham* does not present any of the particular doctrines of the Essenes, but rather represents a 'characterless
Judaism', lacking 'peculiar traits'.[34]

While identifying the *Testament of Abraham* ideologically as an
Essene writing may be perceived as forced due to the widespread
Jewish interest in these subjects, and would require a comprehensive
assessment of its thought, this study will illustrate the author's
indebtedness to Israelite traditions about exalted mediators and throne
scenes, both of which were prominent in the Essene-Qumran community. The depiction of Melchizedek, for instance, in the Qumran
literature, will be shown to be quite similar in comparison to Abel in
the judgment scene of recension A.[35]

Theological Interests

The *Testament of Abraham*'s presentation of a soteriological universalism has been identified as its major theological doctrine. Kohler first
made mention of the *Testament of Abraham*'s 'cosmopolitan humanity'.[36] Sanders, with his interest in the Judaism of the early Roman era,
has followed up on Kohler's work and presented a fourfold case for this
theme: the lack of a distinction between Jew and Gentile; no
specifically Jewish sins; a common standard of judgment for all people;
and repentance as the sole means of atonement for all people.[37]

33. Kohler, 'The Apocalypse of Abraham', pp. 581-606; Ginzberg, 'Abraham',
JewEnc, I, pp. 93-96; Schmidt (ed.), 'Le Testament d'Abraham', I, pp. 54-55;
Delcor, *Le Testament*, pp. 69-72.

34. Sanders, *OTP*, I, p. 876.

35. This similarity will be presented in Chapter 4.

36. Kohler, 'The Apocalypse of Abraham', pp. 581-606. Box admits that the
book is pervaded by a broad humanitarian spirit and uses this quality to defend an
Alexandrian origin (*The Testament of Abraham*, p. xx). Turner agreed with Kohler
but did not give this interest in universalism as much importance with regard to
theological significance. Instead he used it to argue for an early date ('The Testament of Abraham: A Study', pp. 149-50).

37. *OTP*, I, pp. 877-78. Sanders prefers identifying what is traditionally known
as first-century CE Judaism as the 'early Roman era' (*Judaism: Practice and Belief*

Vermes and Goodman take issue with Sanders by suggesting that the author's interest in universalistic moral qualities is not an espousal of Jewish universalism but simply part of his theme of the inevitability of death and divine judgment.[38] G. Boccaccini, in his recent survey of the Judaisms of 300 BCE to 200 CE, presents a strong case for the *Testament of Abraham* being representative of a type of Judaism committed to universalism and 'boundless salvation'.[39] In this regard Boccaccini sets the *Testament of Abraham* alongside the second-century BCE Hellenistic Jewish work, the *Letter of Aristeas*, and illustrates how both documents put forth the same universalistic ideal.[40]

The topic of judgment is a theological interest pertinent to this study of the *Testament of Abraham*. Sanders has observed how one of the main purposes of the author was to depict the judgment scene of recension A 11.1–14.15.[41] He adds that the author's particular theological interest, beyond presenting a judgment free of Jewish advantages over gentiles, is to describe the judgment by bringing together and harmonizing three traditional images: the judgment of individual souls; the nationalistic scheme of Israel's role as a judge; and God's role as a judge.[42] Box was the first to argue for a combination of these different schemes of judgment and referred to *4 Ezra* as an example of a text combining diverse eschatological ideas.[43]

Rather than understanding the author's work as one of reconciling three separate motifs, this study will show how the *Testament of Abraham*'s judgment scene was based upon an earlier Jewish judgment text: Daniel 7. The judgment scene of Daniel 7 already had a unified conception of the judgment and was a major influence on later Jewish expositions of the final judgment.

---

63 BCE–66 CE [Philadelphia: Trinity Press International, 1992], p. ix).

38. Vermes and Goodman, *The History of the Jewish People*, III, p. 762.

39. Boccacini, *Middle Judaism*, pp. 251-65.

40. Boccacini, *Middle Judaism*, pp. 257-59.

41. Sanders, *OTP*, I, p. 878. Vermes and Goodman see the aim of the text as being the apocalyptic vision of judgment (*The History of the Jewish People*, III, p. 761). C. Fishburne argues (in Sanders's understanding, erroneously) that Paul depended upon the *Testament of Abraham* when describing the judgment scene in 1 Cor. 3.10-15 ('I Cor. III 10-15 and the *Testament of Abraham*', *NTS* 17 [1970], pp. 109-15).

42. Sanders, *OTP*, I, p. 878.

43. Box refers to *4 Ezra* 7.78-100 and its interest in a national and individual eschatology (*The Testament of Abraham*, pp. xxiv-xxv).

Relation to Other Literatures

The relation of the *Testament of Abraham*, specifically recension A,[44] to the books in the Christian and rabbinic canons has usually been understood as scant. For Sanders, 'almost nothing of the Old Testament appears except the obvious references to Abraham in Genesis'.[45] Both Kohler and Ginzberg emphasized the text's purely Jewish character, apart from some late Christian interpolations.[46] James opted for the view that the author, a 'Jewish-Christian', actually quotes some New Testament documents, especially in the apocalyptic section.[47] Turner extends James's position and argues for the influence of New Testament documents in three specific instances in the apocalyptic section of recension A of the *Testament of Abraham*.[48]

> *T. Abr.* 11.2: And Abraham saw two ways. The first way was strait and narrow and the other broad and spacious.

> Mt. 7.13: Enter through the narrow gate; for the gate is wide and the road is easy that leads to destruction, and there are many who take it.[49]

> *T. Abr.* 11.11: And when he [Adam] sees many souls entering through the broad gate, then he pulls the hair of his head and hurls himself on the ground crying and wailing bitterly; for the broad gate is [the gate] of the sinners, which leads to destruction and to everlasting punishment.

---

44. Attention here is devoted to *T. Abr.* A because it serves as the focal point of this study.

45. See *T. Abr.* A 1.5; 3.6; 4.11; 6.4; 8.5-7; 11.12; 13.8; *T. Abr.* B 2.8-10; 5.1; 6.10-13 (Sanders, *OTP*, I, p. 879).

46. Kohler was the first to present a systematic portrayal of the *Testament of Abraham*'s Jewish character ('The Apocalypse of Abraham', pp. 581-606); see also Ginzberg ('Abraham', *JewEnc*, I, pp. 93-94). Box (*The Testament of Abraham*, p. xv) is in basic agreement with Kohler. It should be noted that Sanders sees Kohler as exaggerating the text's parallels with rabbinic literature (*OTP*, I, p. 875 n. 30).

47. James says that the apocalyptic section is the kernel of the original book and the chief object of the author (*The Testament of Abraham*, pp. 50-55, esp. pp. 50 and 52.

48. Turner, 'The Testament of Abraham: A Study', pp. 13-143. The passages are *T. Abr.* A 11.2, 10-11, and 13.13 (cf. *T. Abr.* B 8.16). Caragounis believes the *Testament of Abraham* has borrowed New Testament terms and concepts (both by the author and by later copyists), but he admits that it is a Jewish composition (*The Son of Man*, pp. 91-92).

49. Quotations from the Bible are taken from B. Metzger and R. Murphy (eds.), *The New Oxford Annotated Bible: New Revised Version* (New York: Oxford University Press, 1991).

Mt. 7.13: Enter through the narrow gate; for the gate is wide and the road is easy that leads to destruction, and there are many who take it.

Mt. 25.46: And these will go away into eternal punishment, but the righteous into eternal life.

T. Abr. 13.13: But if the fire tests the work of anyone and does not touch it, this person is justified and the angel of righteousness takes him and carries him up to be saved in the lot of the just.

1 Cor. 3.13: the work of each builder will become visible, for the Day will disclose it, because it will be revealed with fire, and the fire will test what sort of work each has done.

Sanders better explains these similarities as primarily those of wording and does not believe the text has been Christianized. For proof of the non-Christianization he points out how Christ does not appear in the apocalyptic section and its description of the judgment.[50] Nickelsburg, in line with Box's earlier comments, argues that the only certain Christian element in the text is the closing doxology of recension A, and explains the phrases reminiscent of the documents of the New Testament as simply reflecting a common Jewish milieu. He adds that the peculiar parallels of recension A to some New Testament documents may be the result of Christian scribal activity as recension A was copied and preserved.[51]

C. Fishburne was the first to argue for dependence of some New Testament texts on the *Testament of Abraham* and believes, on the basis of vocabulary and conceptual parallels, that Paul was familiar with the *Testament of Abraham* when he described the judgment of Christian

50. Sanders, *OTP*, I, pp. 872, 879. While Turner sees definite traces of Christian influence in *T. Abr.* A (esp. 11.1–14.15), he dismisses the possibility of this section being taken from a Christian apocalypse since there is no conceivable motive and the section is fundamentally non-Christian ('The Testament of Abraham: A Study', pp. 13-143). Vermes and Goodman also see the *Testament of Abraham* as intended for a non-Christian, Jewish audience (*The History of the Jewish People*, III, p. 762).

51. Nickelsburg, 'Testament of Abraham', p. 64. Box has shown how one of the texts often singled out as a Christian interpolation—the 'two ways' of *T. Abr.* A 11.2—is a stereotyped idea in Jewish literature well before the Christian era. Even the apocalyptic scene (*T. Abr.* A 11–14) can be paralleled by Jewish materials (Box [ed. and trans.], *The Testament of Abraham*, pp. xvii-xviii, 17 n. 2). Kohler has noted how the apocalyptic section, thought by James to be dependent on the *Apocalypse of Peter* and the *Apocalypse of Paul*, is drawn from earlier Jewish material as are the later Christian apocalypses ('The Apocalypse of Abraham', p. vii).

believers in 1 Cor. 3.10-15.[52] C. Mearns agrees with Fishburne and says several terms in Paul's Corinthian letters provide clear allusions to the *Testament of Abraham*.[53] Given this dependence of some New Testament texts on the *Testament of Abraham*, Fishburne and Mearns date the text to the first half of the first century CE.[54] However, dating the *Testament of Abraham* on the basis of several terms shared with Paul, apart from convincing historical references, is difficult. The shared terms may better reflect a common Jewish milieu. It is certainly possible that Paul was familiar with the Jewish traditions behind the *Testament of Abraham* and drew upon them in his writings. This study will argue that a literary dependency on Daniel can be illustrated which shows a conscious and intentional use of that document.

The *Testament of Abraham*'s literary connection to other Jewish documents is complex because of the difficulty in identifying its genre. Nickelsburg notes how the *Testament of Abraham* begins and ends with a typical testamentary situation (God summoning his messenger of death and Abraham on his deathbed), but Abraham's refusal to make a testament brands the text a non-testament.[55] A. Kolenkow categorizes it as a subtler form of the testamentary literature, prevalent in the Jewish Hellenistic world, which used examples of good and evil deeds (such as Abraham's desires to destroy sinners and then help them) as a teaching device.[56] James believed the text consisted of narrative portions drawn from existing Jewish legends, which go unidentified, and an

---

52. Fishburne, 'I Cor. III 10-15', pp. 109-15.

53. C. Mearns, 'Dating the Similitudes of Enoch', *NTS* 25 (1979), pp. 360-69 (363-64).

54. Fishburne, 'I Cor. III 10-15', p. 114; Mearns, 'Dating the Similitudes', p. 364.

55. See Nickelsburg, 'Structure and Message in the Testament of Abraham', in his *Studies in the Testament of Abraham*, pp. 85-88, esp. p. 88. Vermes and Goodman see the testamentary genre as providing a structure for the narrative, but they also believe the *Testament of Abraham* comes close to being a parody of the genre (*The History of the Jewish People*, III, pp. 761-62). Box first noted the unusual absence of a testament and suggested that the original form may have contained one (*The Testament of Abraham*, p. xi).

56. A. Kolenkow, 'The Genre Testament and the Testament of Abraham', in Nickelsburg (ed.), *Studies in the Testament of Abraham*, pp. 139-52, esp. pp. 141, 152. Earlier thoughts are found in A Kolenkow, 'What is the Role of Testament in the Testament of Abraham?', *HTR* 67 (1974), pp. 182-84.

apocalyptic section drawn from the author's imagination.[57] Similar to James, J. Collins rules out the testamentary category because it lacks a farewell discourse by Abraham. He identifies the *Testament of Abraham* as either a narrative, because of its extended narrative framework, or an apocalypse, because it contains all the defining characteristics of an apocalypse.[58]

Sanders argues that the author uses the testamentary motif, along with other motifs taken from apocalyptic and Mosaic literature, in order to deal with his chief interest: the judgment scene. He agrees with Nickelsburg that the *Testament of Abraham* lacks the basic characteristics of testamentary writings: that is, testament, last words of advice, and paraenetic material. Sanders concludes by saying 'the only real connection [of the *Testament of Abraham*] with the testamentary literature is the emphasis on one virtue', Abraham's hospitality.[59] Indeed, Nickelsburg points out how Abraham's great virtue of obedient faith is so lacking that the text becomes a parody of the biblical Abraham.[60]

The testamentary motif of Abraham being summoned to death by the angel Michael introduces the narrative. The ensuing tour of earth and the view of the judgment, all at the request of Abraham, are apocalyptic in nature.[61] The final section, where Abraham's reluctance to die results in his death through deception, is dependent upon midrashim. This literary connection was first examined by Kohler and later developed by S. Loewenstamm. In these traditions Moses resists death and is given visions of the world.[62] Though there are stories where Abraham

57. James ascribes the work to a second-century 'Jewish Christian' and cites the *Martyrdom and Ascension of Isaiah* as an example of the mix of 'Jewish narrative and Christian apocalyptic genres' after which the author has fashioned his work (*The Testament of Abraham*, p. 55).

58. See J. Collins, 'Testaments', in Stone (ed.), *Jewish Writings of the Second Temple Period*, pp. 325-55, esp. p. 326, and 'The Genre Apocalypse in Hellenistic Literature', in D. Hellholm (ed.), *Apocalypticism in the Mediterranean World and the Near East* (Tübingen: J.C.B. Mohr, 1983), p. 541.

59. Sanders, *OTP*, I, p. 879.

60. Nickelsburg, '*Testament of Abraham*', p. 61.

61. The Jewish Hellenistic apocalyptic text, the *Apocalypse of Abraham*, like the *Testament of Abraham*, describes how Abraham was taken on a tour of the earth and given a glimpse of the judgment (*Apoc. Abr.* 9.1–23.14).

62. Kohler believes the midrashim traditions are dependent upon the *Testament of Abraham* when it was possibly in oral form ('The Apocalypse of Abraham', pp. 581-82). Loewenstamm argues for a reverse relationship and sees the

learns of the future, Sanders places the greatest dependence of the *Testament of Abraham* upon the Moses traditions because they involve more of the text's interests, such as the seer's reluctance to die and the motif of a vision.[63] E. Chazon has produced a recent study detailing the relationship of the Moses tradition to the *Testament of Abraham* and illustrates the author's use of the Moses legend.[64]

This study will argue that the literary category of Jewish mysticism, often overlooked by more recent studies but referred to first by Kohler, and later by Box and Turner, is paramount in understanding the judgment scene of recension A. Kohler suggested that Abraham's chariot ride may have mystical significance.[65] Box developed Kohler's observation and demonstrated how the apocalyptic section of recension A begins with a stereotypical scene (a ride through the heavens in a divine chariot) common in mystical literature.[66] Turner also notes how the portrayal of Adam is similar to those found in Kabbalistic literature.[67] M. Dean-Otting, in her recent dissertation, has categorized the *Testament of Abraham* as one of several Hellenistic Jewish texts centered on the motif of a mystical ascent to heaven.[68]

Conclusion

As this introduction illustrates, the *Testament of Abraham* does not offer much by way of firm insights into its history, but some general

midrashim concerning Moses as more ancient; see 'The Testament of Abraham and the Texts Concerning the Death of Moses' and his earlier study 'The Death of Moses', both in Nickelsburg (ed.), *Studies in the Testament of Abraham*, pp. 219-25, 185-217. Sanders ties this interest to Deut. 34.1-4 and identifies early and later midrashim texts (*Sifre Deuteronomy* and *Gedullat Mosheh*) where Moses is given a tour of heaven and hell (*OTP*, I, p. 879).

63. With regard to Abraham, Sanders refers to *Mek. Amalek* 2, *Pseudo-Philo*, the *Apocalypse of Abraham* and *Targum Neofiti I* (*OTP*, I, pp. 879-80). Delcor is of the position that *Targum Neofiti I* is central to the author's story (*Le Testament*, pp. 39-41). Nickelsburg's article, 'Eschatology in the *Testament of Abraham*', pp. 23-64, also explores the extra-canonical background of the text.

64. E. Chazon, 'Moses' Struggle: *Testament of Abraham*, the Greek Apocalypse of Ezra, and the Apocalypse of Sedrach', *SecCent* 5 (1986), pp. 151-64 (153-58).

65. Kohler, 'The Apocalypse of Abraham', p. 592.

66. Box (ed. and trans.), *The Testament of Abraham*, p. 15 n 1.

67. Turner, 'The Testament of Abraham: A Study', pp. 121-22.

68. M. Dean-Otting, *Heavenly Journeys: A Study of the Motif in Hellenistic Jewish Literature* (JU, 8; Frankfurt: Peter Lang, 1984), pp. 175-217.

observations can be made. In summary, the *Testament of Abraham* can be identified as a first-century CE Hellenistic Jewish document originally written in Greek. It presents a mixed genre of testamentary, apocalyptic and narrative literature. Its author, in all likelihood, wrote from an Egyptian setting (most likely Alexandria), and the book's original contents are probably best represented by recension A. Scholarly consensus has downplayed its literary dependence on any document in the Christian and rabbinic canons and more connections have been made between the *Testament of Abraham* and 'non-canonical' literature. However, as shall be demonstrated in this study, the author of the *Testament of Abraham* made use of Dan. 7.9-27 when he recast its judgment scene into a new vision of the judgment.

Chapter 2

THE JUDGMENT SCENE OF THE *TESTAMENT OF ABRAHAM*

Dan. 7.9-27 exercised considerable influence during the period of Middle Judaism (300 BCE–200 CE).[1] Its descriptions of the 'Ancient of Days', 'one like a son of man' and the 'holy ones of the Most High' resurface even in later rabbinic and Christian writings. The best known and repeatedly discussed references are those that appear in the Parables of *Enoch* and the New Testament Gospels. Interestingly, the interpretation of Dan. 7.9-27 has not been uniform, but rather diverse.[2] This study of the peculiar interpretation of Dan. 7.9-27 in the *Testament of Abraham* needs to be placed in the context of the various interpretations prevalent in Middle Judaism, be they Christian or belonging to other forms of Judaism. The roles of Adam, Abel, the 12 tribes of Israel and the 'Master God of all' in the *Testament of Abraham*'s judgment scene can best be understood as an interpretation of Dan. 7.9-27.

Testament of Abraham *11.1–13.8*

T. Abr. 11.1-12: Michael turned the chariot and brought Abraham toward the east, to the first gate of heaven. And Abraham saw two ways. The first way was strait and narrow and the other broad and spacious. And he saw there two gates. One gate was broad, corresponding to the

---

1.   This term was introduced by Boccaccini and is intended to be of chronological value by referring to a definite period and not to an organic or homogenous system of thought. Its value is twofold. First, it can be used to encompass all the contemporary Judaisms—Christianity included—without any ideological implications. Secondly, it can serve as a bridge between the ancient Judaism of the sixth through the third centuries BCE and the distinct and separate existence, from the second century CE, of the two main Judaisms of modern times: Christianity and Rabbinism (Boccacini, *Middle Judaism*, pp. 24-25).

2.   See the history of Daniel's Jewish interpretation in J. Collins, *Daniel: A Commentary on the Book of Daniel* (Minneapolis: Fortress Press, 1993), pp. 72-89.

broad way, and one gate was strait, corresponding to the strait way. And outside the two gates of that place they saw a man seated on a golden throne. And the appearance of that man was terrifying, like the Master's. And they saw many souls being driven by angels and being led through the broad gate, and they saw a few other souls, and they were being brought by angels through the narrow gate. And when the wondrous one who was seated on the throne of gold saw few entering through the strait gate, but many entering through the broad one, immediately that wondrous man tore the hair of his head and the beard of his cheeks, and he threw himself on the ground from his throne, crying and wailing. And when he saw many souls entering through the strait gate, then he arose from the earth and sat on his throne in great joy, very cheerfully rejoicing and exulting. Then Abraham asked the Commander-in-chief-captain, 'My lord Commander chief, who is this most wondrous man, who is adorned in such glory, and sometimes he cries and wails while other times he rejoices and exults?' The incorporeal one said, 'This is the first-formed Adam who is in such glory, and he looks at the world, since everyone has come from him. And when he sees many souls entering through the strait gate, then he arises and sits on his throne rejoicing and exulting cheerfully, because this strait gate is (the gate) of the righteous which leads to life, and those who enter through it go into Paradise. And on account of this then the first-formed Adam rejoices, since he sees the souls being saved. And when he sees many souls entering through the broad gate, then he pulls the hair of his head, and casts himself on the ground crying and wailing bitterly; for the broad gate is (the gate) of the sinners, which leads to destruction and eternal punishment. And on account of this the first-formed Adam falls from his throne, crying and wailing over the destruction of sinners; for many are the ones who are destroyed, while few are the ones who are saved. For among seven thousand there is scarcely to be found one saved soul saved, righteous and undefiled.

T. Abr. 12.1-18: While he was yet saying these things to me, behold (there were) two angels, with fiery aspect and merciless intention and relentless look, and they drove myriads of souls, mercilessly beating them with fiery lashes. And the angel seized one soul. And they drove all the souls into the broad gate toward destruction. Then we too followed the angels and came inside that broad gate. And between the two gates there stood a terrifying throne with the appearance of terrifying crystal, flashing like fire. And upon it sat a wondrous man, bright as the sun, like unto a son of God. Before him stood a table like crystal, all of gold and byssus. On the table lay a book, whose thickness was six cubits, while its breadth was ten cubits. On its right side and on its left stood two angels holding papyrus and ink and pen. In front of the table sat a light-bearing angel, holding a balance in his hand. [On] (his) left there sat a fiery angel, altogether merciless and relentless, holding a trumpet in his hand, which contained within it an all-consuming fire (for) testing the sinners. And the wondrous man who sat on the throne was the one who judged and sentenced the souls. The two angels on the right and on the left recorded. The one on the right recorded righteous deeds, while the one on the left (recorded) sins And the one who was in front of the table, who was holding the balance, weighed the souls. And the fiery angel, who held the fire, tested the souls. And Abraham asked the Commander-in-chief Michael, 'What are these things that we see?' And the Commander-in-chief said, 'These things which you see, pious Abraham, are judgment and recompense. And behold the angel who held the soul in his hand and brought it before the judge. And the judge told one of the one of the angels who served him, "Open for me this book and find for me the sins of this soul." And when he opened the book he found its sins and its righteous deeds to be equally balanced, and he neither turned it over to the tormentors nor (placed it among) those who are being saved, but set it in the middle.'

T. Abr. 13.1-8: And Abraham said, 'My lord Commander-chief, who is this all-wondrous judge? And who are the angels who are recording? And who is the sunlike angel who holds the balance? And who is the fiery angel who holds the fire?' The Commander-chief said, 'Do you see, all-pious Abraham, the frightful man who is seated on the throne? This is the son of Adam, the first-formed, who is called Abel, whom Cain the wicked killed. And he sits here to judge the entire creation, examining both righteous and sinners. For God said, "I do not judge you, but every man is judged by man". On account of this he gave him judgment, to judge the world until his great and glorious Parousia. And then, righteous Abraham, there will be perfect judgment and recompense, eternal and unalterable, which no one can question. For every person has sprung from the first-formed, and on account of this they are first judged here by his son. And at the second Parousia they shall be judged by the twelve tribes of Israel, both every breath and every creature. And, thirdly, they shall be judged by the Master God of all; and then thereafter the fulfillment of that judgment will be near, and fearful will be the sentence and there is none who can release. And thus the judgment and the recompense of the world is made through three tribunals. And therefore a matter is not ultimately established by one or two witnesses, but every matter shall be established by three witnesses.[3]

---

3.   The translation is taken from *OTP*, I, pp. 880-90.

Questions over Daniel and the Testament of Abraham

Individually none of these characters in the *Testament of Abraham*'s judgment scene in 11.1–13.8 calls to mind a studied dependence on Dan. 7.9-27. In fact, many students of the *Testament of Abraham* have not even considered Daniel 7 as a source for its judgment scene. However, when the characters are seen in their context and proximity to one another, it is hard to dismiss the likelihood of the *Testament of Abraham*'s use of Daniel.

James insisted that the *Testament of Abraham* preserves Jewish legends in its judgment scene but was not specific.[4] G. Macurdy admits that the author of the *Testament of Abraham* has used Daniel and specifically relates how the throne of Abel is similar to the throne of the Ancient of Days in Dan. 7.9, but he fails to draw any further parallels to Daniel 7. Instead, he downplays Jewish influence on the judgment scene of chs. 11–13 and says it was derived from Plato's *Republic*, *Gorgias* and *Phaedrus*.[5] Delcor makes no mention of Daniel when discussing the figures of the judgment vision (chs. 11–13) or triple judgment scene (ch. 13) of the *Testament of Abraham* and opts for an Egyptian court system as the background.[6] Nickelsburg, while arguing for a complex development behind the *Testament of Abraham*, does not take note of any 'substantial similarities' between the *Testament of Abraham* and Daniel 7.[7] Sanders writes that 'almost nothing of the OT

4. James (ed.) *The Testament of Abraham*, pp. 213-26 (55).

5. G.H. Macurdy, 'Platonic Orphism in the *Testament of Abraham*', *JBL* 61 (1942), pp. 213-26 (224-26). Kohler connects the role of Abel as judge to 'Ptolemean syncretism' and seriously considers a connection to Yama of the Aryans and the son of Gayomarth of the Avesta ('The Apocalypse of Abraham', p. 602).

6. Delcor, *Le Testament*, pp. 59-62, 146-47. According to Delcor, the Egyptian court system of the Roman period had three stages of jurisdiction: strategos, epistrategos, and supreme court (p. 61). S. Sharpe refers to the Roman historian Strabo (*lib.* 17), and describes the system as follows: 'Under the prefect was the chief justice of the province, who heard himself, or by deputy, all causes except those which were reserved for the decision of the emperor in person...there was a second judge if the case was too trifling for Rome...under these: freedmen and clerks were entrusted with affairs of greater or less weight' (*History of Egypt* [2 vols.; London: Edward Moxon and Co., 1859], II, p. 80).

7. Nickelsburg, 'Eschatology in the *Testament of Abraham*', pp. 36, 40. Nickelsburg argues that the judgment scene of chs. 11–13 has a complex history and represents an accumulation of traditions, beginning first with the judgment by

appears in the *Testament of Abraham* except the obvious references to Abraham in Genesis'.[8] Dean-Otting, who has published the most recent analysis of chs. 10–14 of the *Testament of Abraham*, identifies its indebtedness to Jewish and Greek literature, but makes no reference to Daniel as a possible source.[9]

These observations would be accurate if *quotations* are what is in mind when discussing the use of Daniel by the *Testament of Abraham*. But 11.1–13.7 strongly suggest that the author used the apocalyptic judgment scene of Daniel 7 as his framework for describing the process of judgment witnessed by Abraham. Sanders has observed that 'one of the main purposes of the original author was to describe the judgment scene'.[10] Dan. 7.9-27 offers one of the most dramatic judgment scenes in all of the Hebrew Bible and would serve as a useful text for an author interested in judgment. While it is unlikely that Daniel 7 was the first (and it is not the only description of judgment), this does not mean that a case for it being a source for the *Testament of Abraham* is unreasonable. C. Rowland notes how 'a *superficial* glance at the eschatological material in the apocalypses [Jewish and Christian] would give an

---

an enthroned Abel, followed by the addition of the Adam throne scene, then the inclusion of the second and third judgments by the tribes of Israel and the Master God of all ('Eschatology in the *Testament of Abraham*', pp. 41-47). What Nickelsburg has overlooked is the possibility that Dan. 7 provides a more than adequate source for these motifs. Box first saw the judgment scene as an combination of different judgment schemes but added that they were originally incompatible (*The Testament of Abraham*, p. xxiv).

8.	Sanders, *OTP*, I, p. 879. Delcor (*Le Testament*, p. 138) lists only one reference to Dan. 7 (*T. Abr.* 12.13).

9.	Dean-Otting, *Heavenly Journeys*, pp. 196-209. Apart from this omission, Dean-Otting provides an excellent survey of the literary background to the *Testament of Abraham*. There are several recent authors who have identified the *Testament of Abraham*'s use of Dan. 7, but they offer no explanation for their observations. Collins, in his study of the Dead Sea scrolls, says that Abel is an adaption of the son of man tradition found in Dan. 7 (J. Collins, *The Scepter and the Star: The Messiah of the Dead Sea Scrolls and Other Ancient Literature* [New York: Doubleday, 1995], p. 143; A. Segal says the same,'The Risen Christ and the Angelic Mediator Figures of the Dead Sea Scrolls', in J. Charlesworth (ed.), *Jesus and the Dead Sea Scrolls* [New York: Doubleday, 1992], p. 311). In his commentary on Daniel, Collins says nothing about the *Testament of Abraham* in his survey of Daniel's influence on Jewish literature and never cites it when discussing the Ancient of Days, one like a son of man, or the holy ones of the Most High.

10.	Sanders, *OTP*, I, p. 878.

impression of having little contact with Scripture'.[11] It must also be remembered that the New Testament Gospels do *not* quote Daniel 7, yet the use of Daniel 7 is undeniable. D. Aune cites the 'tendency to make frequent allusions to, but not quote, the OT' as a major characteristic of apocalyptic literature, and chs 10–15 of the *Testament of Abraham* (recension A) *are* apocalyptic.[12] Rowland observes how Jewish apocalypses do not set out to make obvious connections with specific biblical passages, but he cautions against overlooking their dependence on biblical literature:

> However, the absence of such clearcut connections should not lead us to suppose that the material has only tenuous links with the Scriptures, for the apocalypses do not set out to be in the first instance biblical commentaries. The links that there are will frequently be allusive and indirect. Thus an analysis of the way in which Scripture is used needs to follow a more subtle approach, allowing full weight to the often allusive character of reference to Scripture and the complexity of the relationship.[13]

11. C. Rowland, 'Apocalyptic Literature', in D. Carson and H. Williamson (eds.), *It is Written: Scripture Citing Scripture. Essays in Honour of Barnabas Lindars SSF* (Cambridge: Cambridge University Press, 1988), pp. 170-89 (171). The use of the word 'Scripture' by Rowland might appear to be anachronistic. However, it must be admitted that the communities of Middle Judaism did recognize a body of literature as sacred. The debate is over *which* texts were considered sacred. The use of Daniel in the first century CE gives every indication of it being part of 'scripture' for the vast majority of Jewish groups. There is no doubt that the 'Son of Man' was influential in the first century as the New Testament Gospels and the Parables of *Enoch* attest. That the term disappeared among the later rabbis is probably due to the popularity of Christianity and the reluctance of Jews to use a term associated with Christians. See M. Hengel, *The Son of God* (Minneapolis: Fortress Press, 1976), p. 46.

12. D. Aune, *Prophecy in Early Christianity* (Grand Rapids: Eerdmans, 1983), p. 108. Collins categorizes chs. 10–15 of the *Testament of Abraham* as apocalyptic ('The Genre Apocalypse', pp. 541-44).

13. Rowland, 'Apocalyptic Literature', p. 170. Rowland cautions readers of the apocalypses (among which he includes the *Testament of Abraham*) that with 'the use of Scripture in the apocalypses we do not expect the kind of explicit midrashic activity which is to be found, say, in a rabbinic commentary or a retelling of the biblical passage' ('Apocalyptic Literature', p. 171). M. Bockmuehl notes how apocalyptic literature (specifically *2 Bar.* 38) demonstrates a specific dependence on Scripture without needing to be an explicit 'commentary' and points to several instances of this type of 'implicit' commentary in the Old Testament and New Testament (*Revelation and Mystery* [WUNT, 36; Tübingen: J.C.B. Mohr, 1990],

Rowland does refer to the use of Daniel 7 in the *Testament of Abraham*, but his main interest is to illustrate how Abel has been fashioned after the 'one like a son of man'.[14] Nevertheless, this analysis of chs. 11–13 of the *Testament of Abraham* will demonstrate that the figures identified as the Ancient of Days, the holy ones of the Most High, and the Most High have also been interpreted in the *Testament of Abraham*.

Rowland notes how apocalyptic passages, when subjected to a minute examination, bear out their dependence on various scriptural passages.[15] The *Testament of Abraham* needs to be placed alongside other apocalypses whose subtle use of biblical texts has been detected by a 'minute examination' of specific passages. Ironically, the first serious study of the *Testament of Abraham*, by James in 1892, postulated the 'borrowing' from earlier Jewish texts by the author: 'We must be prepared for any amount of borrowing from earlier documents on the part of apocalyptic writers, and indeed early writers in general.'[16] Unfortunately, James overlooked any dependence on Daniel 7 by the author and went on to write that 'he drew largely on his own imagination' when presenting the judgment section.[17]

Daniel 7.9-27

Dan. 7.9-27: As I watched, thrones were set in place, and an Ancient of Days took his throne, his clothing was white as snow, and the hair of his head like pure wool; his throne was fiery flames, and its wheels were burning fire. A stream of fire issued and flowed out from his presence. A thousand thousands served him, and ten thousand times ten thousand stood attending him. The court sat in judgment and the books were opened.

I watched then because of the noise of the arrogant words that the

---

pp. 30 and 31). See also M. Stone, 'Apocalyptic Literature', in *Jewish Writings of the Second Temple Period*, pp. 390-91, and M. Fishbane, *Biblical Interpretation in Ancient Israel* (Oxford: Clarendon Press, 1985), pp. 292-93. The use of the term 'scripture' does not need to imply that all Jewish communities considered Daniel to be a sacred text. But whether or not it was considered sacred, the Son of Man figure was certainly influential.

14. C. Rowland, *The Open Heaven* (New York: Crossroad, 1982), pp. 107-109. See also C. Rowland's *Christian Origins* (Minneapolis: Fortress Press, 1985), p. 37, and S. Kim, *The Origin of Paul's Gospel* (Grand Rapids: Eerdmans, 1981), p. 211.

15. Rowland, 'Apocalyptic Literature', p. 174.

16. James (ed.), *The Testament of Abraham*, p. 23.

17. James (ed.), *The Testament of Abraham*, p. 55.

horn was speaking. And as I watched, the beast was put to death, and its body destroyed and given over to be burned with fire. As for the rest of the beasts, their dominion was taken away, but their lives were prolonged for a season and a time.

As I watched in the night visions, I saw one like a son of man coming in the clouds of heaven. And he came to the Ancient of Days and was presented before him. To him was given dominion and glory and kingship, that all peoples, nations, and languages should serve him. His dominion is an everlasting dominion that shall not pass away, and his kingship is one that shall never be destroyed.

As for me, Daniel, my spirit was troubled within me, and the visions of my head terrified me. I approached one of the attendants to ask him the truth concerning all this. So he said that he would disclose to me the interpretation of the matter: As for these four great beasts, four kings shall arise out of the earth. But the holy ones of the Most High shall receive the kingdom and possess the kingdom forever—forever and ever.

Then I desired to know the truth concerning the fourth beast, which was different from all the rest, exceedingly terrifying, with its teeth of iron and claws of bronze, and which devoured and broke into pieces, and stamped what was left with its feet; and concerning the ten horns on its head, and concerning the other horn, which came up and to make room for which three of them fell out—the horn that had eyes and a mouth that spoke arrogantly, and that seemed greater than the others. As I looked, this horn made war with the holy ones and was prevailing over them, until the Ancient of Days came; then judgment was given for the holy ones of the Most High, and the time arrived when the holy ones gained possession of the kingdom.

This is what he said: As for the fourth beast, there shall be a fourth kingdom on earth that shall be different from all the other kingdoms; it shall devour the whole earth, and trample it down, and break it to pieces. As for the ten horns, out of this kingdom ten kings shall arise, and another shall arise after them. This one shall be different from the other ones, and shall put down three kings. He shall speak words against the Most High, shall wear out the holy ones of the Most High, and shall attempt to change the sacred seasons and the law; and they shall be given into his power for a time, two times, and half a time. Then the court shall sit in judgment, and his dominion shall be taken away, to be consumed and totally destroyed. The kingship and dominion and the greatness of the kingdoms under the whole heaven shall be given to the people of the holy ones of the Most High; their kingdom shall be given an everlasting kingdom, and all dominions shall serve and obey them.[18]

18. All biblical quotations are taken from *The New Oxford Annotated Bible*.

Daniel 7 divides into two parts: Daniel's vision in 7.1-14 and the angelic interpretation which follows in 7.15-27. The action occurs on two levels—earth and heaven—both of which are described in mythic imagery. The vision narrates a sequence of four beasts which are interpreted as kingdoms in conflict over the sovereignty of the earth. Emphasis is placed on the aggressiveness of the fourth beast. Finally, a white-haired being, the 'Ancient of Days' (Dan. 7.9) takes his seat in the court for judgment. The four beasts are then judged. The closing action turns to the arrival of 'one like a son of man' (Dan. 7.13) who is given 'dominion and glory and kingship' (Dan. 7.14) by the 'Ancient of Days'. According to the angelic interpretation of 7.15-27, the empowerment of the 'one like a son of man' means that 'the holy ones of the Most High' (Dan. 7.18, 22, 27) will receive the everlasting kingdom after the demise of four successive kingdoms.

Types of Interpretation

M. Casey, in his study, *Son of Man: The Interpretation and Influence of Daniel 7*, points out that Daniel 7, a passage typically treated as a text dealing with the judgment, has been interpreted diversely.[19] First, there are interpretations which stand in line with what Casey identifies as the

There are no variants, major or minor, in the Dan. 7.9-27 fragments found at Qumran. For further information see E. Ulrich, 'Daniel Manuscripts from Qumran. Part 1: A Preliminary Edition of 4QDan a', *BASOR* 268 (1987), pp. 17-37, and 'Daniel Manuscripts from Qumran. Part 2: Preliminary Edition of 4QDan b and 4QDan c', *BASOR* 274 (1989), pp. 3-26.

19. M. Casey, *Son of Man: The Interpretation and Influence of Daniel 7* (London: SPCK, 1979), pp. 71-76. Casey's research has been most helpful in detecting the use of Dan. 7.9-27. Jewish and Christian exegetes both interpreted Dan. 7.9-27 as a judgment passage. The use of Dan. 7 has been dealt with in several studies, with the most complete treatment being by Casey. See also D. Juel, *Messianic Exegesis: Christological Interpretation of the Old Testament in Early Christianity* (Philadelphia: Fortress Press, 1988); Caragounis, *The Son of Man*; G. Beale, *The Use of Daniel in Jewish Apocalyptic Literature and in the Revelation of St. John* (Lanham, MD: University Press of America, 1984); J. Theisohn, *Der auserwählte Richter: Untersuchungen zum traditionsgeschichtlichen Ort der Menschensohngestalt der Bilderreden des Aethiopischen Henoch* (SUNT, 12; Göttingen: Vandenhoeck & Ruprecht, 1975); M. Hooker, *The Son of Man in Mark* (Montreal: McGill University Press, 1967). For a thorough bibliography on Dan. 7, see J. Goldingay, *Daniel* (WBC, 30; Dallas: Word Books, 1989), pp. 137-42 and Collins, *Daniel*.

author's 'original intention'. These early interpreters, best represented by the commentator Ephrem (the fourth-century teacher of the Syrian church), interpreted the 'Ancient of Days' as God and the figure identified as 'one like a son of man' symbolically as the 'holy ones of the Most High'. The 'holy ones of the Most High' were viewed as the faithful Jews attacked by Antiochus Epiphanes but promised eventual empowerment.[20]

Secondly, there are ancient interpreters who see the figures of Daniel 7 non-symbolically and alter the author's meaning by means of an 'actualizing exegesis'.[21] This type of interpretation, made possible by the failure of the eschatological events predicted in Daniel 7 to take place,[22] is the most popular and is found in the Parables of *Enoch* where the figures called the 'Ancient of Days' and 'one like a son of man' are cast in a new eschatological scheme representing God and his redemptive agent.[23]

Lastly, Daniel 7 is treated as a major source of scriptural information about the heavenly world, especially among rabbinic interpreters. *b. Ḥag* 13b is a rabbinic text where there is an 'atomistic midrashic' use of Dan. 7.10 in an effort to understand the unknown, in this instance the number of heavenly beings before God.[24]

---

20. Casey, *Son of Man*, pp. 24-26, 64-65. Casey is reflecting the argument of N. Perrin who also interprets the 'son of man' as symbolic of the Maccabean martyrs (*Rediscovering the Teaching of Jesus* [New York: Harper & Row, 1967], pp. 166-67). The 'one like a son of man' has been the subject of intense study and interpretations for this figure are quite varied, ranging from the symbolic to human being to angel to divine hypostasis. For a discussion of the original intention of Dan. 7 and the titles 'one like a son of man' and the 'holy ones of the Most High' see J. Collins, *The Apocalyptic Vision of the Book of Daniel* (HSM, 16; Missoula, MT: Scholars Press, 1977), pp. 123-26; *idem, The Apocalyptic Imagination* (New York: Crossroad, 1989), pp. 81-85; Goldingay, *Daniel*, pp. 167-72.

21. By 'actualizing exegesis' Casey is referring to the exegetical practice of interpreting Dan. 7 in light of one's own historical circumstances and theological interests (*Son of Man*, p. 71).

22. Casey makes this plausible observation (*Son of Man*, p. 136).

23. Especially chs. 46–71 (Casey, *Son of Man*, p. 92). These chapters are found within the part of *1 En.* called the Parables or the Similitudes, i.e. 37–71.

24. *b. Ḥag.* 13b is a discussion about the 'thousands thousands' and 'myriads of myriads' (Dan. 7.10) of heaven. See also *3 En.* 28-30. Casey goes on to add that the 'atomistic' use of scripture allowed 'ancient exegetes [to] appropriate any passage of Scripture and use it atomistically in support of any article of religious belief', and notes how Dan. 7 was one of the best sources of information about the

The *Testament of Abraham* will be seen to share in the characteristics of the last two types of interpretation: it uses Dan. 7.9-27 in an effort to place the figures of this section in a new eschatological framework and to explain the mechanism of judgment.

The second and third uses of Daniel 7 described above, which either treat Daniel 7 in a non-symbolic manner or as a source for information about the heavenly realm, have often been less than explicit. This type of creative, implicit use differs from that of commentaries in that the text is not quoted, but reused through the borrowing of its imagery and ideas in the composition of a new text. An example of this interpretive style can be found in the Parables of *Enoch* and its use of Dan. 7.9-10.

> *1 En.* 47.3: In those days, I saw him—the Antecedent of Time, while he was sitting upon the throne of his glory, and the books of the living ones were opened before him. And all his power in heaven above and his escorts stood before him.[25]

> Dan. 7.9-10: As I watched, thrones were set in place, and the Ancient of Days took his seat. His clothing was as white as snow; the hair of his head was white like pure wool. His throne was flaming with fire, and its wheels were ablaze. A river of fire was flowing, coming out from before him. Thousands upon thousands attended him; ten thousand times ten thousand stood before him. The court was seated, and the books were opened.

The writer of the Parables of *Enoch* never portrays the beings of heaven, other than the Antecedent of Time, as sitting, and he omits any reference to the 'seated' court of Dan. 7.10. Casey observes how this writer has 'reused the imagery of his source material [Daniel 7] with complete freedom' in the writing of a new book, not a commentary on Daniel, and questions 'why every detail of Daniel 7 should be retained for explicit mention' by the author who is recasting an apocalyptic text.[26] This use of Daniel 7 in *1 Enoch* 47 will be seen to parallel the use of Daniel 7 in the *Testament of Abraham*. Like the Parables of *Enoch*, the author of the *Testament of Abraham* creates a new apocalyptic vision through the creative recasting of an older apocalyptic text.

heavenly world available to enterprising rabbis (*Son of Man*, pp. 76, 89).

25. All translations from the Pseudepigrapha are taken from the *OTP*.

26. Casey, *Son of Man*, p. 111. See also *4 Ezra* 11.39-40 for the creative use of Dan. 7 by a different writer. Here Casey says it is 'clear that, like the author of the Similitudes of Enoch, he was a creative writer who reused the Danielic material for his own purposes' (*Son of Man*, pp. 122-23).

A survey of the interpretations of Dan. 7.9-27 also shows it to be a controversial text for interpreters. *b. Ḥag* 14a illustrates how Dan. 7.9 sparked a heated debate among rabbinic interpreters with its ambiguous reference to 'thrones'.

> *b. Ḥag.* 14a II *b. Sanh.* 38b: One passage says, His throne was fiery flames (Dan. 7.9) and another passage says until thrones were placed; and one that was ancient of days did sit—There is no contradiction: one (throne) for Him and one for David: this is the view of R. Akiba. Said R. Yosi the Galilean to him, Akiba, how long will you treat the divine presence as profane! Rather, one for justice and one for grace. Did he accept (this explanation) from him, or did he not accept?—Come and hear: One for justice and one for grace; this is the view of R. Akiba.[27]

Akiba's rebuke by Yosi the Galilean over the question of who occupies the thrones reveals something of the tensions created by Daniel 7. A. Segal sees two factors as instrumental in this instance: current beliefs in the role played by intermediary figures in the last days; and the seriousness of the problem which the rabbis felt was constituted by the plurality of the thrones.[28]

Literary Dependence

Before the interpretation of Dan. 7.9-27 in the *Testament of Abraham* can be surveyed, the issue of literary dependence needs to be clarified. The question of what type of criteria should be used when determining an author's dependence on Daniel 7 is difficult. It is obvious that when an author explicitly quotes a passage from Daniel 7, as in a commentary or midrash (where often the text is even identified by name), there is literary dependence. But determining *when* an author is alluding to Daniel 7 can be hard to establish. Literary allusion by definition refers to an intentional but *tacit* and *covert* evocation in a literary text of another text.[29] Clearly, it is correct to argue that when a text has no

27. All translations of the *Babylonian Talmud* are taken from I. Epstein (ed.), *The Babylonian Talmud* (35 vols.; London: Soncino Press, 1961).

28. A. Segal, *Two Powers in Heaven: Early Rabbinic Reports about Christianity and Gnosticism* (SJLA, 25; Leiden: E.J. Brill, 1977), pp. 66-71. Casey echoes Segal's research (*Son of Man*, p. 87).

29. This definition is taken from W. Harris, *Dictionary of Concepts in Literary Criticism and Theory* (New York: Greenwood Press, 1992), p. 10. L. Newlyn agrees with Harris and describes allusion as a 'conscious echo heard within the

verbal or conceptual similarity with Daniel 7, it can be safely assumed its author did not have this apocalyptic text in mind.[30] Therefore, the difficulty is in deciding when an author is implicitly dependent upon Dan. 7.9-27 and is making conscious use of that text.

Casey has identified two criteria for evaluating cases of possible literary dependence (by means of allusion) upon Daniel 7.[31] The first is verbal similarity, when the vocabulary of Daniel 7 can be detected in a later work, whether it be as explicit as exact word order or wording which is similar to Daniel's text. A second criterion is similarity of thought, when the concepts (i.e. themes or motifs) of a later passage will not only be consistent with Daniel 7, but can be traced to that text.

The strategy used by Casey in discerning literary dependence has been used by other students of Daniel 7. G. Beale works with the same criteria for literary allusion in his study of the influence of Daniel 7 on Jewish apocalyptic literature.[32] D. Juel makes use of the same criteria Casey has identified; in his examination of the Daniel 7 phrase 'son of man' and its use in middle Jewish writings, he states:

> it is improbable that the [phrase] Son of Man always carried an allusion to this passage [Dan. 7.13]... Only when other features [i.e. ideas] of a saying connect it with Dan. 7.13-14 does the phrase necessarily presuppose identification with the Danielic figure.[33]

A third criterion for detecting literary allusions to biblical documents has been carefully demonstrated by C. Stockhausen and offers additional precision. This criterion focuses on the structural parallels between the base text and the dependent text, such as the shared sequence of events or topics. Stockhausen applies the criteria of vocabulary, concepts, and structural parallels to 2 Corinthians when seeking to identify Paul's dependence upon some documents in the Hebrew Bible in her published doctoral dissertation *Moses' Veil and*

---

mind as distinctly recalling or reproducing an original pattern of sound, rhythm or language' (*Coleridge, Wordsworth, and the Language of Allusion* [Oxford: Clarendon Press, 1986], p. viii). See also J. Hollander, *The Figure of an Echo: A Mode of Allusion in Milton and After* (Berkeley: University of California Press, 1981), p. 64.

30. Casey makes this point (*Son of Man*, p. 3).

31. Casey, *Son of Man*, p. 5.

32. Beale, *The Use of Daniel*, pp. 43-44 n. 62.

33. Juel, 'The Risen Christ and the Son of Man: Christian Use of Daniel 7', in *Messianic Exegesis*, pp. 157, 160-61.

the Glory of the New Covenant.[34] When used together, these three tests of literary dependence, though lacking in absolute precision, can give sufficient direction in determining the high probability of an author's dependence on Dan. 7.9-27. Casey has helpfully described the difficult task of locating literary dependence:

> …while it is, both theoretically and practically, impossible to draw an accurate line in a specified place between literary dependence on the one side and lack of it on the other, it is contingently true that it is often possible to place a given document on the one side or the other of that imaginary line.[35]

The interpretation of Dan. 7.9-27 in the New Testament presents an interesting picture. There are no quotations from Dan. 7.9-27 in the New Testament and only a few clear allusions, primarily found in the Gospels, Acts and the Apocalypse.[36] That there are so few allusions in the New Testament to Daniel 7 is strange, given the significance granted to this text in the history of New Testament studies, and especially the long-standing interest in the 'Son of Man' question.[37]

However, what D. Seemuth has observed with regard to Pauline literature, 'In the absence of a specifically cited OT text it is not proper to

34. C. Stockhausen, *Moses' Veil and the Glory of the New Covenant* (Rome: Pontificio Istituto Biblico, 1989), pp. 42-70. For further description and illustration of these criteria, see D. Seemuth, 'Adam the Sinner and Christ the Righteous: The Theological and Exegetical Substructure of Romans 5:12-21' (PhD Dissertation, Marquette University, 1989), pp. 19-20, 141-57, 188-92. Beale makes reference to the criterion of structural parallels when he writes, 'The validity of the reference in each of the categories [of suggested literary dependence] is enhanced if they can be seen to be part of the thought structure of the particular O.T. context from which they have been derived' (*The Use of Daniel*, pp. 43 n. 62, 307-308). See also Beale's comments concerning the dependence of *1 En.* 90.20-27 on Dan. 7.9-13 (*The Use of Daniel*, pp. 84-85). C. Holman and W. Harmon identify how an allusion (a brief reference to another text) can be determined through vocabulary, ideas and structure (*A Handbook to Literature* [New York: Macmillan, 5th edn, 1986], p. 12).

35. Casey, *Son of Man*, p. 5.

36. There are no quotations or allusions to Dan. 7 in Paul's epistles (Juel, *Messianic Exegesis*, p. 152).

37. Besides Casey's study, *Son of Man*, several other studies are insightful for the son of man question: D. Hare, *The Son of Man Tradition* (Minneapolis: Fortress Press, 1990); Caragounis, *The Son of Man*; B. Lindars, *Jesus Son of Man* (Grand Rapids: Eerdmans, 1983); G. Vermes, *Jesus the Jew* (New York: Harper & Row, 1973); C. Colpe, 'ὁ υἱὸς τοῦ ἀνθρώπου', *TDNT*, VIII, pp. 400-77.

assume that no text at all is behind Paul's thought',[38] may be applied to other literatures. With respect to the use of Dan. 7.9-27, allowance must be made for the creative exegesis and integration of a biblical passage in a later text which results in a version of that biblical passage bearing no explicit similarity to its original form. As Juel emphasizes, the 'character of the allusions to Daniel 7 renders unlikely one uniform exegesis of the passage' and thus implies a degree of diversity in the interpretation of this text.[39] The implication for this study is that there may be uses of Dan. 7.9-27 which have been overlooked because of their non-explicit interpretations of Daniel. The *Testament of Abraham*, with its peculiar apocalyptic judgment scene, will be best understood as one such non-explicit use of Daniel 7.

Summary

Despite the influence of Dan. 7.9-27 on Jewish and Christian writings, few interpreters have suggested its use in the *Testament of Abraham*. Most interpreters of this Jewish apocalypse look elsewhere when identifying texts which may have influenced its author. At best, Daniel 7 is cited as a possible source, but no substantiation is ever presented. However, in light of Daniel's judgment scene, and its diverse use by later writers, the *Testament of Abraham*'s judgment scene warrants a serious examination in light of Daniel 7. This examination is heightened if it is the case that apocalyptic writings are often dependent on earlier texts. The question of literary dependence is not restricted to explicit quotations, but may be tacit and covert. Detecting such an incorporation of Daniel 7 is difficult, but not impossible. Students of Middle Jewish literature look for parallels in word use, thought and structure when arguing for literary allusions. What remains is the application of these criteria of literary dependence to the provocative judgment scene of the *Testament of Abraham*.

---

38. Seemuth, 'Adam the Sinner', p. 251.

39. Juel, *Messianic Exegesis*, p. 166. Juel also shows how the 'allusions to Daniel 7 usually, though not always, make use of the phrase "the Son of man". The exception is John's Apocalypse, which in at least one instance uses no title at all, and in other cases uses the biblical "one like a son of man"' (*Messianic Exegesis*, p. 165).

Chapter 3

THE EXEGESIS OF DANIEL 7 IN THE *TESTAMENT OF ABRAHAM*

The judgment scene of the *Testament of Abraham* incorporates figures from the Hebrew Bible, but is it dependent on Daniel 7 and its judgment scene? Only a careful reading, which takes into consideration the various ways that literary allusions can be detected (verbal, thematic and structural parallels), can decide.

The Testament of Abraham *and Daniel 7*

The *Testament of Abraham* describes Abraham's tour through the inhabited world and heaven under the guidance of Michael the archangel. During his heavenly journey, as described in recension A, Abraham learns that Abel will first judge 'every person' (13.5) and then the 12 tribes of Israel will act as judges at the 'second Parousia' (13.6).

> *T. Abr.* 13.5-6: For every person has sprung from the first formed, and on account of this they are first judged here by his son. And at the second Parousia they will be judged by the 12 tribes of Israel, even every breath and every creature.[1]

The reference to 'Parousia' (παρουσία) in *T. Abr.* 13.6 is not connected with the judgment in the LXX, but was probably more common in Jewish literature than what the sources now indicate.[2] The addition of 'second' may represent a Christian addition. But a problem remains as to why a Christian interpreter would add a reference to a 'second' coming yet add no reference to Jesus in the judgment scene.

The *Testament of Abraham* refers to judgments carried out by a 'son' and his empowered associates. This kind of setting is similar to Dan. 7.13-14, 22.

---

1. All translations from the *Testament of Abraham* are mine unless otherwise indicated.
2. R. Robertson, *OTP*, I, p. 890 n. 13a.

Dan. 7.13-14: As I watched in the night visions, I saw one like a son of man, coming with the clouds of heaven. And he came to the Ancient of Days and was presented before him. To him was given dominion and glory and kingship, that all peoples, nations and languages should serve him. His dominion is an everlasting dominion that shall not pass away, and his kingship is one that shall never be destroyed.

Dan. 7.22 (LXX): until the Ancient of Days came and gave the judgment to the holy ones of the Most High, and the time came and the holy ones possessed the sovereignty.[3]

In Dan. 7.22, according to the LXX, the Ancient of Days gives the 'judgment' (κρίμα) to the holy ones of the Most High in Dan. 7.22.[4] κρίμα is also used in Rev. 20.4 for the authority to judge given to the resurrected, enthroned believers who reign with Christ for 1000 years.

Dan. 7.13-14, 22 help illustrate how the conceptual background of the *Testament of Abraham* is drawn from Daniel 7. Both texts deal with scenes of judgment as it is carried out by exalted figures. While the

---

3.   The translation is mine. The LXX is used because it makes the empower-ment of the saints most explicit and the *Testament of Abraham* was probably written in Greek.

4.   Goldingay notes that in Dan. 7.22 'the judgment is given on their [the holy ones of the Most High] behalf rather than exercised by them' (*Daniel*, p. 146). Casey writes that 'At vs. 22, καὶ τὴν κρίσιν ἔδωκεν τοῖς ἁγίοί τοῦ ὑψίστου is a literal translation of the Aramaic, assuming יהב for יהיב. This Greek, like the Aramaic, could, if taken in isolation, mean that the holy ones became the judges, but in the LXX, as in the Aramaic text, the context favors the interpretation "he gave judgment for the holy ones of the Most High"' (*Son of Man*, pp. 132-33). However, Dan. 7.27 has the same lamed preposition as in 7.22 [לקדישׁי] but the meaning is taken (even by Goldingay, *Daniel*, p. 143) to be that the 'kingship and dominion and the greatness of the kingdom under the whole heaven shall be given *to the people* [לעם] of the holy ones of the Most High'. The LXX version of Dan. 7.27 reads: 'the kingdom and the dominion and the greatness of the kingdoms under the whole heaven shall be given *to the holy ones* of the Most High.' Dan. 7.27 in the MT certainly implies that the idea of judgment being given to the holy ones in Dan. 7.22, as suggested by the LXX and its use of the dative of indirect object (ἁγίοις ὑψίστου) in both vv. 22 and 27, is not a forced interpretation. This indeed is the interpretation of Dan. 7.22 in Rev. 20.4. Both Dan. 7.22, 27 in the LXX use the same verb (δίδωμι) to describe how the 'holy ones' are given the 'judgment' (7.22) and the 'kingship and dominion and greatness of the kingdom' (7.27). While the MT may imply a distinction between the 'holy ones' in 7.22 (לקדישׁי) and the 'people' in 7.27 (לעם) the LXX makes no such distinction and uses the word 'holy ones' (ἁγίοις) in both verses.

'one like a son of man' figure in Daniel is not described as being enthroned or specifically entrusted with judgment, the description of the 'son' judging in the *Testament of Abraham* can be understood as inferences from Dan. 7.9 with its reference to 'thrones' and Dan. 7.13-14 where the 'son of man' is given 'authority, glory and sovereign power'.

The judgment carried out by the '12 tribes' in the *Testament of Abraham* is supported by Dan. 7.22. In addition, while it is probably true that the 'one like a son of man' in the vision of Daniel is interpreted in Daniel 7 as 'holy ones' in vv. 22, 27,[5] it is clear that later Jewish readers living in the first century CE, like those of the Jesus community, did not identify the 'one like a son of man' with the 'holy ones'. These two entities were taken as distinct from each other. Mt. 19.28 and Lk. 22.28-30 preserve a Q saying which alludes to Daniel 7 and treats the 'one like a son of man' as distinct from the 'holy ones'.

> Mt. 19.28: Jesus said to them, truly I tell you, at the renewal of all things when the Son of Man is seated on the throne of his glory, you who have followed me will also sit on 12 thrones, judging the 12 tribes of Israel.

> Lk. 22.28-30: You are those who have stood by me in my trials; and I confer on you, just as my Father conferred on me, a kindgom, so that you will sit on thrones judging the 12 tribes of Israel.

Here Jesus is identified with the 'one like a son of man' who was empowered by the Ancient of Days (Luke's version of Q is the clearest in this regard) in Dan. 7.13-14, yet the authority to judge, associated with the 'holy ones' in Dan. 7.22, is applied to Jesus' apostles.[6]

This tendency to distinguish each of the entities of Dan. 7.9-27 is seen again in the *Testament of Abraham*. If the 'son of man' and the 'holy ones' are diversely understood by later interpreters, even the figure known as the 'Ancient of Days' in Dan. 7.9 may be open to interpretation and not necessarily identified with the 'Most High' who is explicitly referred to later in Dan. 7.25: 'He [the horn] shall speak words against the Most High, and shall wear out the holy ones of the Most High.'

---

5.   Rowland has argued that Dan. 7 does not give a clear sense that the 'one like a son of man' is to be interpreted as the 'holy ones' (*The Open Heaven*, p. 180).

6.   In contrast to Mt. 19.28 and Lk. 22.28-30, where the apostles judge, in Mt. 25.3-32 it is the Son of Man who judges. Juel sees the direct influence of Dan. 7 on Mt. 25.31 (*Messianic Exegesis*, p. 158) while Casey argues for indirect influence from Dan. 7 (*Son of Man*, pp. 190-92).

Adam and the Ancient of Days

A closer examination of the context of the *T. Abr.* 13.5-6 reveals something more than an allusion to Dan. 7.13-14, 25. From 11.1 to 13.7 there is a lengthy description of Abraham's visit to heaven during which he gains insight about the judgment of all mankind.[7] He learns that several figures are part of the process of judgment: Adam, before whom all souls must pass; Abel, the son of Adam, who judges the entire creation; the 12 tribes of Israel, who are granted a part in the judgment of mankind at the parousia; and lastly, the 'Master God of all', who will render the final judgment. The way these characters parallel those described in Dan. 7.9-27 is striking. There is a strong possibility that the entire pericope of Dan. 7.9-27 influenced the depiction of the judgment scene in the *Testament of Abraham*. This can be shown by comparing the parallel figures from each text.[8]

---

7.   Delcor (*Le Testament*, pp. 39-42) has listed the texts which deal with the tradition of Abraham's vision of the judgment which appears to be a development of his night-time encounter with God in Gen. 15.17 (*Apoc. Abr.* 15-19; *4 Ezra* 4.14; *LAB* 23.6; *2 Bar.* 4.4; *Midr. Ps.* 16.7; *Yal. Shim.* 77 on Gen. 15.17; *Ber. R.* 44.22; *Pirqe Abot* 2.8). The most striking recasting of Gen. 15.17 is *Targ. Neof.* 15.17 where the influence of Dan. 7.9 can be seen, 'And behold the sun set and there was darkness, and behold Abram looked while seats were being arranged and thrones erected. And behold, Gehenna which is like a furnace, like an oven surrounded by sparks of fire, by flames of fire, into the midst of which the wicked fall, because the wicked rebelled against the law in their lives in this world. But the just, because they observed it, have been rescued from the affliction. All was thus shown to Abram as he passed between the parts.' (All translations from the *Targums* are taken from M. McNamara [ed. and trans.], *The Aramaic Bible: Targum Neofiti I: Genesis* [18 vols.; Collegeville: The Liturgical Press, 1992].) Delcor argues that *T. Abr.* 10–14 and its judgment scene are a midrashic development from the palestinian targums (*Le Testament*, p. 40). This appears unlikely given the second-century CE date of this tradition in *Targ. Neof.* 15.17 (P. Alexander, 'Targum/ Targumim', *ABD*, VI, pp. 320-31 [323]; M. McNamara, 'Targums', *IDBSup*, pp. 856-61). See Boccaccini and his forthcoming book on *Targum Neofiti* for a detailed argument dating this tradition to the second century CE.

8.   Sanders notes how there is evidence of Christian interpolation in both recensions 'but no thoroughly systematic Christianizing of the document was carried out, since it is still easily recoverable as a Jewish document' (*OTP*, I, pp. 872-73). The texts under examination here do not give an indication of being added by Christian interpolators.

Dan. 7.9-10: As I watched, thrones were set in place and the Ancient of Days took his throne. His clothing was white as snow; and the hair of his head was white like pure wool. His throne was fiery flames, and its wheels were burning fire. A stream of fire issued and flowed from his presence. A thousand thousands served him, and ten thousand times ten thousand stood attending him. The court sat in judgment, and the books were opened.

T. Abr. 11.4-5, 9: And outside the two gates of that place, they saw a man seated on a golden throne. And the appearance of that man was terrifying like the master's. And they saw many souls being driven by angels and being led through the broad gate, and they saw a few other souls and they were being brought by angels through the narrow gate...This is the first-formed Adam who is in such glory, and he looks at the world, since everyone has come from him.

Both passages begin with a dazzling figure who is enthroned, accompanied by angels and associated with the judgment. In Daniel, one called the 'Ancient of Days' is described with divine associations like enthronement and an angelic attendant, while in the *Testament of Abraham*, Adam, and later Abel, are described as enthroned in the presence of angels. Clearly, Daniel 7 only depicts the enthronement of the 'Ancient of Days'. However, the plural 'thrones' (Aramaic: כרסון; Greek: θρόνοι) led later interpreters to speculate over the identity of the other enthroned figure(s). According to Mk 14.62, 'You will see the Son of Man seated at the right hand of the Power'; Christian interpreters saw Jesus as being enthroned in light of Daniel 7, as well as Ps. 110.1.[9]

b. Ḥag. 14a is another text which interprets Daniel 7 as referring to several enthroned figures. It quotes Dan. 7.9, 'Until thrones were placed; and One that was ancient of days did sit' and states that Rabbi Akiba identified 'One (throne) for Him [God], and one for David'. As

---

9. Others also see a midrashic combination of Dan. 7.13 with Ps. 110.1 (Juel, *Messianic Exegesis*, p. 159; Casey, *Son of Man*, p. 178). Jesus is portrayed as the 'one like son of man' (Dan. 7.13) who is 'coming on the clouds of heaven' (Dan. 7.13). In addition to Dan. 7, Ps. 110 is also alluded to with the description of Jesus being seated at the 'right hand' of the Power (110.1). The use of 'thrones' in Dan. 7.9 and the ascription of 'kingship' to the 'one like a son of man' in Dan. 7.14 may have facilitated the combination of Dan. 7 and Ps. 110. An allusion to the 'Ancient of Days' (Dan. 7.9) can be inferred from the word 'Power' which is being used as a substitute for the divine name. Therefore, with Jesus 'seated' as the Son of Man besides the 'Power' according to these references, a scene is established which recalls the empowerment and kingship of the 'one like a son of man' before the 'Ancient of Days' in Dan. 7.13-14.

Segal points out, 'Akiba must be identifying the "son of man" with the Davidic messiah'.[10] These interpretations help raise the issue of Daniel 7's significance for the *Testament of Abraham*. The writer of this apocalyptic text, like Mk 14.62 and *b. Ḥag.* 14a, also accepts the idea of two enthroned figures, notably Adam and Abel.

In the *Testament of Abraham*, the presence of Adam is, as Delcor puts it, 'astonishing'.[11] Like the Ancient of Days, Adam is enthroned in the presence of angels and is described as a 'terrifying' being who looks like the 'Master'. These motifs of angelic beings and terror are found in Daniel 7. Dan. 7.10 refers to the thousands of attendants (presumably angels) and 7.15 to the terror of Daniel's visions, 'As for me, Daniel, my spirit was troubled within me, and the visions of my head terrified me.' In the *T. Abr.* 11.4, Adam's appearance is 'terrifying' for Abraham, and later, in *T. Abr.* 13.4, Abel's throne is a 'terrifying' sight for Abraham. Both Daniel 7 and the *Testament of Abraham* use the same Greek adjective for 'terrifying', φοβερός. In Daniel 7 the reference to terror refers to all the seer's visions, whereas in the *Testament of Abraham*, terror typifies the appearances of Adam and Abel. The author of the *Testament of Abraham* has left out any reference to the successive beastly kingdom visions of Dan. 7.2-8. This is in keeping with the judgment interest of chs. 11–13 of the *Testament of Abraham* since Daniel's judgment scene does not begin until 7.9 and the appearance of the Ancient of Days and the 'one like a son of man'.

Rowland argues that in its present context the description of Adam looking like the 'Master' (δεσπότης) can only refer to the appearance of Abel in 12.5.[12] However, the preceding references to God as the 'Master' (δεσπότης) in 1.4, 7; 4.5; 8.2, 3 and 9.6, and later references in 13.7; 15.9; 16.2, 3 and 20.12, appear to rule out any reference to Abel, who himself is compared to a divine being in 12.6. 'Master' (δεσπότης; in LXX for אדון) was a common way of addressing God in the LXX and Josephus. Indisputedly, Adam's appearance is being likened to God's.[13]

10. Segal, *Two Powers in Heaven*, pp. 49-50.

11. Delcor writes, 'The presence of Adam in paradise, from which he had been driven out according to the text of Genesis, is, at first view, astonishing' (*Le Testament*, p. 135). Delcor makes no reference to Daniel as a possible source for this passage. Chapter 4 of this study will deal with the restoration of Adam.

12. Rowland, *The Open Heaven*, p. 468 n. 80.

13. See also Turner, 'The Testament of Abraham: A Study', p. 122, and Kim,

Adam is also described as being 'adorned in such glory' (11.8-9).

> *T. Abr.* 11.8-9: Then Abraham asked the Commander-in-chief, who is this all marvelous man, who is *adorned in such glory*, and sometimes rejoices and exults? Then the incorporeal one said, This is the first-formed Adam *who is in such glory* (emphasis mine).

Glory is characteristic of God in recension A of the *Testament of Abraham* and is associated with the man-like appearance of the glory of God in Ezekiel.[14] By itself Adam's adornment in 'glory' does not render him godlike, but when his glorious appearance is coupled with the 'master's' (God's) appearance, Adam's divine status appears to be implied. No angels in the *Testament of Abraham* have this type of appearance. Segal describes Adam as an exalted angel in the *Testament of Abraham*, but he is overlooking the explicit description of Adam having the 'master's' appearance.[15] The closest angelic resemblance is the being called 'Death', who is described as having 'great glory' and a 'youthful appearance' (*T. Abr.* 16.8).

Thus, Adam's appearance makes him godlike. The Coptic version of the *Testament of Abraham* makes no reference to Adam's divine likeness or glory, but it does describe him as 'a man wearing white garments, seated at the two gates' (8.10),[16] a parallel to the posture (sitting) and 'white as snow' clothing of the Ancient of Days. The

The Origin of Paul's Gospel, p. 211 n. 3. One parallel between the appearance of Adam and the Ancient of Days which may be significant is their hair. Dan. 7.9 and *T. Abr.* 11.6, 11 describe the hair of these enthroned figures. White hair is a distinguishing characteristic for the Ancient of Days and Adam's pulling of his own hair sets him apart. θρίξ (hair) is used in both the Greek version of Dan. 7.9 (LXX) and in *T. Abr.* 11.6, 11. This is an admittedly minor agreement, but along with the other items it illustrates a preponderance of shared interests.

14. Glory (δόξα) appears in 6.6, 8; 7.6; 8.3; 11.8, 9; 16.8, 12; and 18.11 (Schmidt [ed.], *Le Testament grec d'Abraham*, p. 182). Delcor cites Qumran as referring to the 'glory of Adam' (Hebrew: אדם כבוד) in a similar fashion (1QS 23; CD 3.20; 1QH 17.15; *Le Testament*, p. 135). The man-like appearance of God in Ezekiel reads as follows: 'And above the dome over their heads there was something like a throne, in appearance like sapphire; and seated above the likeness of a throne was something that seemed like a human form. Upward from what appeared like the loins I saw something that looked like fire, and there was splendor all around ... This was the appearance of the likeness of the glory of the Lord' (Ezek. 1.26-28).

15. Segal, 'The Risen Christ', p. 311.

16. Translation taken from G. MacRae (ed. and trans.), 'The Coptic Testament of Abraham', in Nickelsburg (ed.), *Studies in the Testament of Abraham*, pp. 327-39.

Coptic translator apparently understood Adam to be the Ancient of Days and added the motif of white clothing from Dan. 7.9.

Besides Adam's divine likeness and divine posture of enthronement, he also appears to possess an all encompassing divine knowledge, as *T. Abr.* 11.9 implies when it describes Adam as 'he looks at the world, since everyone has come from him'. *Ezekiel the Tragedian* describes Moses as an enthroned figure who 'gazed upon the whole earth' and goes on to interpret Moses' 'beholding all the earth' as meaning that 'things present, past, and future you [Moses] shall see' (*Ezek. Trag.* 74-78, 87-89).[17] The motif of omniscience is found in conjunction with other enthroned figures of middle Judaism, like Jesus (Jn 2.25), Enoch (*2 En.* 23.1-2), and Metatron (from the fifth-century CE Jewish text, *3 En.* 11.2).

Adam is not called a judge in the *Testament of Abraham*, but he is part of the judgmental process. This role for Adam is not necessarily inconsistent with Daniel 7, for the Ancient of Days is not explicitly called a judge in Daniel 7, but appears first in the judgment scene, just as Adam does in the *Testament of Abraham*. There are elements in Adam's description which allude to his role in a judicial process.[18] That he is at the 'gates', 'seated' and 'stands' with each passing group of souls (*T. Abr.* 11.4-11) parallels the Israelite setting and procedure of judgment as described by R. de Vaux.[19] Job goes to the city gate and takes his seat when he administers justice: 'When I went to the gate of the city, when I took my seat in the square...' (Job 29.7). The disciples

---

17. L. Hurtado also identifies Moses' acquisition of divine insight in *Ezek. Trag.* 77-78 and relates it to the heavenly secrets given to Enoch in *1 En.* but he says nothing about Adam in the *Testament of Abraham* (*One God, One Lord* [Philadelphia: Fortress Press, 1988], p. 59). This interest in Adam's omniscience will be dealt with later in Chapter 3. All translations from the Pseudepigrapha are taken from the *OTP*.

18. In the Rumanian version, Abraham asks his angelic guide Michael, after he has seen Adam and Abel, 'who are these judges, and these luminous angels' (32.1). The use of the plural 'judges' (giudecatori) may imply that the translator saw two judges up to this point in the narrative—Adam and Abel. The Rumanian version was translated into English by M. Gaster, who identified it as the *Apocalypse of Abraham* (*Studies and Texts: In Folklore, Magic, Medieval Romance, Hebrew Apocrypha and Samaritan Archaeology* [3 vols.; London: Maggs Brothers, 1925–28], I, p. 92).

19. R. de Vaux, *Ancient Israel* (2 vols.; New York: McGraw-Hill, 1965), I, pp. 155-56.

of Jesus will be seated on thrones when they judge the tribes of Israel (Mt. 19.28). In Isaiah the Lord stands when he renders his judgments: 'The Lord rises to argue his case; he stands to judge the people' (Isa. 3.13). Adam may not be called a judge, but he is presented in the context and setting of judgment.

Moreover, even the assumption that the Ancient of Days is acting as the judge in Daniel 7 can be questioned. According to J. Goldingay, when it is a matter of God judging, the scene is normally on earth, and there is some ambiguity over the location of this scene in Daniel.[20] The only clue as to the location of the Ancient of Days is in 7.22—'until the Ancient of Days came'—which is taken by G. Beasley-Murray as denoting an earthly setting.[21] However, the description of God on his throne is usually given a heavenly setting (1 Kgs 22.19-22; Ps. 2.8) and it is clear that other writers who used Dan. 7.9 identified this enthronement as a heavenly one (Rev. 4.2-5; *1 En.* 14.18-22[22]). A heavenly setting would be in line with chs. 11–13 of the *Testament of Abraham* where the judgment scene is placed in heaven. It also needs to be kept in mind that other interpretations of Daniel 7, like the Christian interpretation, had the second figure, the 'one like a son of man', serve as the judge—just as in the *Testament of Abraham* where Abel is the judge. Therefore the lack of an explicit role for Adam in the judgment may not be unusual but in keeping with other interpretations of Daniel 7.

Perhaps even the title given to Adam, 'first-formed', which obviously can be understood as implying his great age or patriarchal stature, can be connected to the title 'Ancient of Days' in Daniel. This conjecture will be examined later in Chapter 3.

Abel and the Son of Man

As suggested above, a connection between 'one like the son of man' in Daniel 7 and Abel, 'the son of Adam', in the *Testament of Abraham* can be established. Both the 'one like a son of man' and Abel are

---

20. See Jer. 49.38; Joel 4.1-2; Zech. 14.1-5; *Daniel*, p. 164.

21. G.R. Beasley-Murray, 'The Interpretation of Daniel 7', *CBQ* 45 (1983), pp. 44-58 (49).

22. The relationship of Daniel to *1 En.* 14.18-22 is debatable. M. Black argues that *1 En.* 14.18-22 is earlier than Dan. 7 (*The Book of Enoch or 1 Enoch* [SVTP, 7; Leiden: E.J. Brill, 1985], pp. 151-52). Collins notes that the direction of influence cannot be settled (*Daniel*, p. 300). Even if *1 En.* 14.18-22 is earlier, it is part of the same trajectory.

empowered over all creation. In each instance their authority is derived from a person who precedes them both in age and in glory.

> Dan. 7.13-14: And he [one like a son of man] came to the Ancient of Days and was presented before him. To him was given dominion and glory and kingship...

> T. Abr. 13.2, 5: Do you see, all pious Abraham, the frightful man who is seated on the throne? This is the son of Adam ... For every person has sprung from the first-formed, and on account of this they are judged here by his son...

While the 'one like a son of man' is not explicitly identified as enthroned and judging like Abel, these prerogatives can be inferred from three passages in Daniel 7. In Dan. 7.9 'thrones' are referred to but only one enthroned figure is identified—the Ancient of Days. Who are the other enthroned figures? Later, in Dan. 7.13-14, the 'one like a son of man' enters the court and is given sovereignty over creation in a ceremony which reads like an enthronement scene.[23] These verses leave room for the idea that the 'one like a son of man' was enthroned as a judge.

Abel is even associated with a 'book', reminiscent of the 'books' of judgment opened in Dan. 7.10. According to *T. Abr.* 12.17, he consults this book when he judges each soul: 'And the judge [Abel] told one of the angels who served him, "Open for me this book and find for me the sins of this soul".' The portrayal of Abel as the judge of humankind is striking.

Why is Abel identified as the judge? James remarked that, 'Here we have a conception which I do not find recurring in Jewish mythology'.[24] James thought that Abel's role as the 'first victim of human sin and God's first martyr' entitled him, in the eyes of the author, to act as the judge of humankind in the *Testament of Abraham*.[25] This view has been supported by Ginzberg, Delcor and Nickelsburg.[26] Nickelsburg adds

---

23. Beale thinks Ugaritic materials may have influenced interpreters like the author of *1 En.* 46.4-6 in the interpretation of the Daniel's 'one like a son of man' as a judge (CTA 5.1.1-3 and 3.3.37-39 in *The Use of Daniel*, pp. 104-105). See also Collins, *Daniel*, pp. 286-94.

24. James (ed.), *The Testament of Abraham*, p. 125.

25. James (ed.), *The Testament of Abraham*, p. 125.

26. Ginzberg (ed.), *The Legends of the Jews* (7 vols.; Philadelphia: Jewish Publication Society of America, 1925), V, pp. 129, 142; Delcor, *Le Testament*, pp. 142-43; Nickelsburg, *Jewish Literature*, pp. 253, 270.

that Abel judges because he is the 'protomartyr' as suggested by Wis. 2.4-5.

However, the *Testament of Abraham* does not say anything which suggests that Abel judges because he is a martyr. Abel surely is the prototype for martyrdom, but the phrase 'son of man' can also be understood as 'son of Adam'. On that basis it is difficult not to see the connection with the 'son of man' who is empowered in Dan. 7.13-14 and take this as the rationale for Abel's authority to judge.

James offered a second explanation for Abel's selection as judge and suggested the possibility of a Sethian basis for Abel's exaltation. He points to the sects which made Adam, Seth and Melchizedek special objects of worship and says some type of confusion between Abel and Seth may have led to Abel's exaltation.[27] Macurdy also notes that Abel as a judge is a conception which does not recur in Jewish mythology. Like James, Macurdy says the exaltation of Abel may be due to Sethian origin, 'since Abel was an object of devotion among the Sethians'.[28]

Perhaps the reason why so little is said about Abel in comparison with Seth in Jewish traditions is because Seth was understood to be a 'replacement' for Abel according to Gen. 4.25. However, neither James nor Macurdy cite any evidence in support of their contention that Abel was an object of devotion among the Sethians and the literature fails to support such a contention. In fact, Epiphanius's account of the Sethians in his *Panarion* says nothing about the worship of Abel and makes it clear that Seth and his line was not an extension of Abel and his line.

> *Pan.* 3.2.7: For as time went on, they say, and the two races were together, that of Cain and that of Abel (and) had relations with each other on account of the great amount of vice and had sexual intercourse together, the Mother of all, noticing this, wanted to effect the purification of human seed, because Abel had been killed, and she chose Seth, showed him to be pure, and in him alone deposited the seed of her power and purity.[29]

It may be that the Sethian exaltation of Seth prompted the author of the *Testament of Abraham* to identify Abel as a judge. G. Strousma has argued that Elisha, one of the four rabbis who went into paradise and

---

27. James (ed.), *The Testament of Abraham*, pp. 125-26.

28. Macurdy, 'Platonic Orphism', pp. 223-24.

29. Translation taken from P. Amidon (ed. and trans.), *The Panarion of St. Epiphanius, Bishop of Salamis: Selected Passages* (New York: Oxford University Press, 1990). Epiphanius's account dates to the fourth century CE.

was subsequently branded a heretic and given the name 'Aher', or 'another, the other, stranger', according to *t. Ḥag.* 2.3, was a rabbi who adopted Sethian Gnosticism.[30] He notes that Sethian Gnostics believed that they were alien to this world and suggests that Palestinian rabbis branded Elisha 'Aher' as a direct allusion to this belief.[31] If Strousma is right, Palestinian rabbis in the early second century were familiar with the gnostic glorification of Seth and were combating its influence among the Jews. Against this background the author's choice of Abel as a judge in the *Testament of Abraham* could be interpreted as a reaction to the Sethian Gnostic threat.

Box traced the explanation for Abel's role as a judge in *T. Abr.* 13.3—'For I do not judge you, but every man is judged by man'—to Gen. 9.6: 'Whoever sheds the blood of a human, by a human shall that person's blood be shed', as it was interpreted by the 'Palestinian Targum'; but he does not cite which Targum.[32] Delcor says the judgment of souls by Abel is 'rather astonishing'.[33] He admits of not knowing any parallel to *T. Abr.* 13.3 in the Hebrew Bible and traces its development from *Targ. Onq.* Gen. 9.6 and especially *Targ. Neof.* Gen. 9.6. 'Whoever sheds the blood of a son of man, his blood will be shed by a son of man.'[34] This type of tradition, if it dates to the first century CE, may have contributed to the formulation of *T. Abr.* 13.3, in conjunction with the use of Dan. 7.13 and its description of the 'one like a son of man' who is given great sovereignty. *Targ. Neof.* Gen. 9.6 and Dan. 7.13 both refer to a 'son of man', who in the context of Genesis could be taken as referring to Abel—the first 'son of man' to have his blood shed.

Abel's identification as 'son of Adam' calls to mind Dan. 7.13 and the 'one like a son of man'. Schmidt suggests that the Greek translator of the Semitic original of the *Testament of Abraham* misunderstood *ben adam* to mean 'son of Adam'; thus Abel as son of Adam equals the empowered son of man in Daniel 7.[35]

30. G. Strousma, 'Aher: A Gnostic', in B. Layton (ed.) *The Rediscovery of Gnosticism* (2 vols.; NumenSup, 41; Leiden: E.J. Brill, 1981), II, pp. 808-18.

31. Strousma, 'Aher: A Gnostic', pp. 812-14.

32. Box (ed. and trans.), *The Testament of Abraham*, p. 21 n. 1.

33. Delcor, *Le Testament*, p. 60.

34. Delcor, *Le Testament*, p. 144.

35. Schmidt (ed.), 'Le Testament d'Abraham', I, p. 64. This phrase reads as οὗτός ἐστιν υἱός (13.2) in Schmidt's edition of the *T. Abr.* He adds that after υἱὸς

F. Borsch, in his study, *The Son of Man in Myth and History*, identifies Abel as a 'kind of version of the Son of Man' who possesses those qualities associated with 'Son of Man' candidates: he is all important and has the right to be judge and ruler because he is the son of Adam.[36]

S. Pétrement, when answering the question of why Valentinian Gnosticism chose Seth as the 'son of man' (*Ap. John* 1.24-25), says the choice of Seth resulted when Adam was recognized as the true man, thus making the son of Adam—Seth—the 'son of man'.[37] This type of literalistic interpretation, but with a preference for Abel, the son of Adam, could help explain the exegetical choices behind the *Testament of Abraham*. Thus the phrase 'son of man' (Dan. 7.13) may have been taken literally in the context of Daniel 7, making Adam the 'man' or 'Ancient of Days' (Dan. 7.9), and his son Abel, the 'son of Adam (man)' (*T. Abr.* 13.2).[38]

Besides this verbal parallel between Daniel's 'son of man' (Dan. 7.13) and the *Testament of Abraham*'s 'son of Adam' (*T. Abr.* 13.2), it should be kept in mind that Abel's role as the judge is justified on the basis of Abel being both a man—'he sits here to judge the entire creation ... For God said, I do not judge you, but every man is judged by man' (13.3)—and the son of Adam: 'For every person has sprung from

MSS G BJQ add ἀδάμ and MS I adds τοῦ ἀδάμ (*Le Testament grec d'Abraham*, p. 136). Collins also observes how 'son of Adam' in *T. Abr.* 13.2 would be equivalent to 'son of man' in Hebrew (*The Apocalyptic Imagination*, p. 249 n. 59).

36. F. Borsch, *The Son of Man in Myth and History* (NTL; Philadelphia: Westminster Press, 1967), p. 170.

37. S. Pétrement, *A Separate God: The Christian Origin of Gnosticism* (San Francisco: Harper & Row, 1990), p. 400.

38. W. Roth, when arguing that Jesus' title 'son of man' renders him 'Abel-Re-Incarnate' in John's Gospel, draws the same conclusion over the literal significance of 'son of man' equalling 'son of Adam' equalling Abel ('Jesus as the Son of Man: The Scriptural Identity of a Johannine Image', in D. Groh and R. Jewett (eds.), *The Living Text: Essays in Honor of Ernest W. Saunders* [Lanham, MD: University Press of America, 1985], pp. 11-26, especially pp. 20-23). Roth brings the *Testament of Abraham* into his discussion when describing the exaltation of Abel and parallels Abel's role as judge with Jesus' claim that he is the judge in Jn 5.26-27 ('Jesus as the Son of Man', pp. 22-23). Roth does not discuss Abel's relationship to the 'one like a son of man' in Dan. 7.13. D. Burkett has questioned Roth's paralleling of Abel and Jesus but fails to give due consideration to the genuine parallels which exist between these two figures within their respective texts (*The Son of the Man in the Gospel of John* [JSNTSup, 56; Sheffield: JSOT Press, 1991], pp. 25-26).

the first-formed, and on account of this they are first judged here by his son' (13.5).[39] There is no doubt that the phrase 'son of man' in Dan. 7.13 (Aramaic בר אנש; Hebrew בן אדם) can simply mean man.[40] This leaves another possibility for explaining Daniel's use in the *Testament of Abraham*. The author understands Abel as both the 'son of man' (Adam; 13.2, 5) and the 'man' (13.3) who is empowered over all people according to Dan. 7.13-14.

This can be paralleled by Jn 5.27, which alludes to Dan. 7.13-14. Here the evangelist explains Jesus' empowerment as a judge on the basis of Jesus being the 'son of man'; 'He has given him authority to execute judgment, because he is the Son of Man' (Jn 5.27).[41] And if Abel is taken to be the 'one like a son of man' in Dan. 7.13, then the

---

39. Delcor sees *T. Abr.* 13.3 as a development of a targumic tradition like *Targ. Neof.* 9.6: 'Whoever sheds the blood of a son of man, by the hands of a son of man shall his blood be shed' (*Le Testament*, pp. 144-45). However, this in itself does not explain why Abel is the judge.

40. For the meaning of 'son of man' as man see G. Vermes, 'The Use of bar nash/bar nasha in Jewish Aramaic', in M. Black (ed.), *An Aramaic Approach to the Gospels and Acts* (Oxford: Clarendon Press, 3rd edn, 1967), pp. 310-28; 'The "Son of Man" Debate', *JSNT* 1 (1978), pp. 19-32; 'The Present State of the "Son of Man" Debate', *JJS* 29 (1978), pp. 123-34.

41. The identification of Jesus with the 'Son of Man' and his delegated 'authority to execute judgment' (from the 'Father' [5.26]) possibly shows the influence of Dan. 7.13-14 on this Gospel. With regard to the absence of an article with the expression 'Son of Man' in Jn 5.27, Casey argues that the phrase cannot point to a specific biblical text because the words 'Son of Man' are too general to point anywhere and such an anarthous expression does not call to mind an allusion to Dan. 7.13-14. This absence of an article, however, does not rule out the strong probability of an allusion to Dan. 7.13. B. Lindars, in his commentary on John, has pointed out how the Greek versions of Dan. 7 leave out the article when translating the expression 'son of man' and even verbally parallel other aspects of Jn 5.27: 'The phrase is unique in John because the article is omitted with both words (*huios anthropou* instead of *ho hu. tou an.*), so that it might be taken to mean "a son of man", i.e. a human being. In this case it would mean that the Father has delegated judgment to the Son because he has experienced the Incarnation, and thus knows the human side as well as the divine side, which could make him strictly impartial. But such considerations never come to the surface in this discourse. Much the more likely explanation is that the verse is a direct allusion to Dan. 7.13f., from which the imagery is derived. For there both LXX and Theodotion have "son of man" without the article, exactly as here, and LXX has precisely the same words for *has given him authority*' (*The Gospel of John* [NCBC; London: Marshall, Morgan & Scott, 1972], pp. 225-26; emphasis his).

preceding figure who looks older and divine, the 'Ancient of Days' in Dan. 7.9, might be seen as Adam, Abel's father and the image of the 'Master'. This would imply that Dan. 7.9-14 was understood by the Jewish interpreter, who was responsible for the judgment scene in the *Testament of Abraham*, as describing an old figure and a young figure.

Segal points out how Dan. 7.9-14, with its court scene involving the 'Ancient of Days' and 'one like a son of man', was cited in rabbinic texts like the *Mekilta* in order to justify their descriptions of God as an *old man* and a *young man*. Apparently the 'Ancient of Days' was understood as an old man (his hair like 'wool' [white] in 7.9 signifying age) and the 'one like a son of man' being taken as a youthful figure. The rabbis denied the appearance of two divine figures, one young and one old, in Daniel 7.

> The proof text for these statements is Dan. 7.9f. which describes a heavenly enthronement scene involving two divine manifestations, 'the son of man' and 'the Ancient of Days'. In this context, the reference from Dan. must be taken to demonstrate that God may be manifested either as a young man or as an old man... Not only does the passage allow the interpretation that God changes aspect, it can easily be describing two separate, divine figures. More than one throne is revealed and scripture describes two divine figures to fill them. One sits and the other seems to be invested with power, possibly enthroned. The Ancient of Days may be responsible for judgment, but delegates the operation to a 'son of man' who accomplishes judgment by means of a fiery stream.[42]

Another first-century Jewish text, the Parables of *Enoch*, draws upon Daniel 7 and infers that the 'one like a son of man' is an enthroned judge, Enoch—just as the Christian community did in identifying Jesus as the enthroned 'son of man' (Mt. 19.28).[43]

---

42. Segal, *Two Powers in Heaven*, pp. 35-36. The rabbinic discussion about God's appearance as a young man and an old man are found in *Mekilta deRabbi Ishmael* Bahodesh 5, Shirta 4.

43. See also Mt. 25.31-46. Hare writes, 'It is, moreover, increasingly clear that Jewish eschatological thought entertained the possibility that one or more human beings would share the role of judge in some phase of God's judgment', and notes the significance of Abel in the *Testament of Abraham*, Jesus in the Christian community, and the 'son of man' in *1 Enoch* (*The Son of Man Tradition*, pp. 16, 163-64). See also J. Dunn, *The Parting of the Ways: Between Christianity and Judaism and their Significance for the Character of Christianity* (Philadelphia: Trinity Press International, 1991), p. 187.

1 En. 69.29: for that Son of Man has appeared and has seated himself upon the throne of his glory; and all evil shall disappear from before his face...

1 En. 71.14: You [Enoch], son of man, who art born in righteousness and upon whom righteousness has dwelt, the righteousness of the Antecedent of Time will not forsake you.

Thus Enoch, Jesus and Abel stand as interpretations of Daniel 7 and its 'one like a son of man' who exercises sovereignty.

Enoch is the name of the third son of Adam in Gen. 4.17 and the name of the seventh son of Adam in Gen. 5.21. The latter is stressed in *1 En.* 60.8; 93.3; *Jub.* 7.39; and Jude 14. Enoch is thus the 'perfect' son of his ancestor, Adam, and serves as an alternative for Abel, who could be understood as the 'true' son of Adam on the grounds that Cain was disqualified for his murder of Abel the righteous son. More discussion of the alternate 'sons of man' will be given later in this chapter.

The Twelve Tribes and the Holy Ones of the Most High

There is also a correspondence between the 'holy ones' of Daniel and the '12 tribes of Israel' of the *Testament of Abraham*. They are given the authority to judge like the 'one like a son of man' and Abel, the 'son' of the 'first-formed', respectively.

Dan. 7.22 (LXX): until the Ancient of Days came and gave the judgment to the holy ones of the Most High, and the time came and the holy ones possessed the sovereignty.

T. Abr. 13.6: And at the second Parousia they will be judged by the 12 tribes of Israel (κριθήσονται ὑπὸ τῶν δώδεκα φυλῶν τοῦ Ἰσραὴλ), even every breath and every creature.

The LXX version makes it explicit that the 'holy ones of the Most High' are given the authority to judge. This motif of empowerment is later repeated in Dan. 7.27 (LXX): 'And the kingdom and the power and the greatness of the kingdoms under the whole heaven will be given to the holy ones of the Most High.' The idea of the tribes 'judging' is an idea drawn from Daniel 7, while the idea of the tribes 'ruling' is not exclusive to Daniel 7. G. Fee has observed that this motif is a common one in Jewish apocalyptic eschatology and he traces its beginning to the

LXX of Dan. 7.22, from which he notes how it was picked up in a variety of texts, including Qumran.[44]

This correspondence between 'holy ones' and 'tribes' is not problematic. It is not difficult to see how Daniel's 'holy ones' could be interpreted as the 'tribes of Israel' in the *Testament of Abraham*. James suggested that the '12 tribes' could be intended to mean the new Israel and may represent a Christianization.[45] However, while Christian redactors could apply the reference to the 12 tribes to themselves, Turner notes how later Christian redactors apparently were not satisfied with the reference to the 12 tribes in *T. Abr.* 13.6. He refers to another reading of 13.6—'at the second coming the twelve tribes of Israel and all the world will be judged by the twelve apostles'—and argues that 13.6 was expanded to include a reference to the role of the apostles.[46]

Box has pointed out how different *T. Abr.* 13.6 is from the Christian tradition in Mt. 19.28 where the tribes of Israel are judged by the apostles, and cites *Yal.* 1065 on Daniel as proof of its Jewishness: 'In the time to come the Lord will sit in judgment, and the great of Israel will sit on thrones prepared by the angels, and judge the heathen nations, together with the Lord'.[47] *Yalqut* is a late text (thirteenth century), but Mt. 19.28 is not. *Yalqut* here is not influenced by Christianity, but is part of a Jewish tradition which shows up in Matthew 19 and elsewhere. It is an illustration of how rabbinic tradition highlights Israel's role in the judgment. Box, when commenting on the idea of the tribes judging in *T. Abr.* 13.6, refers also to the *Sibylline Oracles*: 'Prophets [Israelites] of the great God will take away the sword for they themselves are judges of men and righteous kings' (*Sib. Or.* 3.781).

Delcor identifies a parallel to *T. Abr.* 13.6 from the *Thanksgiving Hymns* of Qumran. Here the people of Israel are understood as the agents of eschatological judgment.

> 1QH 4.23-27: Thou wilt put the fear of them into Thy people and (wilt make of them) a hammer to all the peoples of the lands, that at the judgment they may cut off all those who transgress Thy word.[48]

---

44. G. Fee, *The First Epistle to the Corinthians* (NICNT; Grand Rapids: Eerdmans, 1987), p. 233.

45. James (ed.), *The Testament of Abraham*, p. 54.

46. In MSS B, C, D and E ('The Testament of Abraham: A Study', p. 35).

47. Box (ed. and trans.), *The Testament of Abraham*, pp. 21-22 n. 4.

48. Delcor, *Le Testament*, p. 146. See also 1QS 5.6; 1QM 6.6; 11.13. All translations of the Dead Sea scrolls are taken from G. Vermes (ed. and trans.), *The Dead*

Sanders sees *T. Abr.* 13.6 as a modification of the traditional motif of Israel judging the Gentiles and cites Dan. 7.22.[49] The role of Israel in judging mankind is a common interest in Jewish literature. When speaking of Israel's righteous, Wis. 3.8 says, 'they will govern nations and rule over peoples and the Lord will reign over them forever'.[50] *Jubilees* tells of God's promise that Israel 'will rule in all nations' (32.19).[51] Paul's statement that the 'saints' will judge the world also needs to be recalled, 'Do you not know that the saints will judge the world' (1 Cor. 6.2). In both 1 Cor. 6.2 and Dan. 7.22 (LXX) the same Greek word, ἅγιοι (holy ones or saints), is used to identify those who will judge. C. Barrett, H. Conzelmann and Fee all identify Dan. 7.22 as the basis for Paul's belief that the saints will act as judges.[52] The idea that the 12 tribes would rule (judge) is hardly restricted to Daniel 7. However, when this motif is seen in conjunction with the other elements of Daniel 7 which appear in the judgment scene of the *Testament of Abraham*, it is reasonable to cite Dan. 7.22 as a likely source for this motif.

The Master God and the Most High

The *Testament of Abraham* appears to have found the fourth heavenly figure, the third judge, in Daniel's 'Most High':

> Dan 7.25-26: He [the last adversary] shall speak word against the Most High, shall wear out the holy ones of the Most High, and shall attempt to change the law; and they shall be given into his power for a time, two times, and half a time. Then the court shall sit in judgment, and his dominion shall be taken away to be consumed and totally destroyed.

> *T. Abr.* 13.7: And, thirdly, they shall be judged by the Master God of all...

This last parallel goes without argument. 'Most High' in Daniel and

Sea Scrolls in English (Harmondsworth: Penguin Books, 4th edn, 1995).

49. Sanders, *OTP*, I, p. 890 n. 13 c.

50. All quotations of the Apocrypha are taken from *The New Oxford Annotated Bible with the Apocrypha: New Revised Standard Version.*

51. Also see 1QS 5.6-7.

52. C. Barrett, *The First Epistle to the Corinthians* (HNTC; New York: Harper & Row, 1968), p. 136; H. Conzelmann, *1 Corinthians* (Hermenia; Philadelphia: Fortress Press, 1975), pp. 104-105; Fee, *The First Epistle*, p. 233.

'Master God' in the *Testament of Abraham* are synonymous descriptions of God. Though the 'Most High' is not called a judge in Daniel, the 'court' is described as sitting in 7.26 and this could be taken to imply that the 'Most High', who is referred to in v. 25, presides.

Structure

The use of Daniel 7 by the *Testament of Abraham* can be seen more clearly by noting how the structural sequence of references to each character is identical in both books:

Structural Parallels between the Judgment Scene of Daniel
and the Testament of Abraham

Daniel	*Testament of Abraham*
Ancient of Days (7.9)---------------------	Adam (11.4)
son of man (7.13)-------------------------	Abel (13.2)
holy ones (7.18)--------------------------	tribes of Israel (13.6)
Most High (7.25[53])----------------------	Master God (13.7)

In both judgment scenes the characters are identical in three ways: number, order of appearance, and function. The Ancient of Days and Adam open the judgment scenes as enthroned figures, the 'one like a son of man' and Abel are then identified and highlighted as empowered figures; next follows the holy ones and the 12 tribes who are given the right to judge; and last of all, the Most High and Master God are the overriding powers. This type of structural correspondence among the entities of Daniel 7 could be coincidental, but when these four-character judgment scenes are considered along with their conceptual parallels (judgment, thrones, exalted beings, angelic associates, terror, court scene, books) and the parallel in wording ('son of man' and 'son of Adam'),[54] all within the setting of a vision granted to a pious follower

---

53. 7.25 is being used instead of 7.18 because there is some question over whether or not 'Most High' in 7.18 refers to God or the 'saints'; see A. Lacocque, *The Book of Daniel* (Atlanta: John Knox Press, 1979), pp. 122-23. 7.25 is a clear reference to the 'Most High'. It can also be noted that in 7.26 the court is even referred to, whereas in 7.18 the court is not mentioned. This further evidences how 7.25 refers specifically to God.

54. The other verbal parallels from the LXX include θεωρέω (see), in Dan. 7.9, 11, 13, 21; *T. Abr.* 11.6, 7, 10; 12.5; 13.2; θρόνος (throne), in Dan. 7.9; *T. Abr.*

of God (Daniel and Abraham) who receives angelic assistance, they are best explained by a more or less conscious adaptation of Daniel 7 by the author. The author of the *Testament of Abraham* does not simply parallel Dan. 7.9-27, à la 'parallelomania',[55] but has used the apocalyptic text as a structural prototype for his description of the judgment and filled in this material with his own interpretative outlook. The description of judgment is not merely 'stock' apocalypticism, but is rooted in a borrowing from Daniel 7, which was typical for many Jewish apocalyptic books of this period.[56]

The Ancient of Days

Initially it may seem strange to argue that a Jewish author would so interpret Daniel 7 as to produce an exalted view of Adam and Abel, even substituting the former for the Ancient of Days. However, it has long been known that the Christian community, a distinctly Jewish community at its inception, made significant use of Daniel 7 in its exaltation of Jesus. This tendency of early Christianity to exalt a human figure, Jesus of Nazareth, beyond the status and function of ordinary humanity is understood by L. Hurtado as 'standard fare in post-exilic Judaism' and was paralleled by what Casey calls a 'process of development of

---

11.4, 6, 6, 7, 10, 11; 12.4, 11; 13.2; κάθημαι (sit), in Dan. 7.9, 10, 26; *T. Abr.* 11.4, 6, 9, 10; 12.5, 9, 10, 11; 13.2, 3; θρίξ (hair), in Dan. 7.9; *T. Abr.* 11.6, 11; πῦρ (fire), in Dan. 7.9, 10, 11; *T. Abr.* 12.4, 10, 14; 13.1; βίβλος (book), in Dan. 7.10; *T. Abr.* 12.17, 18; υἱός (son), in Dan. 7.13; *T. Abr.* 12.5; 13.2; φοβερός (frightful), in Dan. 7.19; *T. Abr.* 11.4; 12.4; 13.2, 7.

55. See S. Sandmel for the pitfalls in tracing out parallels between different documents ('Parallelomania', *JBL* 81 [1962], pp. 1-13).

56. Beale has convincingly shown how Dan. 7 was a major source for the judgment scenes of *1 En.*, *4 Ezra* and *Revelation*—all of which used Dan. 7 in their creative rendering of eschatological interests (*The Use of Daniel*, pp. 67-88, 112-44, 154-305; 'The Influence of Daniel Upon the Structure and Theology of John's Apocalypse', *JETS* 27 [1984], pp. 413-23, esp. 421-22). L. Hartman's study, *Prophecy Interpreted: The Formulation of Some Jewish Apocalyptic Texts and of the Eschatological Discourse Mark 13 and Parallels* (ConBNT, 1; Lund: C.W.K. Gleerup, 1966), pp. 111-58, was among the first to argue for Dan. 7 being the source of a Christian 'apocalyptic midrash' which can be detected in Mk 13 and Mt. 24. A. Farrar has argued that Revelation is generally patterned after the form of Daniel's half week (*The Revelation of St John the Divine* [Oxford: Clarendon Press, 1964], pp. 6-8).

purely Jewish figures' also by communities other than Christian in Middle Judaism.[57]

Rev. 1.13-14 demonstrates how the Christian community interpreted *both* the Ancient of Days and the Son of Man of Daniel 7 in light of its allegiance to Jesus of Nazareth. Jesus is given attributes from each figure: the designation 'one like a son of man' and hair like white 'wool'.

> Rev. 1.13-14: and in the midst of the lampstands I saw one like a Son of Man, clothed with a long robe and with a white sash across his chest. His head and his hair were white as white wool, white as snow; his eyes were like a flame of fire.

Concerning this connection of Jesus and the Ancient of Days, Casey writes:

> It is not impossible that John identified the Ancient of Days as Jesus. Some Jewish exegetes saw an angelic figure here, Galipapa identified him as Mattathias, and the identification as Jesus was held by Ephrem ... At this time Jewish authors did reuse such imagery in their descriptions of the intermediary figures characteristic of their apocalyptic works, and it is consistent with John's use of the rest of the OT to suppose that he did the same.[58]

Beside the Christian interpretation of Jesus in the tradition of the Ancient of Days and the one like a son of man, there is the angel Iaoel of the *Apocalypse of Abraham*. In this text Iaoel is described like Jesus was, with characteristics derived from both figures of Daniel 7.[59]

> *Apoc. Abr.* 10.4: The angel [Iaoel] he sent me to me *in the likeness of a man* came... (emphasis mine)

57. Hurtado, *One God, One Lord*, p. 51. Hurtado helpfully surveys the movement towards the glorification of human figures in second-temple Judaism (*One God, One Lord*, pp. 1-69). Casey makes his point when describing the messianic and intermediary figures of second temple Judaism (*From Jewish Prophet to Gentile God: The Origins and Development of New Testament Christology* [Louisville, KY: Westminster/John Knox Press, 1991], p. 78).

58. Casey, *Son of Man*, p. 146. Juel writes that 'John identifies the Ancient of Days with the humanlike figure, thus presupposing the reading *hos* in the Old Greek instead of *heos* in Theodotion's translation' (*Messianic Exegesis*, p. 159).

59. There are points of comparison between Iaoel in the *Apoc. Abr.* 10, 11 and Jesus in Rev. 1. They are not all derived from, but they are part of, a wider exegetical tradition which had Dan. 7 as a pivot (Rowland, *The Open Heaven*, pp. 98-101).

Apoc. Abr. 11.2: The appearance of his body was like sapphire, and the aspect of his face was like chrysolite, and the hair of *his head like snow*... (emphasis mine)

Jesus and Iaoel as the 'Son of Man' and the 'Ancient of Days' illustrates the diversity of opinion over the identity of the ambiguous figures of Dan. 7.9-27.[60] Speculation over the divine status of the 'Son of Man' could be encouraged by the text of Dan. 7.13. A. Feuillet has shown how the accompaniment of clouds at the appearance of the 'one like a son of man' (Dan. 7.13) can be taken to indicate a divine figure since clouds often accompany Old Testament theophanies.[61] Goldingay notes how the 'one like a son of man' comes with or among the clouds, not on them, and adds that clouds came to collect Moses in Josephus (*Ant.* 4.4.48) and Jesus in the New Testament (Acts 1.9).[62] The *Testament of Abraham* adds to the controversy over this text through its near deification of Adam and Abel, both of whom are granted divine characteristics by the author. Even a figure like Adam, known as the fallen head of the human race in Genesis, could be interpreted as the 'Ancient of Days' when the characteristics of this rather ambiguous Danielic figure were interpreted in a broader light.

The title 'Ancient of Days' is enigmatic. Little is known about its background and it is rarely used in later literature, apart from quotations of Daniel 7. Macurdy traced the scene of God on a throne back to 'Greek conceptions' and 'ultimately to such grand Orphic judgment scenes as are found in Plato's *Gorgias* where the sons of Zeus judge souls and in the *Republic*'.[63] In contrast to a Platonic origin, A. Bentzen and J.A. Emerton, have made a case for a Ugaritic heavenly courtroom

---

60. It will be noted later in this chapter how Dan. 7 can be understood to teach the similarity of the 'one like a son of man' with the 'Ancient of Days'. Clues to this idea are given in the Greek versions of Dan. 7 (LXX and Theodotion) and in the text itself (Dan. 7.13 [the 'one like a son of man' comes and is glorified] and Dan. 7.21 [the 'Ancient of Days' comes and glory follows]).

61. A. Feuillet, 'Le fils de l'homme de Daniel et le tradition biblique', *RB* (1953), pp. 170-202 (187-88); also J.A. Emerton, 'The Origin of the Son of Man Imagery', *JTS* 9 (1958), pp. 225-34 (231-32); Colpe, 'ὁ υἱός', p. 420; Kim, *The Origin of Paul's Gospel*, pp. 205-16; *idem, The 'Son of Man' as the Son of God* (WUNT, 30; Tübingen: J.C.B. Mohr, 1983), p. 16.

62. Goldingay, *Daniel*, p. 171.

63. Macurdy depends upon R. Charles's dating of *1 En.* 6-36 to 170 BCE, several years before the writing of Daniel in 168 BCE (*Platonic Orphism*, p. 225).

background which has been built upon by F. Cross and Collins.[64] Several of the Canaanite readings do show close parallels to Dan. 7.9-10.[65] More recently, Rowland, adding to the research of O. Procksch, Feuillet and M. Black, has argued for the influence of Ezek. 1.26-28 and its portrayal of God as a man in Dan. 7.9-13 and its portrayal of the 'one like a son of man'.[66]

'Ancient of Days' (Aramaic: עַתִּיק יוֹמִין), literally 'one aged in days', is used three times in the Hebrew Bible as a divine title with all

64. A. Bentzen's *Daniel* (HAT, 19; Tübingen: J.C.B. Mohr, 1952) presents his groundbreaking insights. Emerton reformulated Bentzen's ideas ('The Origin', pp. 225-34). See F. Cross, *Canaanite Myth and Hebrew Epic: Essays in the History of the Religion of Israel* (Cambridge, MA: Harvard University Press, 1973), pp. 16-17. Collins's chief work on this subject is his book *The Apocalyptic Vision*, esp. pp. 95-118.

65. CTA 2.1.19-21: 'Then the two set their faces toward the mountain of El, toward the gathered council. Indeed the gods were sitting at table... Baal stands by the (enthroned) El...'; CTA 6.1.36: 'Father of Years' (in reference to El); CTA 4.5.66: 'Thou art great O El, verily thou art wise, thy hoary beard indeed instructs you.' Collins translations are being used (*The Apocalyptic Vision*, pp. 100-101). Also see J. Day, 'The Old Testament Utilization of Language and Imagery Having Parallels in the Baal Mythology of the Ugaritic Texts' (PhD Dissertation, Cambridge University, 1977); *God's Conflict with the Dragon and the Sea* (Cambridge: Cambridge University Press, 1985); and M. Korpel, *A Rift in the Clouds: Ugaritic and Hebrew Descriptions of the Divine* (Münster: Ugaritic-Verlag, 1990), pp. 102, 323. The articles by B. Merling Alomia are also helpful for identifying the Near Eastern extrabiblical texts relevant to the setting of Dan. 7 ('Los angeles en el contexto extrabiblico vesterotestamentario: Un estudio exegetico y comparativo', *Theo* 3 [1988], pp. 166-83, *Theo* 4 [1989], pp. 44-99, and *Theo* 4 [1989], pp. 118-205).

66. Rowland, *The Open Heaven*, p. 218. Procksch was the first to argue that the description of the Glory in the Lord in Ezek. 1.26-28 was the derivation of the 'one like a son of man' ('Die Berufungsvision Hesekiels', in *Beiträge zur alttestamentlichen Wissenschaft: Karl Budde zum siebzigsten Geburtstag* [BZAW, 34; Giessen: Lund, 1920], pp. 122-80 (141-48). Feuillet developed Procksch's theory by detailing the connections between Ezek. 1 and Dan. 7 ('Le fils de l'homme', pp. 170-202, 321-46, especially pp. 180-202). M. Black placed Dan. 7.13-14 within the tradition of other biblical throne theophanies and highlighted the ties of Dan. 7 and Ezek. 1 ('The Throne-Theophany Prophetic Commission and the "Son of Man"', in R.G. Hammerton-Kelly and R. Scroggs [eds.], *Jews, Greeks and Christians: Religious Cultures in Late Antiquity* [Festschrift W.D. Davies; trans. J. Smith; SJLA, 21; Leiden: E.J. Brill, 2nd edn, 1976], pp. 56-73). For a complete survey of this subject see the forthcoming article by J. Fossum, 'The Heavenly Man in Recent Research'.

occurrences in Daniel.[67] R. Charles notes that its Hebrew equivalent occurs in Gen. 24.1: 'Abraham was old and well advanced in years' (ואברהם זקן בא בימים).[68] A. Marmorstein, in his monumental work *The Old Rabbinic Doctrine of God*, does not list 'Ancient of Days', but does note 'Ancient of the World' from *Ruth R.* 11.1 as its equivalent.[69] P. Mosca points to several titles in the Bible which he believes are related to this rare title: 'Everlasting Father' (Isa. 9.6), 'everlasting God' (Isa. 40.28), and 'eternal King' (Jer. 10.10).[70] Some middle Jewish books offer similar titles: 'Everlasting' (Bar. 4.10, 14, 20), and 'Antecedent of Time' (*1 En.* 46.1-2; 47.3; 55.1; 60.2; 71.10-14).

A sampling of a few of these occurrences of 'Ancient of Days' and other synonymous titles illustrates how it was usually interpreted as referring to the God of Israel. The Parables of *Enoch* serve as a type of redaction-like interpretation of Dan. 7.9, 13.

> *1 En.* 46.1: At that place, I saw the *One to whom belongs the time before time*.[71] And his head was white like wool, and there was with him another individual, whose face was like that of a human being...

> *1 En.* 47.3: In those days, I saw him—the *Antecedent of Time*,[72] while he was sitting upon the throne of his glory, and the books of the living ones were open before him. And all his power in heaven above and his escorts stood before him.

---

67. Dan. 7.9, 13, 22. Nor does its Greek equivalent (παλαίος ἡμερῶν) appear in the New Testament. H. Seesemann notes this with surprise and observes that outside of the LXX it 'crops up again only in Just. Dial., 31.2-3,5; 32.1; 79.2' ('παλαίος', *TDNT*, V, p. 718). Apart from Ancient of Days, there are other divine names in Dan.: 'God' (אל; 4 times); 'God' (אלה Aramaic; 49 times); 'God' (אלה; 22 times); 'God' (אלו; 4 times); 'Most High' (עלין Aramaic; 4 times), 'most high' (עלי; 9 times).

68. R.H. Charles, *The Book of Daniel* (Edinburgh: T.C. & E.C. Jack, 1913), p. 75.

69. Hebrew: עתיקו שלעולם; A. Marmorstein, *The Old Rabbinic Doctrine of God* (2 vols.; London: KTAV, 1927), I, pp. 94-95.

70. P. Mosca, 'Ugarit and Daniel 7: A Missing Link', *Bib* 67.4 (1986), pp. 496-517 (501).

71. The names for God in these verses (emphasis mine) are the Ethiopic equivalents (*re'sa mawa'el* in 46.1 and *beluya mawa'el* in 47.3) for the Aramaic ימיא עתיק (Lacocque, *Daniel*, p. 143 and Black, *The Book of Enoch*, p. 192). They could also be translated 'Head of days', 'Chief of days', 'the Beginning of days', 'the First of days' and 'he who is of primordial days'. See E. Isaac's note on this title in his translation of *1 Enoch* (*OTP*, I, p. 34).

72. Emphasis mine.

The references in *1 En.* 46.1 and 47.3 to God's 'white like wool' head, a figure who has a human-like face, a throne of glory, open books, and a heavenly entourage make the Parables of *Enoch*'s use of Dan. 7.9-13 unmistakable.[73] The author interprets the 'Ancient of Days' as the Lord of Israel.

A late fourth-century Jewish magical text which describes an ascension to God's throne, *Sepher Ha-Razim* (*The Book of the Mysteries*), does use the title to climatically identify God in the seventh heaven: 'He holds the world as a cluster of grapes, Bearing all that there is, and will be. He is the Ancient of Days.'[74] This usage of 'Ancient of Days' is rare: it is the only Hebrew version of the title apart from a quotation of Daniel 7.

But this was not the only interpretation of the name. A. Lacocque, in his commentary on Daniel, observes how the 'Ancient of Days' was interpreted by the Jewish medieval scholar Jephet as an angel and by his Jewish contemporary Ibn Ezra as the archangel Michael.[75] According to the medieval writer J. Albo, R. Hayyim Galipapa (1310–1380 CE) identified the 'Ancient of Days' as Mattathias Maccabeus, the 'old man', and may imply that Judas Maccabeus is the 'one like a son of man' and the Hasmoneans are the 'holy ones of the Most High'.

> *Sefer Ha-Ikkarim* 4.42: R. Hayim Galipapa also writes in an epistle called, Epistle of Redemption, that all the prophecies of Daniel refer to the second temple only. The words in Daniel: And [he] shall wear out the saints of the Most High; and he shall think to change the seasons and the law; and they shall be given into his hand until a time and times and half a time, all refer to Antiochus. Also the words: But the saints of the Most High shall receive the kingdom, refer he says, to the Hasmoneans. As for the words: And possess the kingdom for ever and ever (*'ad 'alma ve'ad 'alam 'almaya*), he says that *'olam* means one jubilee, a short and definite time during which the Hasmoneans ruled. The words: And one that was Ancient of Days did sit, he refers to Mattathias the high priest,

---

73. Speaking of *1 En.* 46, Hurtado identifies that 'The influence of Dan. 7.9-14 can be seen in the description of God with hair like wool (46.1; cf. Dan. 7.9b) and perhaps most notably in the description of the second figure as "that Son of man" (46.2; cf. Dan. 7.13)' (*One God, One Lord*, p. 149).

74. Translation taken from M. Morgan (ed. and trans.), *Sepher Ha-Razim* (T & T, 25; Chico, CA: Scholars Press, 1983).

75. Lacocque, *Daniel*, p. 136.

who was the head of the Hasmoneans, a very old man, all of whose sons reigned after him.[76]

Galipapa's Maccabean interpretation of Daniel 7 may be one of several ancient trajectories preserved from the period of middle Judaism.[77]

Lacocque writes: 'The powerful Sethian sect identified the "son of man" with Seth "the son of Adam" on the basis of Gen. 4.25-26; 5.3ff.'[78] Seth is called the 'son of man' in *Ap. John* 1.24-25: 'And when Adam had known the image of his own prior acquaintance, he begot the likeness of the son of man, and called him Seth.'[79] If Seth could be seen as the 'son of man', the identification of Adam with the 'Ancient of Days' who empowers the 'one like a son of man' is not unthinkable.[80] Both Seth and Abel are sons of Adam. Since Adam's son was seen as the 'son of man', the next step of interpreting the Ancient of Days, appearing with the son of man in Daniel 7, as Adam, is not a big one.

The sixth-century Jewish text, *Gedullat Mosheh*, is another variation on Daniel 7.

> *Ged. Mos.* 5: I saw further the fiery river *Rigyon*, which comes out before God, from under the throne of glory, and is formed from the perspiration of the holy Creatures who support the throne of glory; and out of dread of God's majesty perspire fire. This river is meant by the saying 'a fiery stream issued and came forth before him; thousand thousands ministered before him, and ten thousand times ten thousand stood before

76. References from Galipapa are taken from I. Husik (ed. and trans.), *Joseph Albo: Sepher ha-Ikkarim: Book of Principles* (4 vols.; Philadelphia: Jewish Publication Society of America, 1929).

77. Porphyry, the Neoplatonist critic of Christianity who was understood by Jerome as holding to Jewish traditions, was associated by Jerome with the view that Judas Maccabeus was the 'one like a son of man'. See Jerome's comments on Dan. 7.14 (G. Archer [trans.], *Jerome's Commentary on Daniel* [Grand Rapids: Baker Book House, 1958]). Aphrahat, the fourth-century leader of the Syrian church, attacked what was probably a Jewish view that the 'holy ones of the Most High' were Maccabean Jews. He rejected that view in favor of triumphant Christians (*Dem.* 5.20-21).

78. Lacocque, *Daniel*, p. 147.

79. All *Nag Hammadi* translations are mine.

80. This possibility was raised earlier in this chapter in connection with the choice of Abel as the 'son of man' and Adam as the 'man' or 'Ancient of Days'. See Pétrement, *A Separate God*, pp. 400-401. Adam, according to the *Apoc. Adam* 8.16-17, 'empowered' Seth by giving him the 'secret knowledge' which is 'the holy baptism of those who know the eternal knowledge through the ones born of the word and the imperishable illuminators'.

him; the judgment was set and the books were opened' (Dan. vii. 10). The Almighty sits and judges the ministering angels, and after the judgment they bathe [sic] in that river of fire...[81]

This text, with decidedly apocalyptic and mystical interests, quotes Dan. 7.10 and interprets it as part of a judgment scene. The author appears to have identified the Ancient of Days, who is not mentioned by name in the passage, with God, who is called 'Almighty' and sits enthroned judging the angels. The reading is quite similar to the fifth-century text, *3 En.* 35.3-5, and may be a development of that portion. *Gedullat Mosheh* goes on to detail the judgment scene it has based upon Daniel 7. In its description of God judging the angels, the text identifies an assistant who is enthroned and judges *with* God. After referring to Michael, Gabriel and Iefefiyah as angels who stand around God's throne, the angel Metatron's position is given: 'he sits and judges all the heavenly hosts before his master. And God pronounces judgment and he [Metatron?] executes it.' Given the setting of Daniel 7 around which this scene is developed, Metatron appears to be an interpretation of the 'one like a son of man'. The two thrones of God and Metatron match the 'thrones' of Dan. 7.9. Like his counterpart in Daniel 7, Metatron has been granted a special status in heaven as God's agent.

The differing interpretations of the figures of Daniel 7 can be more clearly understood by placing them side by side. The judgment scene figures of Daniel, the 'Ancient of Days' and 'the one like a son of man' were interpreted in different ways by Mark, the Parables of *Enoch*, the *Apocryphon of John*, the *Testament of Abraham* and *Gedullat Mosheh*.

Interpretations of the 'Ancient of Days' and the 'one like a son of man'

Daniel	Mark	1 Enoch	Gedullat Mosheh	Ap. John	T. Abr.
Ancient of Days	God	God	God	Adam	Adam
(7.9)	(14.62)	(47.3)	(5)	(1.24-25)	(11.4)
son of man	Jesus	Enoch	Metatron	Seth	Abel
(7.13)	(14.62)	(71.14)	(8)	(1.24-25)	(13.2)

81. All translations of *Gedullat Mosheh* are taken from Gaster (ed. and trans.), *Studies and Texts: In Folklore.*

The point in adding the Parables of *Enoch* is that Enoch, like Seth
and Abel, is a son of Adam. The Ancient of Days is referred to as God
in the Parables of *Enoch*, but the evidence is helpful in that it shows
how the 'son of man' could be taken to be a patriarch, even a 'son' of
Adam. This is also the case in the *Apocryphon of John* where Seth is
taken as the 'son of man'. In the *Testament of Abraham* the interpretation of Daniel 7 matches the kind of speculation seen in the Parables of
Enoch and the *Apocryphon of John*. That Abel looks like a 'son of
man' can hardly be doubted in view of the Parables of *Enoch* and the
Apocryphon of John. That Adam looks like the 'Ancient of Days'
seems reasonable in view of the Parables of *Enoch* and the *Apocryphon
of John*.

Even the late *Gedullat Mosheh*, with its account of God and Metatron
as judges, has much in common with these ancient interpretations since
its candidate for the 'son of man' figure, the angel Metatron, was formerly the patriarch Enoch (*3 En.* 4.1-5). The *Gedullat Mosheh* shows
an interpretation of Daniel 7 which is similar to that of the *Testament of
Abraham*. The Jesus traditions, as represented by Mark, are thus
unusual in their interpretation of Jesus as the son of man, in as far as
Jesus, in contrast to Abel, Seth, and Enoch-Metatron, was not a patriarch.[82] But like those other 'son of man' candidates, Jesus began as a
man.

Black points out how the title 'Ancient of Days' is rendered in both
the LXX and Theodotion by the literal equivalent παλαίος ἡμερῶν (old
of days). He goes on to say that this is not the only possible rendering.
The expression appears fairly often in Syriac literature, meaning simply
'old man', as in Wis. 2.10 (πρεσβύτης).[83] Already Charles observed
that the plain meaning of 'Ancient of Days' simply denotes *'an old
man'*[84] and added

> Hence it is an extraordinary expression to apply to God, and accordingly
> if we take into account the fact that throughout this and all other Jewish
> apocalypses every reference to our description of God is couched in
> terms of the most utmost reverence, we must find it difficult to accept the
> phrase as original in its present form. If this is so it is not improbable

---

82. Other interpretations of Dan. 7 which offer differing interpretations would
be *Ezekiel the Tragedian*, where Moses is a 'son of man' figure, and 1QM 17.6-8,
where Michael is the 'son of man' figure.
83. Black, *The Book of Enoch*, p. 192.
84. Emphasis his.

that instead of 'one aged in days' the text originally read 'one like an aged being or man'.[85]

Despite Charles's reluctance to accept 'Ancient of Days' as the original reading because of its apparent irreverence in identifying God as an old man, this is exactly how the midrashim understand the phrase. Both the *Mekilta deRabbi Simeon ben Yohai* and the *Mekilta deRabbi Ishmael* along with *Pesiqta Rabbati*, use the word 'old man' (Hebrew: זקן) to explicitly describe the Ancient of Days in Dan. 7.9.[86] Probably the reason why the medieval writer R. Galipapa identified Mattathias, the 'old man' (זקן), as the Ancient of Days had something to do with the basic meaning of the title 'Ancient of Days'.[87]

There is even evidence that the highest angel could share a divine name which was associated with the title the 'Ancient of Days'. A figure called the 'Prince of the world', who appears to be related to the traditions of Metatron and Michael, is called 'old man' (זקן) on the basis of Ps. 37.25: 'I have been young, and now am old' (*b. Yeb.* 16b).[88]

In fact, according to Hippolytus, Abraham was indirectly identified with the title 'Ancient of the Days' (παλαιὸς τῶν ἡμερῶν), a slight alteration of the LXX/Theodotion translation (παλαιὸς ἡμερῶν), by the Valentinians. This came about when they identified the demiurge with the 'Ancient of the Days' and then stated that Abraham is the demiurge (*Ref.* 4.32; 34.4).[89] This is important for arguing that the *Testament of Abraham* interprets Adam as the Ancient of Days. It illustrates how in a second-century CE religious system, based on the same scriptures, the Ancient of Days is not the highest God but a patriarch. To the Valentinians, he is Abraham. To others, he is obviously Adam.

The Jerusalem *Talmud* relates the strange story of Simon the Righteous, the High Priest, who was apparently accustomed to see an old man dressed in white when he entered the Holy of Holies on the Day of Atonement.

> *y. Yom.* 5.2: For forty years Simeon the Righteous served as high priest. In the final year, he said to them, This year I am going to die. They said

85. Charles, *The Book of Daniel*, pp. 75-76.

86. See *Mek. SbY*. Bashalah 15; *Mek*. Bahodesh 5, Shirta 4; *Pes. R.* Piska 21.100b.

87. Husik (ed. and trans.), *Joseph Albo*, IV, p. 418.

88. Segal, *Two Powers in Heaven*, p. 67 n. 24.

89. The Greek text is taken from M. Marcovich (ed.), *Hippolytus: Refutatio Omnium Haeresium* (PTS, 25; New York: Walter de Gruyter, 1986).

to him, How do you know? He said to them, Every year I entered the
house of the Holy of the Holies an old man dressed in white and cloaked
in white went in with me and came out with me. This year he went in
with me and he did not come out with me... He [R. Abbahu] said to
them, What tells me that it was a mortal man? I maintain that it was the
Holy One, blessed be he.[90]

This Talmudic account concludes with a discussion over whether this
figure, whose appearance alludes to the Ancient of Days, is God or
simply a human being. R. Abbahu argues for a divine interpretation of
the 'old man', but as the passage reveals, the features associated with
the 'Ancient of Days' (human appearance, age, white dress) could be
taken to refer to someone other than God.

Another Talmudic text describes an encounter in the Holy of Holies
which is very similar to Simon's in *y. Yom.* 5.2. In *b. Ber.* 7a, R. Ishmael b. Elisha enters the innermost part of the temple and sees an
enthroned figure who is explicitly identified as the Lord.

> *b. Ber.* 7a: It was taught: R. Ishmael b. Elisha says: I once entered into
> the innermost part [of the Sanctuary] to offer incense and saw Akathriel
> Jah [Yah] [crown of God], the Lord of Hosts, seated upon a high and
> exalted throne. He said to me: Ishmael, My son, bless me! [91]

G. Scholem remarks that whether the name 'Akathriel Jah [Yah]'
represents an angel or the name of God cannot be determined on the
basis of this passage alone.[92] Other passages illustrate how the name
was used both of God and of an angel. In *3 Enoch* God speaks to
Metatron under the guise of 'Akathriel Jah [Yah] Yahweh': 'Then
'Aktari'el Yah YHWH of Hosts answered and said to Metatron'
(15b.4). In a mystical text called the *Mystery of Sandalphon*, Scholem
illustrates how the name was used of an angel who sat at the entrance to
paradise: 'When I [Elisha ben Abuya] ascended unto Paradise, I beheld
Akatriel YHWH, the Lord of Hosts, who is sitting at the entrance of

90. Rowland, *The Open Heaven*, p. 466 n. 60. The translation is taken from
J. Neusner (ed.), *The Talmud of the Law of Israel* (35 vols.; Chicago: University of
Chicago Press, 1990).

91. Translation taken from Epstein (ed.), *The Babylonian Talmud*. The description of God given in *b. Ber.* 7a is also similar to the glory of the Lord who sits
enthroned upon the cherub (Ezek. 9.3; 10.1, 4).

92. G. Scholem, *Jewish Gnosticism, Merkabah Mysticism, and Talmudic Tradition* (New York: Jewish Theological Seminary of America, 2nd edn, 1965).

Paradise, and 120 myriads of ministering angels surround him.'[93] C. Morray-Jones notes this sharing of a divine name and Elisha's description of Akatriel's position at the gate of Paradise after his (Elisha's) ascent to heaven as quite similar to Adam's role in the *Testament of Abraham*.[94]

Strousma is convinced that ancient Jewish conceptions of God as an 'old man' and a 'young man' influenced Christian conceptions of Jesus and says, 'The Christian and Gnostic speculation on the dual forms (young man and old man) of Christ take their source in the Jewish esoteric traditions dealing with the figure of the "lover" in Canticles 5 and the "Ancient of Days" in Daniel 7.'[95] A. Green presents a convincing case for this less well-known Jewish tradition that God has the form of a young man *and* an old man.[96] He refers to the following haggada to make his case.

> *Pes. R.* 21.6: Face to face the Lord spoke to you (Deut. 5.4). Rabbi Levi said: In many images He appeared to them. To one He appeared standing; to another, seated. To one as an old man; to another as a youth. How is this? When God was revealed at the Sea of Reeds to do battle for His children and to demand of the Egyptians their due, He appeared as a youth, for battle is appropriate only to the young. But when God revealed Himself at Sinai to give Torah to Israel, He appeared as an elder. Why? For it is written: Wisdom is with the aged, and length of days is understanding (Job 12.12). Thus Daniel says: I kept looking until the thrones were set in place and the Ancient of Days took his seat (Dan. 7.9).[97]

---

93. Translation taken from Scholem, *Jewish Gnosticism*, p. 53. Akatriel is also described as an angel like Michael, Gabriel and Metatron (Scholem, *Jewish Gnosticism*, p. 53).

94. C. Morray-Jones, 'Transformational Mysticism in the Apocalytpic-Merkabah Traditon', *JJS* 43 (1992), pp. 1-31.

95. G. Strousma, 'Polymorphie divine et transformations d'un mythologène l'Apocryphon de Jean et ses sources', *VC* 35 (1981), pp. 426-27. That Jesus takes on the likeness 'of a servant' can also be traced back to Jewish sources. Scholem shows how 'youth' (נער) can be translated 'servant' and proves that it was used in this capacity of the principal angel Metatron (*Jewish Gnosticism*, p. 50). See also J. Fossum, 'The Magharians: A Pre-Christian Jewish Sect and Its Significance for the Study of Gnosticism and Christianity', *Hen* 9 (1987), pp. 303-44 (342 n. 136).

96. A. Green, 'The Children in Egypt and the Theophany at the Sea', *Jud* 24 (1975), pp. 446-56.

97. Quoted from Green, 'The Children in Egypt', p. 455.

In a second-century CE Christian text preserved by Tertullian, *The Martyrdom of Perpetua and Felicitas*, Saturus relates his vision of heaven prior to his martyrdom. In it an enthroned man has the appearance of great age, yet has a youthful face. Its recasting of Dan. 7.9 is plain.

> *Mart. Perp.* 4.2: And in the midst of that place we saw as it were a hoary man sitting, having snow-white hair, and with a youthful countenance: and on his right hand and on his left were four and twenty elders, and behind them a great many others were standing. We entered with great wonder, and stood before the throne...[98]

Mart. Perp. 4.2 blends the images of the Ancient of Days (enthronement and 'snow-white hair') and the son of man ('youthful countenance') from Daniel 7, when depicting an enthroned man. The influence of the LXX, with its description of one like a son of man coming 'as' (ὡς) the Ancient of Days, may explain the transference of both characteristics to one figure: 'as' implies that the youthful figure (the 'one like a son of man') took on the appearance of the old figure (the 'Ancient of Days'). The chapter summary found in R. Wallis's translation of *The Martyrdom of Perpetua and Felicitas* identifies the enthroned figure as God.[99] However, given the Christian setting of the account and the figure's similarity to the portrayal of the exalted Jesus in Rev. 1.13-14, where he is both 'one like a Son of Man' and has hair 'white as white wool', it may be more accurate to see in *Mart. Perp.* 4.2 a description of Jesus in his glorified state.[100] Yet, *Mart. Perp.* 4.2 depicts the figure as 'sitting', in keeping with Dan. 7.9 and different

98. Translation taken from Roberts and Donaldson (eds.), *The Ante-Nicene Fathers*.

99. Roberts and Donaldson (eds.), *The Anti-Nicene Fathers*, III, p. 702.

100. Another relevant passage is Mk 9.2-13. In the transfiguration of Jesus there are several elements which may imply a dependence on Dan. 7 and a transference of the attributes of the Ancient of Days and the son of man to Jesus: Jesus' clothes 'became dazzling white' (Dan. 7.9), a cloud overshadows Jesus and those with him (Dan. 7.13), Jesus is called the 'Son' and the 'Son of Man' (Dan. 7.13), and the Father is implicitly identified by the voice from the cloud (Dan. 7.9). See Fossum's 'Partes posteriores dei: The "Transformation" of Jesus in the *Acts of John*', in *The Image of the Invisible God: Essays on the Influence of Jewish Mysticism on Early Christology* (NTOA, 30; Freiburg: Universitätsverlag; Göttingen: Vandenhoeck & Ruprecht, 1995), pp. 95-108, which deals with the topic of Jesus' transfiguration and its motif of ascent to heaven and transformation into the form of the glory of the Lord.

from Rev. 1.13-14 where Jesus is standing. Daniel 7 appears to be the basis for this text.[101]

This conclusion is borne out by *Mart. Perp.* 1.3 where the man ('white-haired') in the midst of a garden has the dress of a *shepherd* and is of a *large stature*. These characteristics make an identification with Christ certain. This figure also has some similarity to the description of Abel and Enoch in recension B of the *Testament of Abraham*. In *T. Abr.* 11.2 Abel is in παράδεισος (Greek), 'paradise', which is used in the LXX for גן (Hebrew), 'garden'. In 10.8, Abel's assistant, Enoch, is described as being of enormous stature.

The Nag Hammadi text, the *Apocryphon of John*, describes John's encounter with the resurrected Christ in which he appears as a youth, an old man, and a servant:

> *Ap. John* 1.31–2.5: Immediately, while I was thinking about these things, behold, the heavens opened and the whole creation which is below heaven shone, and the world was shaken. I was afraid, and behold I saw in the light a youth who stood by me. While I looked at him he became like an old man. And he changed his likeness again becoming like a servant.

Christ's appearance as a youth and an old man, found in both *The Martyrdom of Perpetua and Felicitas*, the Revelation of John and the *Apocryphon of John*, appears to be borrowed from the Jewish tradition of God appearing as both a youth and an old man. In all three texts the authors were applying divine attributes to Jesus.

Of particular significance for the issue of Daniel's use in the *Testament of Abraham* is the use of Daniel 7 in the rabbinic texts discussing the appearance of God as an 'old man' and a 'young man'. In all the significant passages found in the *Mekiltas* and *Pesiqta Rabbati* which deal with this topic, Dan. 7.9 and its surrounding context is referred to and is important to the debate.[102] Its figures were of obvious interest and concern to Jewish interpreters.

Green argues that the popularity of Jesus as the 'youthful' God of Christianity prompted rabbinic Judaism to give up the image of a youthful manifestation of the deity. It is also true that Enoch came to be known as the 'youth' (נער; *3 En.* 2.2) and after his transformation into

---

101. Rowland notes the similarity of *Mart. Perp.* 4.2 to Rev. 1.14 and Dan. 7.9. He goes on to say that it owes much to the Jewish apocalyptic tradition (*The Open Heaven*, pp. 398-99).

102. *Mek. SbY.* Bashalah 15; *Mek.* Bahodesh 5, Shirta 4: *Pes. R.* Piska 21.100b.

the exalted angel Metatron was enthroned and called the 'lesser Yahweh' (*3 En.* 12.5), thus sharing in the attributes of God. M. Hengel puts forth the hypothesis that because of rabbinic Judaism's conflict with Christianity and Christianity's understanding of Jesus as the 'son of man', the title 'youth' was used for Enoch-Metatron instead of 'son of man'.[103] These developments concerning Jesus and Enoch-Metatron leave open the possibility that another biblical figure, like Adam, could share a traditional characteristic of God.[104]

There are other texts, besides *The Martyrdom of Perpetua and Felicitas* and the *Apocryphon of John*, which show a dependence on Dan. 7.9 by describing an aged figure on a throne, but go on to identify the enthroned being as someone other than God. In the second-century CE Nag Hammadi text, the *Apocalypse of Paul*, Paul meets an unnamed old man who threatens to block his ascension beyond the seventh heaven.

> *Apoc. Paul* 22: Then we went up to the seventh heaven and I saw an old man...light and whose garment was white, His throne, which is in the seventh heaven, was seven times brighter than the sun.[105]

G. MacRae correctly argued that the judgment scene of the Coptic *Apocalypse of Paul*, with its references to the judgment of a single soul, to angels who drive the souls, and to the book used in judgment 'offers an interesting parallel to that in the *Testament of Abraham*, more specifically the Coptic version of the shorter recension'.[106] MacRae also suggests that the 'old man' (Coptic: *zllo rome*) on the throne in the seventh heaven has been drawn from two apocalyptic texts: Dan. 7.13 and *1 En.* 46–47.[107] His citing of Dan. 7.13 must be a mistake since the

---

103. Taken from Hengel's book, *The Son of God*, found in *The Cross and the Son of God* (London: SCM, 1986), p. 44.

104. And if Adam is identified as the aged figure by the author of the *Testament of Abraham*, who else would fit as the 'one like a son of man' other than Adam's son Abel?

105. The motif of a old man in heaven who is not identified with God can also be found in the fifth-century CE *Apocalypse of Paul* (20.1) and the second-century CE *Acts of Pilate* (25.2-3).

106. G. MacRae, 'The Judgment Scene in the Coptic Apocalypse of Paul', in Nickelsburg (ed.), *Studies in the Testament of Abraham*, pp. 285-88.

107. See his comments in the preface to his translation of the text in J. Robinson (ed.), *The Nag Hammadi Library* (San Francisco: Harper & Row, rev. edn, 1988), p. 257.

obvious reference is to the 'Ancient of Days' in Dan. 7.9.[108] *1 En.* 46–47 should also be ruled out because there are no references to the *apparent* age of the enthroned figure in *1 Enoch*. MacRae is not specific about the parallels, but the age of the figure, his white garment, his throne, and the later reference to the 'principalities and authorities' (23; Dan. 7.10) around the 'old man' make an allusion to the 'Ancient of Days' in Dan. 7.9 certain.

This blending in the *Apocalypse of Paul* of Daniel 7 with a judgment scene which is dependent upon the *Testament of Abraham* bodes well for recognizing the use of Daniel 7 in the *Testament of Abraham*. The *Testament of Abraham* understood the 'Ancient of Days' to be Adam; the *Apocalypse of Paul*, due to gnostic influence, interpreted the God of Israel as a hostile figure and not the highest God.

In the Hermetic writings[109] G. Widengren has identified a series of texts dealing with a 'literary *topos* of a highly fixed form' which narrate a heavenly ascension with the recurring image of an old man on a throne.[110] In an Arabic work, *Tabula Smaragdina*, Balinas (Apollonios of Tyana) descends into a dark chamber where he meets with just such a figure who gives him a tablet which preserves an ancient revelation.

> *Tabula Smaragdina*: When I entered the chamber over which the talisman was set, I came upon an old man sitting on a throne of gold, a tablet of emerald being in his hand. And behold, on it was written in the primordial language...[111]

108. Perhaps MacRae drew a parallel between Paul approaching the 'old man' and the 'one like a son of man' approaching the 'Ancient of Days'.

109. The Hermetic writings can be found in several languages and get their name by being associated with Hermes Trismegistos ('thrice-greatest', an epithet borrowed from the Egyptian god Thot, with whom the Greek god Hermes was identified), the Greco-Egyptian deity, though some are attributed to his alleged disciples. They represent a mixture of Platonic, Stoic, Neo-Pythagorean and Jewish ideas, and are usually dated between the first and fifth centuries CE, though the traditions they preserve may be much earlier. They are often called by the name *Corpus Hermeticum*, which specifically represents a collection of 17 documents, written in Greek. There are no explicit references to Christianity in the *Corpus Hermeticum*, but there may be some allusive statements indicating an acquaintance with Christianity. For a fuller description see J. Trumbower's article 'Hermes Trismegistos' and the attached bibliography (*ABD*, III, pp. 156-57).

110. G. Widengren, *The Ascension of the Apostle and the Heavenly Book* (UUÅ, 7; Uppsala: A.-B. Lundequistska Bokhandeln, 1950), pp. 77, 78-85.

111. All translations of the originally Arabic texts are quoted from Widengren,

The motif of a descent in the Hermetic literature is traced by Widengren to Egyptian conditions and conceptions, for it is only there that the idea of a descent into an underground edifice in order to acquire understanding is found.[112] This Hermetic text is not necessarily directly dependent on Daniel 7, but there does appear to be a literary topos undergoing modifications.

In another Hermetic work, the *Book of Apollonios, the Sage, on the Causes*, a nearly duplicate account of the *Tabula Smaragdina* appears. Here Apollonios tells how he came across a book containing all the mysteries of nature.

> *Book of Apollonios*: Then I entered the chamber, and behold, I met with an old man sitting on a throne of gold, a tablet of gold, a tablet of green emerald being in his hand: It was written on this tablet...This is the description of nature...

In the so-called *Krates-Book*, the initiate, Krates, does not descend into a chamber, but is elevated to heaven and has an experience of the same kind as Apollonios. In this text the old man is finally identified, not as God, but as Hermes Trismegistos—the composite being, who was originally thought of as a man and the recorder of divine revelation, but came to be seen as a god, enthroned in heaven with a holy book.[113]

> *Krates-Book*: And behold, an old man, the most beautiful of men, sitting on a throne-stool and wearing white garments, in his hand a shining tablet, containing a writing...And I inquired about the old man, and it was said to me: this is Hermes Trismegistos.

The Ascension of the Apostle.

112. Widengren, *The Ascension of the Apostle*, p. 80. There are Greek oracles in caves and underground chambers, but there is no white-haired man upon a throne as in this text. The similarity to the idea of a 'descent' to the chariot in order to gain a vision of God in the Hekhalot literature is striking. P. Schafer identifies what he believes to be unsatisfactory explanations for this Hekhalot description (terminological explanations for the reversal of *yarad* and *'alah*; analogies with 'descending' to the Torah shrine; parallels with the descent of the Israelites to the Red Sea), but says nothing about the possibility of Egyptian influence (*The Hidden and Manifest God: Some Major Themes in Early Jewish Mysticism* [Albany: State University of New York Press, 1992], pp. 2-3 n. 4).

113. Widengren details the transmutation of the character of Hermes in Syrian thought where he was probably conceived of as a god, enthroned in heaven (*The Ascension of the Apostle*, pp. 81-84).

As pointed out by Widengren, the similarities of the enthroned figure to the Ancient of Days are most obvious and this implies that this literary *topos* has its source in Dan. 7.9.[114] One would expect the enthroned figure to be none other than God himself, but Egyptian-Hellenistic speculation replaces God with Hermes.[115] And like Adam, who in the *Testament of Abraham* has an unusual appearance (like the 'master's' [God]), a 'golden throne' and a 'world' gazing knowledge (*T. Abr.* 11.4, 9), Hermes Trismegistos is unique in his appearance (being 'the most beautiful of men' [*Krates-Book*]), is seated on a 'throne of gold' (*Tabula Smaragdina; Book of Apollonios*), and possesses a 'tablet' of great knowledge (*Tabula Smaragdina; Book of Apollonios; Krates-Book*). Lastly, it must be remembered that Hermes, like Adam, was originally a man, but now sits enthroned like a god in heaven. These parallel motifs are significant and suggest that the author of the *Testament of Abraham* and the Hermetic tradition had similar exegetical insights in their interpretations of Daniel 7.[116] Perhaps their similarity can be related to their common Egyptian provenance.

The Ancient of Days and the Most High

There is a textual element suggesting a connection between the Ancient of Days and Adam which involves the other name of God in Daniel 7. In the vision and interpretation of Daniel 7, God is unmistakably

114. Widengren's view carries weight in that Jewish texts like Daniel were known in Egypt and there are no other prominent texts where an enthroned, aged, white-clad figure are presented.

115. Widengren, *The Ascension of the Apostle*, p. 81.

116. The *Shepherd of Hermas* has an aged enthroned figure who is identified as a woman, yet there may be parallels to Dan. 7.9: 'While I was advising and discussing these matters in my heart, I saw before me a great white chair of snow white wool; and there came an aged lady in glistening raiment, having a book in her hands, and she sat down alone, and she saluted me...' (Hermas, *Vis.* 1.2). In Hermas the female figure represents the church and her age is interpreted as representing both the church's creation 'before all things' and the narrator's (Hermas) poor spiritual condition (Hermas, *Vis.* 2.4; 3.11). However, the motifs of a sitting on a throne (chair), an aged figure, dazzling garb, wool-like whiteness and a book within the setting of a vision make Hermas's use of Dan. 7.9-10 possible. There is strong doubt, though, over Hermas's dependence on the Ancient of Days figure. E. Peterson argues that the Sibyl and the revealer in Hermetic literature may be a better source for the vision (*Frühkirche, Judentum und Gnosis* [Freiburg: Herder, 1959], pp. 254-56).

identified by the title 'Most High' (Aramaic: עלי; Greek: ὕψιστος) in v.
25. All biblical occurrences of this Aramaic term are in Daniel and it
always functions as a divine title.[117] In fact, it is the only *familiar* divine
title used in Daniel 7.

In the interpretation of the vision given to Daniel by 'one of those
standing there' (7.16), the titles 'Ancient of Days' and 'Most High'
appear.

> Dan. 7.21-22: As I looked, this horn made war with the holy ones and
> was prevailing over them, until the Ancient of Days came; then judg-
> ment was given for the holy ones of the Most High, and the time arrived
> when the holy ones gained possession of the kingdom.

> Dan. 7.25: He [the last adversary] shall speak words against the Most
> High, and shall wear out the holy ones of the Most High, and shall
> attempt to change the sacred seasons and the law.

An interpreter could realistically treat 'Ancient of Days' and 'Most
High' as two different persons. This is a possibility since 'Most High'
has been established earlier in Daniel as a divine title and the unique
'Ancient of Days' only appears in Daniel 7. By interpreting the
'Ancient of Days' as Adam, the author of the *Testament of Abraham*
may be revealing his own familiarity with the 'two or more powers' in
heaven controversy.[118]

These textual elements give support for an 'Adam' interpretation.
Adam has been shown to have been a genuine interpretive possibility
given first-century Jewish traditions when the *Testament of Abraham*
was written.

Conclusion

The observation of O. Cope that Matthew uses the scriptures as a
'source' by modeling a passage on a familiar biblical text, with the text

---

117. Dan. 3.26; 4.2, 17, 24, 25, 32, 34; 5.18, 21; 7.25. עלין (Dan. 7.18, 22, 25,
27), a plural adjective, is being distinguished from עלי, a singular adjective.
According to Lacocque, עלין modifies 'saints' and should be translated 'the most
haughty saints'(*Daniel*, pp. 122-23).

118. This is the kind of dilemma faced by the Jewish opponent of Justin in *Dial.*
56: 'Then the fourth of those who had remained with Trypho said, "It must therefore necessarily be said that one of the two angels who went to Sodom, and is
named by Moses in the Scripture Lord, is different from Him who also is God and
appeared to Abraham".' Translation taken from Roberts and Donaldson (eds.), *The
Ante-Nicene Fathers*.

providing the logical framework for the Matthean passage,[119] can also be said of the *Testament of Abraham. T. Abr.* 11.1–13.7 offers clear allusions to Dan. 7.9-27 which illustrate how one judgment scene was used as the pattern for another, more explicit, judgment scene. Parallels in vocabulary, themes and structure can be established. More precisely, *T. Abr.* 11.1–13.6 can be identified as a haggadic midrash in which the biblical text being adapted, Dan. 7.9-27, is taken as authoritative and used as the springboard for a 'new revelation' about the judgment of the dead.[120] Beale's designation of 'apocalyptic midrash' would also fit, since the *Testament of Abraham* has used Daniel 7 in the same manner as the Parables of *Enoch*—in a creative apocalyptic description of the judgment.[121] The figures of the Daniel text have been dealt with in the order of their appearance and have been interpreted to represent Adam, Abel, Israel and the God of Israel.

119. O. Cope, *Matthew: A Scribe Trained for the Kingdom* (CBQMS, 5; Washington: Catholic Biblical Association, 1976), pp. 11-12.

120. P. Miller observes, 'The minimum requirement for the usage of this term [midrash] as a substantive will be the presence of a literary unit to which the biblical citations or allusions clearly belong as formative elements at some stage in the development of that literary unit' ('Targum, Midrash and the Use of the Old Testament in the New Testament', *JSJ* 2 [1971], pp. 29-82 [44]). A. Wright adds that the allusions to a biblical text must be obvious and the biblical context needs to be preserved if the work is to be considered as an example of the literary genre of midrash (*The Literary Genre Midrash* [Staten Island: Alba, 1967], p. 130). Neusner has written extensively on the Midrashim, with special attention being given to the development and character of the Midrashim in the Talmud (*Midrash in Context: Exegesis in Formative Judaism* [Philadelphia: Fortress Press, 1983]). His description of talmudic midrash is fourfold: close exegesis, amplification, illustration, and anthological collection (*Midrash in Context*, pp. 82-83). While the use of Daniel in the *Testament of Abraham* is similar to what Neusner would call the amplication of the meaning of Scripture, allowance should be made for the presence of midrash in apocalyptic literatures like *1 Enoch* and the *Testament of Abraham* which predate the Talmud.

121. Beale uses this phrase when describing the use of Dan. 7 in *1 En.* 90.9-27 (*The Use of Daniel*, p. 86).

Chapter 4

ADAM AND ABEL AS EXALTED FIGURES IN THE *TESTAMENT OF ABRAHAM* AND MIDDLE JUDAISM

The *Testament of Abraham* is related to the Adam literature because of its shared interest in Adam and Abel as exalted figures. These texts illustrate a growing tendency to restore and glorify these patriarchs, with special interest being given to Adam. However, there are also other texts which prove that the status granted to a figure like Adam could be held by others. This chapter will deal with those documents of Middle Judaism which throw light on the position given to Adam and Abel in the *Testament of Abraham*. Adam and Abel will be examined with regard to the motifs associated with them in *T. Abr.* 11.1–13.7, along with other figures who have been exalted in a similar fashion.

Adam

Adam as the 'Ancient of Days' is the most unusual parallel proposed between the *Testament of Abraham* and Daniel. Initially it seems strange to argue that a Jewish author would interpret the 'Ancient of Days' as Adam, who is known in Genesis as the fallen head of the human race. Yet there are persistent Jewish speculations which view Adam as a glorified divine agent. The first-century CE work *2 Enoch* bears witness to this interest in Adam's glorification by describing his original position at creation in dazzling terms.

> *2 En.* 30.11-12: And on the earth I assigned him to be a second angel, honored and great and glorious. And I assigned him to be a king, to reign on the earth, and to have my wisdom. And there was nothing comparable to him on the earth, even among my creatures that exist.[1]

It is clear from *2 Enoch* that Adam's stature was epic in nature. His

---

1. All translations from the Pseudepigrapha are taken from the *OTP*.

position on a throne of glory in the *Testament of Abraham* is compatible with the enthroned 'Ancient of Days' in Dan. 7.9. M. Stone, in his survey of the Adam literature, states the following about the growing interest in Adam in Second Temple Judaism:

> It is a striking fact which we shall not address here that, apart from the beginning of Genesis, Adam and Eve play almost no role in the scriptures of the Hebrew Bible, and certainly the legendary aspects of their doings are not developed in any way in its writings. From the period of the Second Temple on, however, the figures of Adam and Eve, the protoplasts, have always fascinated the nations and cultures whose primordial history is that of Genesis.[2]

The study of Adam has grown in sophistication over the past two centuries.[3] In the eighteenth century, J. Fabricius produced the first significant collection of Adam traditions in his collection of Old Testament Pseudepigrapha, *Codex Pseudepigraphus Veteris Testamenti*.[4] A. Dillman and E. Renan, with their studies of the Adam literature in

---

2. M. Stone, *A History of the Literature of Adam and Eve* (SBLEJL, 3; Atlanta: Scholars Press, 1992), p. 1. For similar comments see W.D. Davies, *Paul and Rabbinic Judaism* (Philadelphia: Fortress Press, 4th edn, 1980), pp. 94-95; J. Danielou, *The Theology of Jewish Christianity* (London: Darton, Longman & Todd, 1964), p. 309; R. Scroggs, *The Last Adam* (Philadelphia: Fortress Press, 1966), p. 16; Segal, *Two Powers in Heaven*, p. 189; and Hurtado, *One God, One Lord*, pp. 51-69.

3. The best bibliographic guides to the Adam materials can be found in J. Dunn, *Romans 1–8* (WBC, 38a; Dallas: Word Books, 1988), pp. 269-70; J.R. Levison, *Portraits of Adam in Early Judaism: From Sirach to 2nd Baruch* (JSPSup, 1; Sheffield: JSOT Press, 1988), pp. 233-40; and Stone, *A History of the Literature of Adam and Eve*, pp. 127-53. For rabbinic views see Ginzberg (ed.), *The Legends of the Jews*; A. Altmann, 'The Gnostic Background of the Rabbinic Adam Legends', *JQR* 35 (1944–45), pp. 371-91; U. Bianchi, 'Gnostizismus und Anthropologie', *Kairos* 11 (1969), pp. 6-13; and P. Schafer, 'Adam in der judischen Uberlieferung', in W. Strolz (ed.), *Vom alten zum neuen Adam* (Freiburg: Herder, 1986), pp. 69-93.

4. J. Fabricius, *Codex Pseudepigraphus Veteris Testamenti* (Hamburg and Leipzig: Liebezeit, 1713), pp. 1-95. Fabricius's second volume, *Codicis Pseudepigraphi Veteris Testamenti volumen alterum accedit Josephi veteris christiani auctoria hypomnesticon* (Hamburg: Felginer, 1723), contains supplements to the first volume. J.-P. Migne, in his *Dictionnaire des Apocryphes ou collection de tous les livres apocryphes relatifs à l'ancien et au nouveau testament* (Troisième et dernière encyclopédie théologique, 23–24; Paris: Migne-Ateliers catholiques, 1856–58), preserves useful information on the early history of collections.

1853, inaugurated the modern study of the Adam books.[5] Since then numerous studies of the Adam traditions and documents have been produced, chief among the more recent ones being *Portraits of Adam in Early Judaism* by J. Levison, the most thorough study yet of the Adam traditions,[6] and Stone's *A History of the Literature of Adam and Eve*, the most complete accounting of the Adam books.[7] Stone, in conjunction with G. Anderson, is editing a synopsis of the primary Adam books, in collaboration with W. Lechner-Schmidt. [8]

5.   A. Dillman published 'Das christliche Adambuch des Morgenlandes aus dem Äthiopischen mit Bemerkungen übersetzt', in *Jahrbücher der biblischen Wissenschaft 5* (Göttingen: Vandenhoeck & Ruprecht, 1853), pp. 1-144, and E. Renan published 'Fragments du livre gnostique intitule Apocalypse d'Adam, ou Penitence d'Adam ou Testament d'Adam', *JA* 5 (2) (1853), pp. 427-71.

6.   Levison's study (*Portraits of Adam in Early Judaism*, p. 29) is restricted to nine authors which he identifies as Jewish and originating between the years 200 BCE and 135 CE (these authors include *Sirach, Wisdom of Solomon, Philo, Jubilees, Josephus, 4 Ezra, 2 Baruch, Apocalypse of Moses* and the *Life of Adam and Eve*). Adam texts which are not included are reckoned to be either too late, not sufficiently Jewish, or have too few references to Adam (*Portraits of Adam in Early Judaism*, pp. 29-31). Boccaccini argues for a more inclusive approach to what he terms 'Middle Judaism' which would result in both an earlier and later date for what Levison calls 'early Judaism' and more literature from other Jewish communities (i.e. Christian) being considered (*Middle Judaism*, pp. 7-25). Interestingly, Levison does not include the *Testament of Abraham* in his survey even though he dates it from the 'second century BCE to the second century CE' (*Portraits of Adam in Early Judaism*, p. 30).

7.   Levison believes many Adam studies are flawed because of their dependence on either the theory of an Adam myth which in turn influences the Adam traditions, or the theory of a Adam *Vorlage* from which the Adam books were drawn (*Portraits of Adam in Early Judaism*, pp. 13-14). He rejects both presuppositions and instead argues for a 'plethora' of views on Adam which were drawn from each author's interests and 'tendenz', and not some Adam myth or Semitic Adam book (*Portraits of Adam in Early Judaism*, p. 14). Stone notes Levison's desire to illustrate how Adam materials were diverse from ancient times but points out how some or all of this diversity may still have had a Semitic *Vorlage* (*A History of the Literature of Adam and Eve*, p. 64). See also C. Hayward for a recent criticism of Levison ('The Figure of Adam in Pseudo-Philo's Biblical Antiquities', *JSJ* 23 [1992], pp. 1-20). For a brief but helpful survey of the Adam literature see S. Robinson's *The Testament of Adam: An Examination of the Syriac and Greek Traditions* (SBLDS, 52; Chico, CA: Scholars Press, 1982), pp. 3-18.

8.   As announced by Stone (*A History of the Literature of Adam and Eve*, p. 62). The primary Adam literature consists of the *Apocalypse of Moses*, the Latin

A sampling of both the Adam literature and other related texts dealing with Adam's glorification reveals how Adam was believed by some to be exalted over all creation, great in size, innocent of sin, and even the creator.[9] An examination of those texts dealing with Adam's enthronement, his position at the gate of Paradise and Hell, his divine likeness, and his overseeing of creation will provide a context which makes an Adam-Ancient of Days interpretation feasible. Such a survey will demonstrate how Adam's favored place in the judgment scene of the *Testament of Abraham* is not an anomaly for its era.

Adam's Heavenly Enthronement

Abraham's encounter with an enthroned Adam is in keeping with several descriptions of the first man. Ezek. 28.2, 11-15, a very difficult text, demonstrates how speculation over Adam enthroned in heaven can be traced back to Biblical traditions.

> Ezek. 28.2, 12-14: I am a god, a seat of the god(s). I sit upon/in the midst of the sea...Thou wast a sealer of the preserved (thing), full of wisdom and accomplished in beauty. In Eden, the garden of God, thou wast, every precious stone being thy cover, ruby, chrysolith, diamond, topaz, shoham, jasper, sapphire, malachite, beryl, hyacinth, agate, amethyst and gold. The work of thy settings and thy trappings on thee, the day thou wast created they were prepared. Thou wast a cherub, oh, what an anointed of the Shadower, and I placed thee on the holy mountain. A god thou wast, in the midst of stones thou walked.[10]

Commentators have long argued that the king of Tyre has been

Vita Adam et Evae, the Slavonic *Vita Adam et Evae*, the Armenian *Penitence of Adam* and the Georgian *Book of Adam*. All later Jewish and Christian writings are categorized as secondary Adam books.

9.   For Adam as exalted over creation see Sir. 49.16; Philo (*Op. Mund.* 136-41); *Apoc. Adam* 1.3; for his great size see *Apoc. Abr.* 23.5; Philo (*Quaest. in Gen.* 1.32); for his innocence from sin see *Adam and Eve* 18.1-2; Philo (*Op. Mund.* 151-52); *Ep. Apos.* 39; For his role as creator see Philo (*Conf. Ling.* 14); *Greek Magical Papyri* 1.195-97; 4.1167-68; *t. Sanh.* 8.7. J. Fossum, in his study, 'Colossians 1.15-18a in the Light of Jewish Mysticism and Gnosticism' (*NTS* 35 [1989], pp. 193-96), summarizes some of the evidence for the Jewish belief that Adam was viewed as the creator. For a survey of exalted Adam traditions see Fossum, *The Name of God and the Angel of the Lord* (WUNT, 36; Tübingen: J.C.B. Mohr, 1985), pp. 226-91.

10.   Widengren's translation of Ezek. 28.2, 12-14 has been used (*The Ascension of the Apostle*, p. 97). All other translations from the Bible are taken from the *New Oxford Annotated Bible: New Revised Standard Version*.

described in terms of a myth about the primal man and his enthronement on God's mountain.[11] Ezek. 28.11-15 has several references
which allude to the Genesis account: 'Eden, the garden of God' (cf.
Gen. 2.8, 15; 3.23), the day the primal man was 'created' (Hebrew:
ברא; cf. Gen. 2.4; 5.2), 'cherub' (cf. Gen. 3.24), and the 'stones of fire'
(cf. Gen. 2.10-14) . Especially pertinent is the position of the primal
man on the 'mountain of God'. In Isa. 14.13 the mountain of God is
called the 'mount of assembly (of the gods)' and is identified by J. Gray
as 'a kind of Canaanite Olympus'.[12] Ps. 48.1-3 identifies Zion as the
'holy mountain' on which God dwells. Widengren points out that this
mountain was where God had his seat, 'on the top of the cosmic
mountain which is, as it were, His throne'.[13] In light of Ezek. 28.2, 14,
it is correct to identify the primal man as dwelling in the abode of God,
even the throne of God, called heaven.[14]

There are other biblical passages which share Ezekiel's interest in the
enthronement of a human being upon God's throne. According to 1
Chron. 28.5, David knew that the Lord had chosen Solomon 'to sit
upon the throne of the kingdom of the Lord over Israel'. In 2 Chron. 9.8
God sets Solomon on his throne: 'Blessed be the Lord your God, who
has delighted in you and set you on his throne as king for the Lord your
God.' Ps. 110.1 describes how the Lord has seated the king at his right
hand: 'The Lord says to my lord, "Sit at my right hand until I make

11. H. Gunkel was the first to demonstrate this with a wealth of evidence
(*Genesis übersetzt und erklärt* [Göttingen: Vandenhoeck and Ruprecht, 1922],
pp. 25-40). G. Cooke followed with further insights about its Near-Eastern setting
('The Paradise Story of Ezekiel 28', in *Old Testament Essays* [London: Charles
Griffin and Co., 1927], pp. 37-45). Widengren has given a detailed commentary on
Ezek. 28 in the light of Near-Eastern traditions ('The Ascension of the Apostle',
pp. 94-97), and related the figure of Ezek. 28 to the corresponding Mesopotamian
figure, the primordial man called Adapa (*The King and the Tree of Life* [UUÅ, 4;
Uppsala: A.-B. Lundequistska Bokhandeln, 1951], pp. 4, 11, 44-45, 56-57, 64-66).
See also Widengren's essay 'Early Hebrew Myths and their Interpretation', in S.
Hooke (ed.), *Myth, Ritual, and Kingship: Essays on the Theory and Practice of
Kingship in the Ancient Near East and in Israel* (Oxford: Clarendon Press, 1958),
pp. 165-69.

12. J. Gray, *The Legacy of Canaan* (VTSup, 5; Leiden: E.J. Brill, 2nd edn,
1965), p. 21 n. 7.

13. Widengren, 'Early Hebrew Myths and their Interpretation', pp. 164-65.

14. See also O. Kaiser, *Isaiah 13–39: A Commentary* (TOTL; Philadelphia:
Westminster Press, 1974), pp. 142-43.

your enemies your footstool".' While this text does not specify whether the king is seated on God's throne or a separate throne, the motifs of enthronement and exaltation are clear.

Rabbinic tradition assumed that Ezekiel 28 served as a description of the first man. The third-century CE midrash, *Pesiqta deRab Kahana*, discusses the glory of Adam against the background of Ezek. 28.13.

> *Pes. K.* 26.3.2: R. Levi in the name of R. Hama b. R. Hanina: Thirteen canopies did the Holy One, blessed be He, weave for the first man in the Garden of Eden. This is in line with the following verse of scripture, Ez. 28.13: You were in Eden, the Garden of God; every precious stone was your covering, carnelian, topaz, and jasper, chrysolite, beryl, and onyx, sapphire, carbuncle, and emerald; and wrought gold were your settings and your engravings.[15]

This glorified view of the first man in Ezekiel 28 has prompted several commentators to argue for differing views of Adam in Israelite thought. W. Eichrodt argues that Ezekiel 28 is evidence that the Paradise story 'was told in all sorts of variations'.[16] W. Zimmerli adds that 'from a traditio-historical point of view this account has close connections with Genesis 2f, the Yahwehistic paradise narrative, and that it reveals an independent form of the tradition'.[17]

Ezekiel's view of Adam as enthroned on the mountain of God may be connected with another biblical passage. In Job 15.7-8 Eliphaz asks Job, 'Are you the first man ever born? Were you brought forth before the hills? Do you listen in on God's council? Do you limit wisdom to yourself?' These verses allude to a legend that the first man was a kind of demi-god, created before the hills, who had access to the council of God and acquired extraordinary knowledge of the mysteries of the world.[18] T. Kronholm, when describing the source of the belief of Ephrem, the Syrian church leader, that paradise was a world 'highly spanning the terrestrial world', cites *Targ. Ps.-J.* on Gen. 2.15: 'And Yahweh God took the man from the mountain of worship, from which

---

15. Translation and date taken from J. Neusner (ed. and trans.), *Pesiqta de Rab Kahana* (2 vols.; Atlanta: Scholars Press, 1987).

16. W. Eichrodt, *Ezekiel: A Commentry* (OTL; Philadelphia: Westminster Press, 1970), p. 392.

17. W. Zimmerli, *Ezekiel* (2 vols.; Hermenia; Philadelphia: Fortress Press, 1983), II, p. 90.

18. See F.R. Tenant, *The Sources of the Doctrine of the Fall and Original Sin* (Cambridge: Cambridge University Press, 1903), pp. 61-62.

he had been created, and caused him to dwell in the garden of Eden.'[19] Syrian iconography even portrays Adam being seated upon a throne in Paradise in a manner which assimilates him to Christ.[20]

Adam's enthronement in the *Testament of Abraham* can be set within this tradition of an enthroned Adam, which existed alongside other Adamic traditions. From Ezekiel to *Pseudo-Jonathan* and the fifth-century CE Syrian church there was an idea that Adam's original position was in a heavenly sphere, in the very dwelling of God. He was even enthroned according to several documents.

Although there was the common belief that Adam sinned and fell, some Jewish traditions maintained that he would be reinstituted to his original position. The first-century CE *Apocalypse of Moses* teaches that God promised Adam enthronement and dominion.

> *Apoc. Mos.* 39.2: Yet now I [LORD] tell you [Adam] that their joy shall be turned into sorrow, but your sorrow shall be turned into joy; and when that happens, I will establish you in your dominion on the throne of your seducer. But that one [Satan] shall be cast into this place [ground], so that you might sit above him. Then he himself and those who listen to him shall be condemned, and they shall greatly mourn and weep when they see you sitting on his glorious throne.

The notion of Adam's future glorious enthronement is explicit in this text and is compatible with his position in the *Testament of Abraham*.

The *Testament of Adam*, which may date as early as the second century CE, represents a Syriac Christian redaction of some old Jewish traditions.[21] In *T. Adam* 3.4 God, after telling Adam about his future incarnation, death and resurrection, promises him: 'And after three days, while I am in the tomb, I will raise up the body I received from you. And I will set you at the right hand of my divinity.' This promise referring to Adam's future enthronement 'at the right hand' shows a welding of Adam and Christ: 'Jesus said, "I am; and you will see the Son of Man seated at the right hand of the Power", "coming with the clouds of heaven"' (Mk 14.62). An additional inference, in light of the *Testament of Adam* alluding to Ps. 110.1 and Adam's enthronement at

---

19. T. Kronholm, *Motifs from Genesis 1–11 in the Genuine Hymns of Ephrem the Syrian* (ConBOT, 2; Lund: C.W.K. Gleerup, 1978), p. 68.

20. See M.-T. and P. Canivet, 'La mosaïque d'Adam dans l'église syrienne de Huarte (Ve S)', *CahArch* 34 (1975), pp. 49-69.

21. See Robinson, *The Testament of Adam*, pp. 135-60.

God's right hand, would be the idea of Adam sharing God's throne.

In a fourth-century CE discourse by Timothy, the patriarch of Alexandria, Adam is dramatically presented as an enthroned king at the time of his creation: 'Thereupon, my Father set him upon a great throne, and he placed upon his head a crown of glory, and he put a royal scepter [in his hand].'[22] This patriarch's high view of Adam in all likelihood goes back to Jewish traditions in Alexandria. For Philo of Alexandria the first man was heavenly, called a second God (even *Lord* and *God*), made after God's image, and served as the model for the second man who was earthly.[23] Levison argues that Philo is creating his own interpretation of Adam on the basis of Genesis and Greek concepts.[24] While Philo's view of Adam may be the result of his own independent exegesis, it is difficult to dismiss the possibility that Philo is reacting against Adam traditions prevalent in Alexandrian Jewish communities which depicted the heavenly Adam as the embodied glory of God as G. Quispel proposes.[25]

Further illustration of a Jewish tradition detailing Adam's future enthronement surfaces in a sixth-century CE Armenian Adam book, *The Death of Adam*. This late work represents mixed traditions and probably draws on Greek and Syriac sources. It has its greatest affinities with the two Jewish works of the first century CE—the *Apocalypse of Moses* and the *Life of Adam and Eve*.[26] In this writing Eve has a dream in

22. The translation is by W. Budge as it was quoted by Fossum, *The Name of God*, p. 272.

23. See *Op. Mund.* 136-41; *Quaest. in Gen.* 2.62; *Cher.* 27-28.

24. Levison, *Portraits of Adam in Early Judaism*, pp. 74, 85.

25. G. Quispel, 'Ezekiel 1:26 in Jewish Mysticism and Gnosis', *VC* 34 (1980), pp. 4-7. Quispel quotes Philo's work *Quis rerum divinarum heres sit*, '"God made man", he says "made him after the image of God". Male and female He made—not now "him" but "them". He concludes with the plural, thus connecting with the genus mankind the species which had been divided, as I said, by equality' (*Rer. Div. Her.* 164), and adds 'Philo's polemic against the androgyny of heavenly Man seems to show that there existed in Alexandria a Jewish circle which proclaimed that the heavenly Adam was both male and female' ('Ezekiel 1:26', p. 5). Quispel suggests in the same article that the Platonic idea of man was integrated into Jewish conceptions of Adam ('Ezekiel 1:26', p. 3). Fossum has detailed this insight with regard to the LXX and the Alexandrian Jews in the time of Philo ('Colossians 1.15-18a', p. 188). The *Testament of Abraham* also testifies to the influence of Platonic ideology with the words of 11.4, καὶ ἦν ἡ ἰδέα τοῦ ἀνθρώπου ἐκείνου φοβερὰ (and the idea of the man was fearful).

26. See M. Stone (ed. and trans.), 'The Death of Adam—An Armenian Adam

which she sees Adam seated on a throne with three 'shining men'
(presumably the members of the trinity) in a 'tall shining Temple'.

> *The Death of Adam* 16-22: And in her dream Eve followed to see where
> Adam was being taken. And he was taken up into a tall shining Temple
> and there with a (on a) throne, on high shining seats, were three shining
> men in bright garments. And Adam was brought close to the door of the
> Temple and (again) hastily turned around and driven away as if by force.
> And Adam went sadly. Suddenly one of the three men who were sitting
> on the throne arose and interceded with his companions. And in hiding
> from the other servants, the three took secret counsel. And the man who
> had risen from the throne descended and came quickly after Adam, and
> he found Adam as if sad near Eve, and taking his hands he called him.
> And he brought and led him into the Temple and seated him on a throne
> and spoke to him sweetly.[27]

E. Preuschen argued that Adam was seated with the 'three shining
men' and shared their throne.[28] Stone does not dispute Preuschen's
position and the passage does refer to only one 'throne', on which there
are several 'seats'. At the least, this Adam text teaches that Adam was
enthroned in heaven in the presence of divine beings.[29]

Book', *HTR* 59 (1966), pp. 283-91 (291).

27. The translation used here is taken from Stone ('The Death of Adam') and all
words in parentheses are his. The most recent edition and translation of the Armenian Adam literature is by W. Lipscomb, *The Armenian Apocryphal Adam Literature* (ATS, 8; Philadelphia: University of Pennsylvania, 1990). The three men may
not necessarily be representative of the trinity as Stone argues ('The Death of
Adam', p. 289). According to P. Perkins, they could be the related to the three
angels who visited Adam in the *Apocalypse of Adam* ('Apocalypse of Adam: The
Genre and Function of a Gnostic Apocalypse', *CBQ* 39 [1977], pp. 382-95 [386
n. 17]). It does seem more likely that the Christian idea of the trinity is in view,
though, especially in a sixth-century CE book.

28. E. Preuschen (ed. and trans.), 'Die apokryphen gnostischen Adamschriften',
in W. Diehl (ed.), *Festgruss Bernhard Stade* (Giessen: Ricker's, 1900), pp. 186-88.
D. Issaverdens understands the passage to be referring to several thrones (*The
Uncanonical Writings of the Old Testament* [Venice: Armenia Monastery of
St Lazarus, 1907], p. 58).

29. *B. Sukk.* 52b places Adam in the company of other biblical figures in its
midrash depicting the time of the Messiah as based on Mic. 5.4: 'And this shall be
peace: when the Assyrians shall come into our land, and when he shall tread in our
palaces, then shall we raise up against him seven shepherds and eight princes
among men. Who are the 'seven shepherds? David in the middle, Adam, Seth,
Methuselah on his right, and Abraham, Jacob and Moses on his left' (all translations of the *Babylonian Talmud* taken from Epstein (ed.), *The Babylonian Talmud*).

The sharing of the divine throne is a development of traditions in which God shares his throne with others. As cited above, 1 Chron. 28.5, 2 Chron. 9.8, and, possibly, Ps. 110.1 describe the king as sharing God's throne. The *Wisdom of Solomon* positions Lady Wisdom on God's throne (Wis. 9.4, 10).

Several writings provide explicit portrayals of the enthronement of human figures. Moses replaces a male figure on a throne, who gives his crown and scepter to Moses, in *Ezek. Trag.* 68-76.[30]

> *Ezek. Trag.* 68-76: On Sinai's peak I [Moses] saw what seemed a throne so great in size it touched the clouds of heaven. Upon it sat a man of noble mien, becrowned, and with a scepter in one hand while with the other he did beckon me. I made approach and stood before the throne. He handed o'er the scepter and bade me to mount the throne, and gave me the crown; then he himself withdrew from off the throne.

Moses takes God's (or the Glory's[31]) place and is seated on his throne in a heavenly setting. Especially intriguing is the description of the divine occupant of the throne leaving it so that Moses can be enthroned. This scene is similar to the depiction of Adam in the *Testament of Abraham*. In both texts patriarchs are exalted to heaven and enthroned.

Other men and even angels were portrayed as enthroned in heaven. Heb. 1.13 applies Ps. 110.1 to Jesus when describing his enthronement at God's right hand. Heb. 1.18 quotes Ps. 45.8 and identifies Jesus' enthronement and exaltation with the words, 'Your throne, O God is forever and ever'. Both Ps. 110.1 and Ps. 45.1 were originally addressed to the king of Israel, who was thought of as an enthroned son of God (Ps. 2.8). *1 En.* 51.3 identifies the 'Son of Man', known also as the 'Elect One' (and later as Enoch the patriarch; 71.14), as sitting on God's throne in the future time of deliverance: 'In those days, the Elect One shall sit on my throne'[32] (cf. *1 En.* 61.8). In *3 En.* 10.1, Enoch-Metraton, the exalted angel, describes the throne God has prepared him: 'the Holy One, blessed be he, made for me a throne like the throne of glory.'

30. Interestingly, in Samaritan works Adam and Moses are glorified together (*Codex Gothanus* 963; *Mermar Marqah* 6.3).

31. Ezek. 1.26-28 says the appearance of the 'glory of the Lord' was that of a human form upon the throne.

32. Manuscript A omits 'the Elect One', while manuscripts B and C include it. See *OTP*, I, p. 36.

In the sixth-century CE *Gedullat Mosheh*, David's ascent to heaven is described.[33] Following his ascent David is enthroned on a huge 'throne of fire': 'David went up to the heavenly temple, where a throne of fire stood ready for him, whose height is of 40 parsangs.' And like the enthronement of Moses in *Ezekiel the Tragedian*, David receives some of the trappings of enthronement such as a crown, which surpasses all others.[34] At his enthronement David's throne is positioned in front of God's: 'When David took his throne upon the throne prepared for him, facing that of his Creator, all the kings of Judah ranged themselves before him, and the kings of Israel stood behind him.'

This picture of the enthronement of both God and David in heaven not only parallels the dual enthronements of Adam and Abel in the *Testament of Abraham*, it also calls to mind the debate between Akiba and Jose over the interpretation of the 'thrones' of Dan. 7.9.

> *b. Ḥag.* 14a II; *b. Sanh.* 38b: One scripture says, His throne was flames of fire (Dan. 7.9) and another scripture says until thrones were placed and an Ancient of Days took his seat (Dan. 7.9). There is no contradiction: one for him and one for David. As it was taught, one for him and one for David, according to R. Akiba. Rabbi Jose the Galilean said to him, Akiba, for how long will you profane the Presence? Rather, one is for Judgment and one for Vindication. Did he accept this opinion from him or not? Come and hear! One for Judgment and one for Vindication, this is the opinion of Akiba!

Gedullat Mosheh, with its enthronement of David in the presence of God, is proof that Akiba's dual enthronement interpretation persisted in some Jewish circles.[35] Like Daniel 7, *Gedullat Mosheh* refers to God as an enthroned figure and assumes the existence of 'thrones' (Dan. 7.9) in heaven (for God and David).

---

33. Both versions are taken from Gaster (ed. and trans.), *Studies and Texts: In Folklore*. All translations of *Gedullat Mosheh* are taken from Gaster.

34. Another possible connection between David and Moses is the association of David's arrival in heaven with the declaration in *Gedullat Mosheh* that '"The heavens declare the glory of God" (Ps. 19.1)'. This raises the question of David's relation to the 'glory of the Lord' (Ezek. 1.26-28).

35. As noted by Casey, who goes on to observe how Akiba's opinion was not only rejected but even suppressed in a parallel passage, *Tanḥ. Qed.* 1 (*Son of Man*, p. 87). 'The rabbis were so worried about this problem that several discussions of it have been preserved, some partial parallels to others, providing no less than eight distinct, if largely related, solutions' (*Son of Man*, p. 88).

The *Babylonian Talmud* also records a story which relates to the controversy over the enthroned intermediary angel named Metatron. It concerns the mistake Elisha b. Abuya (110–135 CE), contemptuously called Aher ('Another') in the story, made when he saw two seated beings in heaven.[36]

> *b. Ḥag.* 15a: Aher mutilated the roots. Of him Scripture says: (Ecc. 5.5). Suffer not thy mouth to bring thy flesh into guilt. What does it refer to? He saw that permission was granted to Metatron to sit and write down the merits of Israel. Said he: It is taught as a tradition that on high there is no sitting and no emulation, no back and no weariness. Perhaps God forfend!—there are two divinities (powers). Thereupon they led Metatron forth, and punished him with sixty fiery lashes, saying to him: Why didst thou not rise before him when thou didst see him? Permission was (then) given to him to strike out the merits of Aher. A Bath Kol went forth and said: Return ye backsliding children (Jer. 3.22)—except Aher.

The story in *b. Ḥag.* 15a appears again in *3 En.* 16.1-5 where additional details bring out not only its use of Daniel 7, but also its similarity to *T. Abr.* 11.1–13.7.

> *3 En.* 16.1-5: At first I sat upon a great throne at the door of the seventh palace, and I judged all the denizens of the heights on the authority of the Holy One, blessed be he. I assigned greatness, royalty, rank, sovereignty, glory, praise, diadem, crown, and honor to all the princes of kingdoms, when I sat in the heavenly court. The princes of kingdoms stood beside me, to my right and to my left, by authority of the Holy One, blessed be he. But when Aher came to behold the vision of the chariot and set eyes upon me, he was afraid and trembled before me. His soul was alarmed to the point of leaving him because of his fear, dread, and terror of me, when he saw me seated upon a throne like a king, with ministering angels standing beside me as servants and all the princes of kingdoms crowned with crowns surrounding me.

In *3 En.* 16.1-5 Metatron sits on a throne, by the door of the seventh heaven, judging with the assistance of angels, strikes fear in Aher because of his appearance, and is mistaken for God. In *T. Abr.* 11.1-12 Adam sits enthroned outside the gates of heaven and hell, has the

---

36. Aher is infamous in Jewish tradition. His observation that there might be 'two divinities' in heaven and its implied criticism of monotheism got him branded a heretic by the rabbis and earned for him the name 'Aher' (Another). Strousma argues that the name 'Aher' was an allusion to Abuya's adoption of Sethian gnosticism ('Aher: A Gnostic', II, pp. 808-18).

appearance of God himself which Abraham finds 'terrifying', is surrounded by angels leading souls through the gates, and like a judge sits
and rises.

The enthronement of Adam in the *Testament of Abraham* appears to
be part of a broader Jewish interest in enthroned figures. Moses, Jesus,
Abraham, Jacob, David and Metatron were all enthroned with varying
degrees of exaltation.[37] Many rabbis opposed the idea of a human
enthroned in heaven, but the strength of this tradition has shown itself
in several documents.

Adam's Position at the Gate of Heaven and Hell

The first-century CE book, *4 Ezra*, besides presenting a negative picture
of Adam as a sinner who contributed to human misery, also preserves a
tradition which places Adam in a heavenly paradise. Its description of
Adam's position in a heavenly paradise is reminiscent of the primal
man's dwelling in Ezekiel 28 and Adam's placement in heaven outside
the gate of Paradise in the *Testament of Abraham*. In 3.4-6 Adam is
depicted as an immortal figure residing in a heavenly paradise, prior to
the earth's creation.

> *4 Ezra* 3.4-6: O sovereign Lord, did you not speak at the beginning when
> you formed the earth—and that without help—and commanded the dust
> and gave you Adam, a lifeless body? Yet he was the workmanship of
> your hands, and you breathed into him the breath of life, and he was
> made alive in your presence. And you led him into the garden which
> your right hand had planted before the earth appeared.

Though *4 Ezra* appears to suppress the idea of Adam's celestial setting within the text, there are clues within the text which allude to it.

---

37. Regarding the multiplicity of the enthronements, *Gedullat Mosheh* says that
in paradise, 'the greatest of all the thrones is Abraham's' (quoting Ginzberg's
translation, *The Legends of the Jews*, V, pp. 418-19). This reference illustrates the
belief of some Jews that there were a number of enthronements in heaven. Even
Adam's glorious appearance (*T. Abr.* 11.8-9) is matched by Abraham, who, in the
Apocalypse of Abraham, is clad in garments of glory in heaven (17.1). Yet, in
Zohar 1.97, it is Jacob's throne which has the distinction of being the greatest
throne. Apparently the question of who among the patriarchs enjoyed the most
glorious enthronement was a live issue for some Jewish groups. These late Jewish
texts testify to the persistent Jewish belief in patriarchal enthronement and the
question of who had the grandest enthronement.

Levison notes how this 'garden' (Latin: paradisum; cf. 6.4) planted before the earth's creation is in heaven by virtue of 'paradise' being positioned above hell according to *4 Ezra* 4.7-8, 7.36-37.[38] He also cites *4 Ezra* 6.54—'and over these you placed Adam as ruler over all the works which you had made'—as illustrating how Adam's dominion included the heavenly creations since the context is a careful narration of God's creation of heaven and earth (6.38-53, esp. v. 46).[39]

The *Apocalypse of Moses* presents an interesting contrast with the *Testament of Abraham*. In *Apoc. Mos.* 25.2–26.2 Adam tells Seth how he was taken to 'Paradise' by Michael in a chariot where he saw God enthroned and there he received a judgment of death.

> *Apoc. Mos.* 25.2–26.2: After your mother and I had been driven out of Paradise, while we were praying, Michael the archangel and messenger of God came to me. And I saw a chariot like the wind and its wheels were fiery. I was carried off into the Paradise of righteousness, and I saw the Lord sitting and his appearance was unbearable flaming fire. And many thousands of angels were at the right hand and at the left of the chariot. I was disturbed when I saw this; fear laid hold of me and I worshiped in the presence of God on the face of the earth. And God said me, Behold, you shall die, because you have disregarded the command of God...

Later in the narrative Eve asks Seth to look up to heaven where can be seen the body of Adam with all the holy angels interceding on his behalf: 'She said to him, "Look up with your eyes and see the heavens opened, and see with your eyes how the body of your father lies on its face, and all the holy angels are with him praying for him..."' (35.2).

Still later, in 37.4-5, God orders Michael to bring Adam up to 'Paradise', to the third heaven.

> *Apoc. Mos.* 37.4-5: ...and so the LORD of all, sitting on his holy throne, stretched out his hands and took Adam and handed him over to the archangel Michael, saying to him, Take him up into Paradise, to the third heaven, and leave (him) there until that great and fearful day which I am about to establish for the world.

---

38. Levison, *Portraits of Adam in Early Judaism*, pp. 116-17. Levison takes issue with Stone who distinguishes a pre-existent paradise (3.6; 6.4) from eschatological paradise (7.38, 123; 8.52), and from a paradise of mystical associations (4.7-8) (Stone, 'Features of the Eschatology of IV Ezra' [Doctoral Dissertation, Harvard University, 1965], pp. 77-79).

39. Levison, *Portraits of Adam in Early Judaism*, p. 120.

This tradition places Adam in Paradise in a way which parallels Adam's position in the *Testament of Abraham*. In both texts Adam is to be found in heaven, either in Paradise, or outside its gates.

The Mandeans, the gnostic-baptist sect whose Jewish roots appear to predate the fall of Jerusalem in 70 CE,[40] preserve variations of the Adam materials. In the *Ginza* (*The Treasure*; also known as *The Book of Adam*), Adam is taken to heaven where he is asked to await the 'Day of Judgment' in the company of Eve (Hawa) and Abel (Hibil-Ziwa).

> GRl [Ginza Rba]: Then spoke the Great First Life to Adam, Head of the Race [of mankind]. O Adam, rest at ease in thy glory: let the calm of the good come upon thee. Hibil-Ziwa is here, thy brethren the uthras are here and the Jordan; it is all here. Here wilt thou dwell, Adam! Thy spouse Hawa is coming hither. Thy whole race will rise upward following after thee. This is the abode prepared for thee, Adam, and the spouse Hawa, in the presence of the Great Life until the Day, the Day of Judgment.[41]

Adam's invitation to rest in his 'glory' in the company of Abel is clearly similar to Adam's place in the *Testament of Abraham*. In the judgment scene of *T. Abr.* 11.1–13.7, Adam is 'adorned in such glory' (*T. Abr.* 11.8) outside the gates of heaven, while Abel is between the gates of heaven (*T. Abr.* 11.4; 12.4).

In the second-century CE work, the *Martyrdom of Isaiah*, there is a scene taking place in the seventh heaven which has several similarities to the exalted, ascended and glorified status of Adam and Abel in the *Testament of Abraham*.

> *Mart. Isa.* 9.6-10: And he took me up into the seventh heaven, and there I saw a wonderful light, and also angels without number. And there I saw all the righteous from the time of Adam onwards. And there I saw the holy Abel and all the righteous. And there I saw Enoch and all who (were) with him, stripped of (their) robes of the flesh; and I saw them in their robes of above, and they were not sitting on their thrones, nor were their crowns of glory on them.[42]

Even with the explicit Christian additions to the immediate context of

---

40. For a concise introduction to the Mandeans see K. Rudolph, *Gnosis: The Nature and History of Gnosticism* (San Francisco: Harper & Row, 1987), pp. 343-66.

41. Translation taken from E. Drower, *The Secret Adam: A Study of Nasoraean Gnosis* (Oxford: Clarendon Press, 1960).

42. Recension B of the *Testament of Abraham* identifies Adam, Abel and Enoch in its judgment scene (8.5–11.10).

this passage (9.11-12), a knowledge of and reaction to exalted patriarch traditions, and perhaps even the *Testament of Abraham*, cannot be ruled out.[43] Adam and Abel are the patriarchs referred to in recension A of the *Testament of Abraham*, while in recension B Adam, Abel and Enoch are all identified, as in *Mart. Isa.* 9.6-10. And in 9.28 it reads, 'And Adam and Abel and Seth and all the righteous approached first and worshiped him' (Jesus, whose 'glory' is described as surpassing them all [9.27]). A later author appears to be reworking exalted patriarch traditions in the service of his own Christian ideology.[44]

A provocative work for the exalted Adam traditions is the second-century CE text *Acts of Pilate*. While it has clearly been redacted from a Christian perspective, it presents a view of Adam similar to that of the *Testament of Abraham*. In ch. 25 'our forefather Adam' is led into paradise by Jesus. Later, in ch. 26, a man, who asks Michael the archangel to lead him to the gate of paradise, is told to wait for the arrival of Adam, 'the forefather of the race', who will presumably allow the righteous to enter.[45]

Similar to *Acts Pil.* 26 is *b. Ta'an* 1.21 and 4.124. In these texts the deceased are brought to Adam as soon as they die, and Adam, in his capacity as a judge, confronts them with their guilt: 'I committed one trespass. Is there any among you, and he be the most pious, who has not been guilty of more than one.'[46] With reference to a similar tradition, Kohler refers to an 'old *Gan Eden* treatise' in *b. Hammid.* vv. 42-51. The passage is attributed to the old Shammite mystic, R. Eliezer b. Hyrcanos, and says Abraham and Isaac sit as judges at the gate in place of Adam and Abraham in the Abrahamic vision.[47]

The *Apocalypse of Paul*, a fifth-century CE Christian work which shows some dependence on earlier Jewish materials, may be alluding to the *Apocalypse of Moses*. In it Paul describes his ascent to the third heaven where he sees 'another who surpassed them all, very beautiful.

---

43. See the comments of M. Knibb (*OTP*, II, pp. 147-49).

44. A 'Christian' recasting of Adam traditions may be found in the second-century CE text, the *Acts of Pilate*, where Christ descends into Hades and raises Adam up (*Acts Pil.* 24).

45. All quotes from the New Testament Apocrypha are taken from W. Schneemelcher (ed.), *New Testament Apocrypha* (2 vols.; Philadelphia: Westminster Press, 1963).

46. See Ginzberg (ed.), *The Legends of the Jews*, I, p. 102.

47. Kohler, 'The Apocalypse of Abraham', p. 603.

And I said to the angel: who is this, my lord? He said to me: This is Adam, the father of you all' (*Apoc. Paul* 51). Ginzberg cites *Seder Rabba di-Bereshit* 7–8 which says 'Adam was permitted to ascend to the highest heaven to take part in rejoicing over the Sabbath' and was permitted by God to sit upon a throne of glory after his creation.[48]

Turner, when discussing the magnificent appearance of Adam in the *Testament of Abraham*, ties in the kabbalistic midrashic thesaurus work *Yalquṭ Hadash* where Adam is seated on a throne at the gate of Paradise surrounded by many souls of the righteous.[49] According to Jewish tradition Abraham was told that on the day of judgment he would sit at the gate of hell and keep all who kept the law of circumcision from entering therein (*b. 'Erub.* 19a; *Ber. R.* c. 48).

An even closer parallel to Adam's placement at the gates of heaven is found in the late text *Mystery of Sandalphon*.[50] In this text Elisha b. Abuya says, 'When I ascended to Paradise, I beheld Akatriel YHWH, the Lord of the hosts, who is sitting at the entrance of Paradise, and 120 myriads of ministering angels surrounded him'.[51] The parallel of the angel Akatriel YHWH to Adam is obvious. Both sit outside the gate(s) of heaven in the company of angels and are the first figure met by those ascending to heaven (*T. Abr.* 11.4). And unlike Abraham in the *Yalquṭ Hadash* passage, there is no explicit statement about judgment in the *Mystery of Sandalphon*.

Adam's Divine Likeness

In the *Testament of Abraham* the appearance of Adam is described as being 'like the Master's' (11.4). There are two textual elements in Daniel 7 which are relevant when dealing with the subject of Adam's likeness to God. The first involves the connection between Ezek. 1.26-28 and Dan. 7.9.

---

48. Ginzberg (ed.), *The Legends of the Jews*, I, p. 84.

49. Turner, 'The Testament of Abraham: A Study', p. 122.

50. Morray-Jones cited this text in connection with the *Testament of Abraham* ('Transformational Mysticsm', p. 17). The *Mystery of Sandalphon* is found in the Oxford manuscript (1531) of the Hekhalot. Scholem dates the Hekhalot texts to the Talmudic period ('Merkabah Mysticism or Ma'aseh Merkavah', *EncJud*, XI, pp. 1386-89). Schafer argues that the Hekalot texts were in circulation no later than the tenth century (*Übersetzung der Herkhalot-Literatur* [2 vols.; Tübingen: J.C.B. Mohr (Paul Siebeck), 1987], II, pp. xx-xxi).

51. Translation taken from Scholem, *Jewish Gnosticism*, p. 53.

Ezek. 1.26-28: And above the dome over their heads there was some-thing like a throne, in appearance like sapphire; high above on the throne was a figure like that of a man. I saw that from what appeared to be his waist up he looked like glowing metal, as if full of fire, and that from there down he looked like fire: and brilliant light surrounded him... This was the appearance of the likeness of the glory of the Lord.

Dan. 7.9-10: As I watched, thrones were set in place and the Ancient of Days took his throne. His clothing was white as snow; and the hair of his head was white like pure wool. His throne was fiery flames, and its wheels were burning fire.

Commentators have long noticed how Dan. 7.9 has built upon Ezek. 1.26-27.[52] What needs to be singled out especially is the description of God as a 'figure like that of a man' who is 'high above on the throne' in Ezek. 1.26. What Ezekiel lends to Daniel is the idea that the enthroned being is man-like in appearance.[53] The LXX version of the enthroned deity reads as ὁμοίωμα ὡς εἶδος ἀνθρώπου, and J. Fossum has pointed out that this phrase is alluded to in the description of the enthroned Adam, ἡ ἰδέα τοῦ ἀνθρώπου, in *T. Abr.* 11.4.[54] Gen. 1.26-27 adds fur-ther light.

Gen. 1.26-27: Then God said, Let us make man [אדם] in our image, in our likeness...So God created man [adam] in his own image, in the image of God he created him...

God and Adam look alike. The *Apocalypse of Moses* refers to the prayer of the angels on Adam's behalf in which Adam is identified as

52. See Rowland, 'The Influence of the First Chapter of Ezekiel on Judaism and Early Christian Literature' (Doctoral Dissertation, Cambridge University, 1974), pp. 90-98. Daniel being addressed as the 'Son of Man' in 8.17 may also be taken as evidence of Ezekiel's influence on the book of Daniel. See Colpe, 'ὁ υἱός', p. 418; Kim, 'An Exposition of Paul's Gospel in the Light of the Damascus Theophany' (Doctoral Dissertation, University of Manchester, 1977), pp. 302-10).

53. C. Newman notes how Ezek. 1.26, with its anthropomorphic portrayal of God as an enthroned king, has influenced Dan. 7, but he does not make its relation-ship to the 'Ancient of Days' explicit and instead dwells on the 'one like a son of man' ('"Lord of Glory", "Glory of the Lord": Tradition and Rhetoric in Paul's Doxa-Christology' [paper read to the International SBL; August, 1990], pp. 6-10). Interestingly, he identifies 'Glory' as denoting God in a throne vision where apoca-lyptic information is given ('"Lord of Glory"', p. 8). This is significant for the enthroned Adam who is described as adorned in 'glory' (*T. Abr.* 11.8-9). See also Rowland, *The Open Heaven*, pp. 95-98, 218-24.

54. Fossum, *The Name of God*, p. 171.

the image of God: 'all the holy angels are with him, praying for him and saying, "Forgive him, O Father of all, for he is your image"' (35.2).

Rabbinic literature also includes some elaborations upon this Genesis motif. R. Banaah came to the grave of Adam after having seen the grave of Abraham and was told, 'You have seen the likeness of my image; My image itself you are not allowed to see' (*b. Bat.* 58a).[55]

The Jewish Christian work *Pseudo-Clementine Homilies* echoes the same emphasis on Adam *being* the image of God: 'For he who insults the image and the things belonging to the eternal King, has the sin reckoned as committed against Him in whose likeness the image was made (*Ps.-Clem. Hom.* 3.17.2).[56] That Adam was 'the image' of God has been correctly observed by Fossum, who adds, 'since the concept of *eikon* always involves an archetype, this representation must mean that Adam was the manifestation of God or of a divine aspect'.[57]

The first-century CE document the *Life of Adam and Eve* maintains that Adam was worshiped by Michael and the angels because he was *the* image of the Lord.

> LAE 14.1-2: And Michael went out and called all the angels, saying, Worship the image of the Lord God, as the LORD God has instructed. And Michael himself worshiped first, and called me and said, Worship the image of God, Yahweh.

The emphasis on the adoration of Adam is brought by the repeated use of the verb 'worship' (Latin: adorare; 13.3; 14.1, 2 [2 times], 3 [4 times]; 15.1, 2 [2 times]). In addition, the rationale for worshiping Adam, being the 'image of God', is referred to five times (13.3 [2 times]; 14.1, 2; 15.2). This distinction between Adam being the image of God in contrast to being made in the image of God (Gen. 1.27) is part of the 'heavenly man' ideology witnessed to by Philo and the Gnostics. Fossum was the first to note how Adam as the image reveals a rapprochement between the first earthly man and the heavenly man and says, 'When the earthly Adam is glorified and called the divine "image", he is described like the heavenly Man, the Glory.'[58]

The *Life of Adam and Eve* underscores the motif of Adam being the

55. As quoted by Fossum ('Jewish-Christian Christology and Jewish Mysticism', *VC* 37 [1983], pp. 260-87 [277] n. 57).

56. Translation taken from Roberts and Donaldson (eds.), *The Ante-Nicene Fathers*.

57. Fossum, 'Jewish-Christian Christology', p. 269.

58. Fossum, *The Name of God*, p. 278.

visible image of God by identifying how it involves his 'countenance and likeness'—that is, as Levison puts it, 'The image itself consists of physical similarity to God'.[59]

> *LAE* 13.3: When God blew into you the breath of life and your counte-
> nance and likeness were in the image of God, Michael brought you and
> made (us) worship you in the sight of God, and the LORD God said,
> Behold Adam! I have made you in our image and likeness.[60]

In *Genesis Rabbah* Adam's likeness to God is so exact that Adam must be put to sleep so that the angels might worship the right person.

> *Gen. R.* 8.10: And God created man in his own image (Gen. 1.27).
> R. Hoshaia said: At the time the Holy One created the first man, the
> ministering angels mistook him [for God Himself] and were about to say
> Holy before Him. What did the Holy One do? He put him into a deep
> sleep, and all the angels realized that he was no more than a man. [God
> and man together in the world were then] like a king and a governor
> riding together in a state carriage. The people of the province were about
> to cry, Hail, Domine! but did not know which one was the king. What
> did the king do? He pushed aside the governor and put him out of the
> carriage, whereupon all realized that that one was no more than a mere
> man.[61]

The subject of Adam receiving worship also relates to the aggressive rabbinic opposition to the doctrine of the 'two powers' (the multiplicity of divine beings), explored by Segal.[62] In *Yal.* 1.20 on Gen. 2.9 the angels exclaim when they notice Adam's resemblance to God, 'Are there two powers in heaven?'[63] *Gen. R.* 8.10 also connects the doctrine of the worship of Adam with the 'two powers' teaching and vigorously opposes them both.

---

59. Levison, *Portraits of Adam in Early Judaism*, p. 178.

60. Later, in 20.1, Adam, through some means not identified in the text, but perhaps indicative of special abilities which were his due to being the image of God, learns of Eve's plight without being told.

61. Translation taken from H. Bialik and Y. Ravnitsky (eds.), *The Book of Legends: Sefer Ha-Aggadah* (New York: Schocken Books, 1992). M. Smith, in his article 'On the Shape of God and the Humanity of the Gentiles', in J. Neusner (ed.), *Religions in Antiquity: Essays in Memory of Erwin Ramsdell Goodenough* (SHR, 14; Leiden: E.J. Brill, 1968), pp. 315-26, shows how many rabbis saw the *imago dei* in terms of a bodily likeness to God.

62. Segal, *Two Powers in Heaven*. *Mek.* Bahodesh 5, Shirta 4, connects the 'two powers' argument with Dan. 7.9.

63. As quoted by Segal, *Two Powers in Heaven*, p. 112.

Besides their appearances, God and Adam could be thought to share the same name, even Adam. Marmorstein cites an example from R. Judah b. Simon who sees in Eccl. 2.21 one of God's names, Adam (Hebrew: אדם), as based on Ezek. 1.26.[64]

> Eccl. 2.21: For a man may do his work with wisdom, knowledge and skill, and then he must leave all he owns to someone who has not worked for it. This too is meaningless and a great misfortune.

> Ezek. 1.26 And above the dome over their heads there was something like a throne, in appearance like sapphire; and seated above the likeness of a throne was something like a human form [אדם].

Marmorstein also notes how R. Simon b. Johai saw in Prov. 15.23 and its reference to a 'man' (Hebrew: איש) finding joy an allusion to God.[65] Lacocque, when discussing how Gnostic speculations about 'Man' were anchored in the 'older Israelite mentality', quotes *Corpus Hermeticum* 10.25 to illustrate how God could be understood as a man: 'Man on earth is a mortal god; God in the heavens is an immortal man.'[66] The Alexandrian provenance of *Corpus Hermeticum* makes it a valuable witness in light of the *Testament of Abraham*'s Egyptian origin.

Another text which follows Alexandrian Jewish teaching, the Nag Hammadi work the *Apocryphon of John*, also gives the name 'man' to

---

64. *V. Tanḥ.* 1.24, *Gen. R.* 27.1, *Eccl. R.* 2.21 (Marmorstein, *The Old Rabbinic Doctrine*, II, pp. 64-65). Justin (*Dial.* 128) reveals how his Jewish audience were familiar with the teaching that 'the power sent from the Father of all' was sometimes called 'angel... Glory... Man'. 'Man' therefore could also designate an empowered being who was called by a divine name (Glory). All quotations of Justin are taken from Roberts and Donaldson (eds.), *The Ante-Nicene Fathers*. Pétrement traces the Gnostic use of 'man' as a name for God (*Ap. John* 1.14) to Christian traditions. She theorizes that because Christ, the 'son of God', was called the 'son of man', gnostic adherents came to the conclusion that God must be a man (*A Separate God*, pp. 105-107).

65. 'Man' (איש) is taken for God in light of Exod. 15.3 where God is called a 'man of war' (Marmorstein, *The Old Rabbinic Doctrine*, II, pp. 65-66). Marmorstein notes how early Christian and late pagan readers of the Bible were delighted to discover in such anthropomorphisms some support of their ideologies (*The Old Rabbinic Doctrine*, II, p. 9). The rejection of the literal use of this name of God is traced to the school of R. Ishmael. This school was opposed to exegetical methods followed by R. Akiba and his school who took such anthropomorphisms literally as the identification of man (איש) with God.

66. Lacocque, *Daniel*, p. 147.

God. In the *Apocryphon of John*, the Demiurge is rebuked for thinking that he is the true God with the words, 'Man exists and the Son of Man' (14.14). This type of statement, if interpreted in a non-Gnostic manner, could mean that Adam (Man) and Abel (the Son of Man) were higher powers. Or perhaps it was derived from an exalted Adam tradition at Alexandria.

Stronger biblical support for 'man' (אִישׁ) as a divine name can be drawn from Exod. 15.3, 'The Lord is a man (אִישׁ) of war'. This motif of God as a man of war is later reflected in 1QM 12.2; 1QM 19, where it reads,

> 1QM 12.2; 1QM 19: Rise up, O Hero! Lead off thy captives, O Glorious One. Gather up thy spoils, O Author of mighty deeds! Lay Thy hand on the neck of Thine enemies and Thy feet on the pile of the slain! Smite the nations, Thine adversaries, and devour the flesh of the sinner with thy sword.[67]

This Qumran identification of God as a 'glorious man' (Hebrew: אִישׁ כבוד) can be placed alongside the man-like figure of Ezek. 1.26-28 who is 'the appearance of the likeness of the glory of the Lord', and *T. Abr.* 11.8 where Adam is described as a 'wondrous man, who is adorned in glory (δόξα)'. Adam is depicted in a manner typical of God or his glory in the Hebrew Bible and Dead Sea scrolls.[68]

In a fashion which recalls the Qumran description of God as a 'glorious man', the Qumran texts use the phrase 'glory of Adam' when speaking about the fulfillment of eschatological hope (1QS 4; CD 3; 1QH 17). And in a fragment of 4Q504, Adam is described as made in the likeness of God's 'glory': [Remember, O Lo[r]d that... Thou hast fashioned A[dam], our [f]ather in the likeness of [Thy] glory.' The *Testament of Abraham*'s description of Adam having the appearance of the 'Master' and being 'adorned in such glory' (11.4, 8) is part of a greater Jewish interest in associating Adam with God's 'likeness' and 'glory'.

The *Shepherd of Hermas*, a second-century CE Christian text, uses the same Qumran description of God as a 'glorious man' when speaking about Jesus:

---

67. All quotations from the Dead Sea scrolls are taken from Vermes (ed. and trans.), *The Dead Sea Scrolls in English*.

68. 1QS 4.23; 1QH 17.15; CD 3.20.

Hermas, *Sim.* 9.12.7-8: so you see, saith he, the six men, and the glorious
and great man in their midst, who is walking round the tower and
rejected the stones from the building? Yes, Sir, said I. I see him. The
glorious man, said he, is the Son of God, and those six are glorious
angels supporting him on the right hand and on the left.[69]

Hermas describes Jesus as the principal angel in the way that God is
described in Qumran as a 'glorious man' (1QM 12). Adam's likeness to
God in the *Testament of Abraham* is thus paralleled by Jesus' likeness
to God in the *Shepherd of Hermas*. The description of a human being as
godlike was not unheard in Jewish communities. With this in mind, the
'Ancient of Days' could be taken for Adam, since Adam has God's
likeness.

The second textual element to examine is the 'white like wool' hair
of the 'Ancient of Days'. This simile is usually understood to empha-
size how the 'Ancient' is either patriarchal or pure.[70] The canonical
writings support these associations as Job 15.10 and Ps. 51.7 demonstrate.

Job 15.10: The gray-haired and the aged are on our side, men even older
than your father.

Ps. 51.7: Cleanse me with hyssop, and I will be clean; wash me, and I
will be whiter than snow.[71]

Both patriarchal stature and purity were applied to Adam. In Wis.
10.1-2 Adam is called the 'first formed father of the world'.[72] In addition to the description of Adam as the 'father' in Wis. 10.1, 2 *En.* 58.1
gives a description of Adam as the father of Israel.

---

69. All quotations from the *Shepherd of Hermas* are taken from *The Loeb
Classical Library: The Apostolic Fathers* (2 vols.; eds. T. Page and W. Rouse; New
York: Macmillan, 1913). Hermas, *Sim.* 9.12 has several interesting elements: Jesus
is the 'glorious man', the 'Son of God', the 'ancient' one (9.12.2), the 'gate'
through which all who wish to enter the kingdom must pass (9.12.1), and he is surrounded by angels (9.12.8). Jesus' appearance as a glorious man and his function as
the 'gate' call to mind Adam's glorious appearance and his placement outside the
gates of heaven. Like the scene of *T. Abr.* 1.1–13.7, Hermas, *Sim.* 9 is a tour conducted by an angel who explains the process of judgment.

70. Lacocque, *Daniel*, p. 143.

71. For another text associating white with purity see Isa. 1.18.

72. All translations of the Apocrypha are taken from *The New Oxford Annotated Bible: New Revised Standard Version*.

> *2 En.* 58.1: Listen, children! In the days of [y]our father Adam, the
> LORD came down onto the earth and he inspected all his creatures
> which he himself had created.[73]

With reference to Adam's purity, Wis. 10.1-2 says that Wisdom
'delivered him from his transgression, and gave him strength to rule all
things'. These verses could be interpreted to mean that Adam recovered
from his fall through the agency of wisdom.[74] However, another interpretation has been suggested. Levison observes how the verb translated
'preserved' in 10.2 (διαφυλάσσειν), is used elsewhere in the *Wisdom
of Solomon* where it is understood as 'preserved from' rather than
'rescued from' (10.12; 17.4).[75] On this basis Adam is understood not to
have transgressed. This interpretation is supported by the *Wisdom of
Solomon*'s allusions to Cain as the one who is to be blamed for death's
entrance (2.24) and the flood (10.3-4).[76]

The *Life of Adam and Eve* makes it emphatic that Eve is responsible
for the fall and ensuing judgment and thus clears Adam of any wrong-
doing.

> *LAE* 18.1-2: And Eve said to Adam, You live on my lord. Life is granted
> to you, since you have done neither the first nor the second error, but I
> have been cheated and deceived, for I have not kept the command of
> God.[77]

In *De opificio mundi* Philo reflects an interest in safeguarding

---

73. This *2 Enoch* reading is from manuscript A as translated by F. Anderson
(*OTP*, I, p. 183). Sanders writes that 'The most striking feature of the *Testament of
Abraham* is the one that has just been noted: the lowest-common-denominator universalism of its soteriology' (*OTP*, I, p. 877). This theological universalism of the
author would naturally gravitate towards Adam. He is the patriarchal head of the
human race. As such he would be a logical interpretation for the figure called the
'Ancient of Days'.
74. Wis. 9.6, 'For though a man be never so perfect among the children of men,
yet if thy wisdom be not with him, he shall be nothing regarded', could imply the
same.
75. Levison, *Portraits of Adam in Early Judaism*, p. 60. In a puzzling remark,
Levison admits that Sirach 'exonerates Adam [from sin]...he does not exalt him'
(*Portraits of Adam in Early Judaism*, p. 133). Such a depiction of Adam necessarily
implies some degree of exaltation.
76. Levison, *Portraits of Adam in Early Judaism*, p. 62. In *Jubilees*, Gen. 3.8-
13 with its description of Adam as guilty before God is left out.
77. See also *Apoc. Mos.* 14.1-2.

Adam's status and places the blame for the entrance of evil on Eve while leaving Adam blameless.

> *Op. Mund.* 53: But since no created thing is constant, and things mortal are necessarily liable to changes and reverses, it could not but be that the first man too should experience some ill fortune. And woman becomes for him the beginning of blameworthy life.[78]

The second-century CE work *Epistula Apostolorum* enlarges upon Wis. 10.1-2 and makes Adam's innocence plain.

> *Ep. Apos.* 39: Adam was given the power to choose one of the two. He chose the light and put his hand upon it; but he forsook the darkness and cast it from him. So have all men the power to believe in the light which is life and which is the Father who sent me.[79]

White hair is not an exclusive attribute of God in Jewish literature. In the *Apocalypse of Abraham*, which may date as early as the first century CE, the angel of God Iaoel has hair 'like snow'(11.2). In fact, 11.2-5 describes Iaoel in terms borrowed from several Old Testament theophanies.

> *Apoc. Abr.* 11.2-5: The appearance of his body was like sapphire, and the aspect of his face was like chrysolite, and the hair of his head like snow. And a kidris (was) on his head, its look that of a rainbow, and the clothing of his garments (was) purple; and a golden staff (was) in his right hand. And he said to me, Abraham. And I said, Here is your servant! And he said, Let my appearance not frighten you, nor my speech trouble your soul. Come with me![80]

Iaoel's appearance calls to mind John's description of Jesus—'the one like a son of man'—in Rev. 1.14, where the latter's head and hair 'were white like wool'. This modeling of Iaoel and even Jesus, 'the one like a son of man', after the 'Ancient of Days' may have been anticipated by the LXX version of Dan. 7.13, where the 'one like a son of man' is identified with the 'Ancient of Days'. Concerning the LXX Rowland observes:

---

78. All translations of Philo are taken from F. Colson and G. Whitaker (eds. and trans.), *The Loeb Classical Library: Philo* (10 vols.; 2 suppls.; Cambridge, MA: Harvard University Press, 1929). *LAE* 35.1-3 and *Apoc. Mos.* 9.1-2 both present Adam as suffering for Eve's sin.

79. *Hom.* 3.17 of the late second-century Clementina also makes the same claim about Adam's innocence.

80. Iaoel also has the appearance of a man and is called by the divine name (*Apoc. Abr.* 10.3-4).

Whereas Theodotion follows the Hebrew and translates 'and he came to [ἕως] the Ancient of Days', the LXX translates the same Hebrew phrase in the following way, 'he came as [ὡς] the Ancient of Days', a variant which was probably known to at least two Jewish writers (Rev. 1.14 and *Apocalypse of Abraham* 11).[81]

Fossum argues that it would appear that the LXX version intends to present the Son of Man as God's delegate in much the same way as the Angel of the Lord often is represented as indistinguishable from God himself.[82]

Both the *Apocalypse of Abraham* and Revelation demonstrate how divine attributes like God's appearance could be shared with other figures, whether they be angelic or human. That Adam looks like God is matched by the descriptions of Iaoel and Jesus. The identification of Adam with the 'Ancient of Days' is in keeping with Jewish exegetical practices of the first century CE.

The Nag Hammadi writings also raise the possibility of a tradition which used the name 'old Adam' for a heavenly figure other than God. In *Steles Seth* 118.25-31 Seth praises his father (Adam apparently) with the words,

> *Steles Seth* 118.25-31: I praise you, O Father Geradamas—I your own son Emmakha Seth, whom you have ingenerately produced for the praise of our god. I am your own son. And it is you who are my own mind, my father.[83]

Geradamas as a designation for Adam occurs also in the *Ap. John* 8.28, *Zost.* 6.21 and *Melch.* 6.6.

> *Ap. John* 8.28: from prior acquaintance of the perfect mind through disclosure of the invisible spirit and the will of the self-originate, the perfect man appeared, the first manifestation and the true person, was named 'the Geradamas'...

---

81. Rowland, *The Open Heaven*, p. 98. E. Lust thinks ὡς reflects an early, pre-Masoretic Hebrew text ('Dan. 7.13 and the Septuagint', *ETL* 54 [1978], pp. 62-69). Goldingay sides with F. Bruce, who argues that ὡς reflects an old Greek midrash, and Goldingay adds that it was probably subsequent to the translation of the LXX since it does not suggest anywhere else in Dan. 7 that the 'one like a son of man' is divine (Goldingay, *Daniel*, p. 145; F. Bruce, 'The Oldest Greek Version of Daniel', *OTS* 20 [1977], pp. 25-26).

82. Fossum, *The Name of God*, p. 319.

83. All Nag Hammadi translations are mine.

Zost. 6.21: the first parent, the Geradamas, an eye of the self-originate aeon, the first perfect man; Seth Emmakha Seth, the child of Adamas, the father the immovable race...

Melch. 6.6: you Man of Light, immortal aeon the Geradamas.

Geradamas is a peculiar name. It appears to be a compound of Adamas prefixed with ger-. B. Layton favors explaining the prefix as the Greek hier- from ἱερός, 'holy'.[84] M. Tardieu opts for the Greek noun γέρας, 'venerable', and H.-M. Schenke thinks the adjective form γεραρός, 'stately', is a better choice for the prefix.[85] A. Bohlig looks elsewhere and derives Ger- from the Greek γέρων, 'old man', a choice which best fits the contexts where Geradamas is used.[86] In each instance the motif of Geradamas being the first, and by implication the oldest, is present.

Though there are no uses of Geradamas outside of the Nag Hammadi texts, there is a similar compound in Hippolytus. When describing the divine and human aspects of Jesus, in his work *Against Noetus*, Hippolytus describes Jesus' nature as, 'having from the Father (ἐκ τοῦ πατρός) that which is heavenly, since he is the Word, and [having] from ancient Adam (ἐκ παλαιοῦ Ἀδάμ) that which is earthly, since he is born by the Virgin' (17.9)[87] The parallelism of the phrases 'from the Father' and 'from ancient Adam' implies that 'ancient Adam' served as a title for the first man, Adam. There is even a similarity between this

84. B. Layton (ed. and trans.), *The Gnostic Scriptures* (New York: Doubleday, 1987), p. 34 n. f.

85. M. Tardieu (ed. and trans.), 'Les trois steles de Seth-Un écrit gnostique retrouvé à Nag Hammadi, introduit et traduit', *RSPT* 57 (1973), pp. 545-75 [567]; H.-M. Schenke, 'The Phenomenon and Significance of Seth', in B. Layton (ed.) *The Rediscovery of Gnosticism* (2 vols.; NumenSup., 41; Leiden: E.J. Brill, 1978–81), II, p. 594 n. 17. Schenke admits that he finds none of the explanations, including his own, convincing. For further discussion about the name Geradamas see B. Pearson (ed.), *Nag Hammadi Codices IX and X* (NHS, 15; Leiden: E.J. Brill, 1981), pp. 36-37.

86. A. Bohlig, 'Zum "Pluralismus" in den Schriften von Nag Hammadi', in M. Krause (ed.), *Essays on the Nag Hammadi Texts in Honour of Pahor Labib* (Leiden: E.J. Brill, 1975), p. 26. See also J.D. Turner's article, 'Sethian Gnosticism: A Literary History', in C. Hedrick and R. Hodson (eds.), *Nag Hammadi, Gnosticism, and Early Christianity* (Peabody, MA: Hendrickson, 1986), pp. 61-62.

87. Translation mine. The Greek text with a French translation can be found in P. Nautin, *Hippolyte: Contre les hérésies* (Paris: Cerf, 1949).

Greek title of Adam (παλαιός Αδάμ) in Hippolytus and the title 'Ancient of Days' in the Greek version of Dan. 7.9 (παλαιός ἡμερῶν).

If 'old Adam' is the correct meaning of Geradamas and rests upon an older Jewish tradition,[88] then the possibility of the author of the *Testament of Abraham* taking 'Ancient of Days' as a title for Adam would seem even more plausible.[89]

Adam Overseeing the World

In the *T. Abr.* 11.9, Adam sits on a golden throne outside the gates of Paradise and 'looks at the world'. This type of description appears in the Jewish Hellenistic work *Ezekiel the Tragedian*, where Moses sits enthroned like Adam and also gazes down upon the earth. In this Hellenistic work, Moses' vision of the earth is interpreted to signify the god-like knowledge Moses will receive.

> *Ezek. Trag.* 77-78: I gazed upon the whole earth round about: things under it, and high above the skies.

> *Ezek. Trag.* 87-89: As for beholding all the peopled earth, and things below and things above God's realm: things present, past, and future you shall see.

The tradition of Moses' grand knowledge is also found in Samaritan traditions. In the Samaritan commentary, *Memar Marqah* (*The Teachings of Marqah*), which dates to the third century CE, Moses is taught about the past and the future when he meets God at the burning bush.

---

88. An older Jewish tradition about Adam may have circulated among the Jews of the first century which eventually became part of Gnostic speculations. An example of this would be Josephus's identification of the first-century Jewish belief that Seth left some information for his descendants in tablet form on a mountain in *Ant.* 1.2.3. See A. Klijn, *Seth in Jewish, Christian, and Gnostic Literature* (NovTSup, 46; Leiden: E.J. Brill, 1977).

89. Quispel suggests that Geradamas 'seems to be the Greek translation of *Adam Qadmaia*, or *Adam Kadmon*' and connects it to the Mandean concept of the primeval man called Adam Qadmaia and the term Adam Kadmon of medieval Jewish mysticism. He believes all of these terms are old and of Jewish origin ('Ezekiel 1:26', pp. 3-4). Fossum ties in Manicheism by observing how 'the heavenly Man who is sent forth to fight against the powers of darkness is called Nasha Qadmaia in Theodore bar Konai's summary in Part XI of his *Book of Scholia*' (*The Name of God*, p. 278 n. 59).

> *Mem. Mar.* 1.1: He [God] taught Moses secrets in the bush (Ex. 3.2),
> which manifest His majesty and His glory. An Angel came up to him
> and stood before him; he discoursed with him about what had been and
> what was yet to be… Great was the miracle seen there, containing three
> quite distinct features: shooting flames; the bush standing up promi-
> nently in it; the angel proclaiming, while Moses listened fearfully. He
> said Moses, Moses, and he replied Here am I (Ex. 3.4, et seq.). Wonder-
> ful mysteries and all revelations were sent down.[90]

The idea of a human being looking down on the earth as a way of
gaining knowledge can also be found in the *Apocalypse of Abraham*. In
Apoc. Abr. 9.6 the angel Iaoel is sent to Abraham in order to give him
the knowledge of 'guarded things' and 'great things'. The means of
revelation used by Iaoel to give Abraham this special understanding is
similar to that used in *Ezekiel the Tragedian* and the *Testament of
Abraham*. After having ascended to heaven, Abraham looks down on
creation.

> *Apoc. Abr.* 21.1-2: And he said to me, look now beneath your feet at the
> firmament and understand the creation that was depicted of old on this
> expanse, (and) the creatures which are in it and the age prepared after it.
> And I looked beneath the firmament at my feet and I saw the likeness of
> heaven and the things that were there in.

Abraham, Moses and Adam all gain an understanding of creation
from their positions in heaven.

Rabbinic tradition records in *Genesis Rabbah* how Adam, when he
was still just a *golem* (an unarticulated lump), was given a knowledge
of the future pertaining to each generation of Israelites.

> *Gen. R.* 24.2: This is the book of the generations of Adam (Gen. 5.1).
> R. Judah bar Simon said: While the first man lay prone as a golem [an
> unarticulated lump] before Him who spoke and the world came into
> being, He caused to pass before him each generation with its expounders
> of Scripture, each generation with its sages, each generation with its
> scribes, and each generation with its leaders, as is said, O [Adam], when
> thou was still a golem, thine eyes did see all [the worthies whose names]
> were inscribed in thy book (Ps. 139.16).[91]

Gen. R. 11.1 and 12.6 also express this interest in the expansive

---

90. The translation is taken from J. MacDonald (ed. and trans.), *Memar
Marqah: The Teaching of Marqah* (2 vols.; Berlin: Alfred Töpelmann, 1963), I,
p. 3.

91. Translation taken from Bialik and Ravnitsky (eds. and trans.), *The Book of
Legends: Sefer Ha-Aggadah*. See also *Pes. R.* 115a.

knowledge of Adam by referring to the celestial light whereby Adam could survey the world from one end to the other. Unfortunately for Adam, this gift of celestial light was taken away when he sinned. In its place Adam was given two stones and the knowledge of making fire so that he might illuminate the darkness, thus protecting himself from the serpent. Only in the Messianic era will the enlightening celestial light return to man.[92] The phrase 'glory of Adam', used to describe the eschatological restoration at Qumran (1QS 4; CD 3; 1QH 17), appears to be related to the celestial light theme of *Genesis Rabbah*.[93]

This type of divine knowledge was associated with several other figures who carried out mediatorial duties as enthroned beings. In the Gospel of John, Jesus tells Nicodemus that he has both earthly and heavenly knowledge, operating as the heavenly 'Son of Man'.

> Jn 3.12: If I have told you about earthly things and you do not believe, how can you believe if I tell you about heavenly things? No one has ascended into heaven except the one who descended from heaven, the Son of Man.

The patriarch Enoch is given a cosmic understanding of creation in *1 En.* 60.

> *1 En.* 60.10: And he [the second angel] said to me [Enoch], You, son of man, according (to the degree) to which it is permitted, you will know the hidden things. Then the other angel who was going with me was showing me the hidden things: what is first and last in heaven, above it, beneath the earth, in the depth, in the extreme ends of heaven, the extent of heaven.[94]

In *2 Enoch* the theme of Enoch's knowledge is continued. In this text he is taught by the angel Vrevoil about all things.

> *2 En.* 23.12: And he [Vrevoil the Archangel] was telling me [Enoch] all the secrets of heaven and earth and sea ... and every kind of human thing, and every kind of language (and) singing, and human life and riles and instructions and sweet-voiced singing, and everything that it is appropriate to learn.

92. See Ginzberg (ed.), *The Legends of the Jews*, I, p. 86, V, p. 112 n. 104.

93. See Delcor for a discussion of the Qumran phrase 'glory of Adam' and its relationship to the idea of the restoration of Adam's privileges in the literature of Middle Judaism (*Le Testament*, p. 135).

94. The case for Enoch's knowledge can be supplemented if he is identified with the redeemer figure known as the 'Elect one—Son of Man' (49.13; 50.3) as *1 En.* 60.10 and 71.14 imply.

In *3 En.* 48 c.1-4 Enoch-Metatron is given great wisdom when he is brought up to heaven and made God's witness.

> *3 En.* 48 c.1-4: Alep: The Holy One, blessed be he, said: I made him strong, I took him, I appointed him, namely Metatron my servant, who is unique among all the denizens of the heights...Lamed: I took him— Enoch the son of Jared, from their midst, and brought him up with the sound of the trumpet and with shouting to the height, to be my witness, together with the four creatures of the chariot, to the world to come... I committed to him wisdom and understanding, so that he should behold the secrets of heaven above and beneath.

Adam's vast knowledge is best seen against this context of intermediary figures who shared in the divine attributes like Moses, Jesus, Enoch and Metatron—all of whom were enthroned in heaven. Adam's likeness to God extents beyond his appearance and name and includes his knowledge.

Abel

In comparison to Adam, Abel is rarely spoken about in Jewish literature.[95] E. Goodenough refers to a collection of liturgical fragments in the *Apostolic Constitutions*, first identified by W. Bousset, which were apparently drawn from a Hellenistic Jewish background.[96] Among these fragments, now entitled the *Hellenistic Synagogal Prayers* and dated to the second to third century CE, is a prayer which includes a list of priests. Prominent among the priests listed is Abel, who is identified along with several other notable patriarchs:

---

95. Abel is most often dealt with in conjunction with Cain. The study of V. Aptowitzer, *Kain und Abel in der Agada, den Apokryphen, der hellenistischen, christlichen, und muhammedanischer Literatur* (Vienna: R. Lowit, 1922), remains the definitive examination of the traditions about Cain and Abel.

96. E. Goodenough, *By Light, Light: The Mystic Gospel of Hellenistic Judaism* (Amsterdam: Philo Press, 1969), pp. 306-58. Bousset published these fragments in 'Eine jüdische Gebetssammlung im siebenten Buch der apostolischen Konstitutionen', in *Nachrichten von der königlichen Gesellschaft der Wissenschaften zu Göttingen: Philologische-Historische Klasse*, 1913–16, pp. 435-85. See also R. Eccles, 'The Purpose of the Hellenistic Patterns in the Epistle to the Hebrews', in J. Neusner (ed.), *Religions in Antiquity: Essays in Memory of Erwin Randall Goodenough* (SHR, 14; Leiden: E.J. Brill), pp. 207-26, esp. pp. 214, 220-21.

Thou who hast foreordained priests from the beginning for the govern-
ment of Thy people—Abel in the first place, Seth and Enos, and Enoch
and Noah, and Melchizedek and Job.[97]

Abel's role as first among priests is striking. Goodenough argues that
such a list of priests could only have come from a Jewish mystical
community closely akin to that of Philo and suggests 'that this prayer is
taken from the consecration of a "priest" Presbyter, or hierophant in the
Jewish Mystery'.[98] The idea of a chain of priests is comparable to the
idea of the 'seven pillars (Adam, Enoch, Noah, Abram, Isaac, Jacob
and Moses) of the world' who were granted a special revelation
according to the *Pseudo-Clementine Homilies*.[99]

The association of Adam and Abel in the *Testament of Abraham* is
found in *Apocalypse of Moses*. According to *Apoc. Mos.* 40.2-4, God
orders the angels to anoint both of their dead bodies.

> *Apoc. Mos.* 40.2-3: And God said to Michael, Gabriel, Uriel, and
> Raphael, Cover Adam's body with cloths and bring oil from the oil of
> fragrance and pour it on him. And thus they did and prepared his body.
> And the Lord spoke, Let also Abel's body be brought. And they brought
> other linens and prepared him also.[100]

In early Christian literature Abel is primarily portrayed as a righteous
man. Mt. 23.35 refers to 'the blood of righteous Abel'.[101] In 1 Jn 3.12
Abel's righteous deeds are contrasted with the evil deeds of his brother
Cain: 'why did he [Cain] murder him? Because his own deeds were
evil and his brother's righteous.'

An interesting account about Abel appears in Heb. 11.4: 'By faith
Abel offered to God a more acceptable sacrifice than Cain's. Through
this he received approval as righteous, God himself giving approval to
his gifts; he died, but through his faith he still speaks.' Abel is
described as 'righteous', and also said to be 'still' speaking after his
death. Gen. 4.10, 'Listen, your brother's blood is crying out to me', is

97. Translation taken from Goodenough, *By Light, Light*, p. 330.
98. Goodenough, *By Light, Light*, p. 331.
99. See *Ps-Clem. Hom.* 18.13, 14.
100. See also the Georgian *Book of Adam* 48.40, edited and translated by
J. Mahé, 'Le Livre d'Adam georgien', in M. Vermaseren (ed.), *Studies in
Gnosticism and Hellenistic Religions: Presented to Gilles Quispel on the Occasion
of his 65th Birthday* (EPRO, 91; Leiden: E.J. Brill, 1981).
101. See also *T. Levi* 5.4; *Apoc. Sedr.* 1.18; *Hellenistic Synagogal Prayers* 6.4;
Ps-Clem. Hom. 2.16.

being alluded to in Heb. 11.4 and has puzzled interpreters. Philo urged that a literal interpretation of Abel's crying was most correct and held that Cain slew himself and Abel actually lived on.

> *Det. Pot. Ins.* 14: So the words that follow 'Cain rose up against Abel, his brother, and slew him' (Gen. 4.8), suggest, so far as superficial appearance goes, that Abel has been done away with, but when examined more carefully, that Cain has been done away with by himself. It must be read in this way, 'Cain rose up and slew himself', not someone else. And this is just what we should expect to befall him. For the soul that has extirpated from itself the principle of the love of virtue and the love of God, has died to the life of virtue. Abel therefore, strange as it seems, has both been put to death and lives: he is destroyed or abolished out of the mind of the fool, but he is alive with the happy life in God. To this the declaration of Scripture shall be our witness, where Abel is found quite manifestly using his 'voice' and 'crying out' (Gen. 4.10) the wrongs which he has suffered at the hands of a wicked brother. For how could one no longer living speak?

Gen. 4.10, and its interest in the righteous dead, may be one of the starting points for Rev. 6.9-11, which refers to the souls of martyrs who are in heaven, clothed in white and crying out for justice.

> Rev. 6.9-11: When he opened the fifth seal, I saw under the altar the souls of those who had been slaughtered for the word of God and for the testimony they had given; they cried out with a loud voice, Sovereign Lord, holy and true, how long will it be before you judge and avenge our blood on the inhabitants of the earth? They were each given a white robe and told to wait a little longer...

The description in Revelation of the heavenly abode of the righteous dead who urge God to carry out his judgment is germane to the setting of Abel in the *Testament of Abraham*.

A second-century CE targum on Gen. 4.8, Neofiti, describes the conflict of Cain and Abel in ways which can be taken as supplemental to Abel's appearance in the *Testament of Abraham*.

> *Targ. Neof.* Gen. 4.8: Cain answered and said to Abel: There is no judgment, and there is no Judge and there is no other world. There is no giving of good reward to the just nor is vengeance exacted of the wicked. Abel answered and said to Cain: There is judgment, and there is a judge, and there is another world, and there is a giving of good reward to the just and vengeance is exacted of the wicked in the world to come.[102]

---

102. Translation taken from McNamara (ed. and trans.), *The Aramaic Bible*.

In this reading Cain argues with Abel over the issue of the afterlife, the judge, and the final judgment. Abel, in the *Testament of Abraham*, is placed in the 'judgment', as the 'judge', dispensing 'good reward' and 'vengeance', all in accordance with the interests of *Neofiti*.

The *Martyrdom of Isaiah*, which dates to the second century CE, offers a glimpse of heaven wherein Abel is present.

> *Mart. Isa.* 9.6-10: And he took me up into the seventh heaven, and there I saw a wonderful light, and also angels without number. And there I saw all the righteous from the time of Adam onwards. And there I saw the holy Abel and all the righteous. And there I saw Enoch and all who (were) with him, stripped of (their) robes of the flesh; and I saw them in their robes of above, and they were not sitting on their thrones, nor were their crowns of glory on them.[103]

Like the description of Abel in the *Testament of Abraham*, Abel has a throne (though it is unoccupied in *Mart. Isa.* 9.10). And akin to the *Testament of Abraham*, which infers the sanctity of Abel by contrasting him with 'Cain the wicked' (13.2), the *Martyrdom of Isaiah* identifies Abel as the 'holy Abel'. One further parallel exists when *Mart. Isa.* 9.6-9 is set alongside recension B of the *Testament of Abraham*. In both heavenly scenes the same figures, Adam, Abel and Enoch, are presented (*T. Abr.* B 8.5–11.10).[104]

One recension of the Syriac text of the *Testament of Adam* adds a word on the future resurrection of Adam's son Seth, who was the replacement for Abel.

> *T. Adam* 3.4: And after three days, while I am in the tomb, I will raise up the body which I received from you. And *I will raise it up and I will set it at the right hand of my divinity*. And I will make you a god as you desired. *And you also, my son Seth, and he will raise up*, (must) keep the

---

103. Paul's vision of heaven in the Christian *Apocalypse of Paul* includes an encounter with many biblical figures, including Abel and Adam (51).

104. Fossum argues that Abel, in recension B of the *Testament of Abraham*, should be identified with the man of great stature who is wearing three crowns: 'And behold, (there came) cherubim bearing two books, and with them was a very enormous man. And he had on his head three crowns' (*T. Abr.* B 10.8 [*The Name of God*, p. 277 n. 55]). However, a close reading of the text leads to the conclusion that this enormous man with three crowns is the judge's (Abel) assistant, Enoch. Both the immediate context, where the man *assists* the judge (10.7-10), and the following chapter, where Michael identifies the judge as Abel and the man as Enoch (11.1-4), make this clear.

commandments of God and not despise his words because he is going to come [emphasis mine].[105]

Here Adam tells Seth about his future resurrection, and the parallelism of the passage suggests that Seth too will be seated (at the left hand of the divinity?). This implied enthronement of Adam and his son Seth parallels that of Adam and his son Abel in the *Testament of Abraham*.[106] Seth as Adam's son is comparable to Abel.

When commenting on the whereabouts of Abel according to Syriac sources, S. Brock cites a fifth-century CE Syriac text which he believes is dependent on a very early Jewish tradition about Abel. This tradition, preserved in a homily by Jacob of Serugh (d. 521), makes it likely that Abel was believed to have ascended to heaven.

> *Hom. of Jacob of Serugh*: Indeed truly he [Cain] did not know where Abel was, and all unaware the truth thundered forth from his lips; for he did not know that at his murder Abel had departed to the land of the watchers, and that he had ascended and cried out in heaven before the divine majesty; and he was not aware that Abel had been raised to the abode of angels, and had battered the dwelling place of the heavenly beings with his cries; no, he did not realize that Abel had seen the face of the supernal king...[107]

Brock goes on to cite Ephrem, who polemicized against this type of tradition:

> *C. Gen.* 3.5: Once Cain had slain his brother, he then persuaded his parents that Abel had in fact entered Paradise because he had pleased God; proof of his entry there was his offering that had been accepted: for the keeping of the commandment effects entry into Paradise, just as your transgressing of it caused your departure from thence. Cain imagined that he had deceived his parents, and that Abel had no avenger, but at that point God was revealed over him and said 'Where is Abel your brother?'[108]

---

105. See Robinson, *The Testament of Adam*, p. 99.

106. There is also a similarity to the request of Jesus' disciples, James and John, in Mk 10.35-37: 'Teacher, we want you to do for us whatever we ask of you.' And he said to them, 'What is it you want me to do for you?' And they said to him, 'Grant us to sit, one at your right hand and one at your left, in your glory.' Their request for an enthronement with Jesus supports the idea of many enthronements in heaven.

107. S. Brock, 'Jewish Traditions in Syriac Sources', *JJS* 30 (1979), pp. 212-32 (226-27).

108. Brock, 'Jewish Traditions', p. 226.

Cain's explanation for Abel's entrance into Paradise is similar to what is found in the Christian *Apocalypse of Paul*. In his vision of the heavenly city of Christ, Paul sees men on golden thrones at the gates of the city who are wearing golden crowns and gems: 'And I turned and saw golden thrones which are set at the several gates, with men on them who had golden diadems and gems' (29). He is told that the enthroned figures are glorified on account of their innocence and goodness (29). These 'gate' enthronements on account of innocence and goodness are obviously similar to Abel's in the *Testament of Abraham*.

The promise of enthronement is a common theme in early Christian literature (Mt. 19.28; Eph. 2.6; Rev. 3.21). Paul may even have been assuming an enthronement of Christian believers when he told them that they are to judge angels (1 Cor. 6.2), since the posture of judgment was usually that of sitting (2 Cor. 5.10).

In the Hermetic text, *Kore Kosmou*, the idea of enthronement for faithfulness to God is also found. Here God tells the souls of heaven prior to their stationing on earth, 'If you are steadfast in obedience, heaven shall be your reward; you shall sit on thrones that are charged with potent forces' (17).[109] The Alexandrian provenance for *Kore Kosmou* and other Hermetic texts, along with the recognized influence of Judaism on Hermeticism, makes them invaluable for the *Testament of Abraham*, another Jewish-Egyptian text.[110]

Abel, who is known as Hibil in the Mandean texts, functions as a savior spirit in Ginza. According to one account, Hibil descends to the underworld in order to bring back imprisoned souls.[111] In order to return to his celestial home, Hibil must undergo purifying rites.

---

109. Translation taken from W. Scott and A. Ferguson (eds. and trans.), *Hermetica: The Ancient Greek and Latin Writings which Contain Religious or Philosophic Teachings Ascribed to Hermes Trismegistus* (4 vols.; Oxford: Clarendon Press, 1924–36).

110. See B. Copenhauer (ed. and trans.), *Hermetica: The Greek Corpus Hermeticum and the Latin Asclepius in a New English Translation, with Notes and Introduction* (Cambridge: Cambridge University Press, 1992), pp. xvi-xxxii, for information about the Alexandrian setting for the *Hermetica*. For an examination of the Jewish influence on Hermeticism see Pearson, 'Jewish Elements in Corpus Hermeticum I (Poimandres)', in Vermaseren (ed.), *Studies in Gnosticism*, pp. 336-48; and Quispel, 'Hermeticism and the New Testament, especially Paul', in W. Haase (ed.), *ANRW* 2.22 (Berlin, New York), forthcoming.

111. See Drower, *The Secret Adam*, pp. 36, 56-59.

> GR: Uthras rose up from their throne, baptized me with their baptism,
> and made me firm with their wonderous voice. Shitil-Uthra went for-
> ward and addressed me, Hibil-Ziwa: He said: Thy garment be shining
> and thy figure honored with thy Father, the Lord of Greatness. He twined
> for me a pure wreath, preserving me from everything detestable. It made
> me take place in its *skina*, where it itself already was.[112]

After his baptism by the Uthras (celestial spirits), Hibil-Ziwa (Abel
the Glory) is then welcomed by Shitil-Uthra (Seth), readmitted to
heaven, and thus established in the *skina* (the dwelling of the highest
deity). This conception of Abel as a heavenly intermediary who is
glorified is quite striking. After a ceremony which reads like an
enthronement ceremony—he is washed, dressed in a shining garment
and given a crown—Hibil takes his place with God and dwells in the
highest heaven, all of which may suggest his enthronement.[113]

In another Mandean text Abel touts his 'baptism' which promises
resurrection and ascension: 'Everyone that is baptized with my baptism, Hibil-Ziwa's, shall be erected with me, and shall be like me and
be a dweller in my world, Hibil-Ziwa's.'[114] In this passage Abel reaches
his greatest exaltation as heavenly mediator and exceeds the status
given to him in the *Testament of Abraham*.[115]

Together these Mandean texts have much in common with the conception of a heavenly Abel who serves as God's agent of judgment in
the *Testament of Abraham*. These parallel interests may serve as evidence that the Mandean traditions preserved old Jewish traditions about
Abel. The exaltation of Abel in the *Testament of Abraham* appears to
be just one example of a diverse tradition.

Other figures were given duties much like Abel's in the *Testament of
Abraham*. Melchizedek offers an interesting parallel to Abel's role as a

112. Translation taken from Widengren, 'Heavenly Enthronement and Baptism:
Studies in Mandean Baptism', in Neusner (ed.), *Religions in Antiquity*, p. 566.

113. Widengren identifies this scene as an enthronement ceremony ('Heavenly
Enthronement and Baptism', p. 566).

114. The text has been edited and translated by Drower in her book *The Haran-
Gawaita and the Baptism of Hibil-Ziwa* (Studi e Testi, 176; Citta del Vaticano:
Biblioteca Apostolica Vaticana, 1953). The translation given is taken from Widen-
gren ('Heavenly Enthronement and Baptism', p. 567).

115. Rudolph has illustrated how Abel carried out a judging function in Man-
deism through his selection of a judge (the personified Sunday) and destruction of
evil (*Die Mandäer* [2 vols.; FRLANT, 75; Göttingen: Vandenhoeck & Ruprecht,
1961], II, pp. 324-25). This evidence, however, is very late.

heavenly judge. In 11QMelch, Melchizedek is identified as a heavenly judge who as Elohim has taken his place in the divine council.

> 11QMelch: For this is the moment of the Year of Grace for Melchizedek. [And h]e will, by his strength, judge the holy ones of God, executing judgment as it is written concerning him in the Songs of David, who said, ELOHIM has taken his place in the divine council; in the midst of the gods he holds judgment.

The reference to Melchizedek 'executing judgment' and taking his 'place in the divine council' may serve to imply his enthronement since sitting was the posture of judgment (Job 29.7).

The Gospel of Matthew identifies Jesus as the 'Son of Man', who, like Abel in the *Testament of Abraham*, sits on a throne, in the company of angels, and judges all people as God's intermediator.

> Mt. 25.31-32: When the Son of Man comes in his glory, and all the angels with him, then he will sit on the throne of his glory. All the nations will be gathered before him, and he will separate people one from another as a shepherd separates the sheep from the goats.[116]

In *1 En.* 61.8 the 'Elect One', who is also known as the 'Son of Man' (*1 En.* 46.3), 'Messiah' (*1 En.* 52.4), and later identified as the patriarch Enoch (*1 En.* 71.14), is placed by God on a heavenly throne from which he judges the angels as God's intermediary: 'He placed the Elect One on the throne of glory; and he shall judge all the works of the holy ones in heaven above, weighing in the balance their deeds.' His judgment of human beings may be inferred from *1 En.* 46.4, where he is the one 'who would remove the kings and the mighty ones from their seats and the strong ones from their thrones'.

In a little known Jewish Hellenistic text called *Sepher Ha-Razim*, the *Book of the Mysteries*, there are several heavenly enthronement scenes which cast light on that of Abel's enthronement. This work, which dates to the third century CE, describes the seven firmaments of heaven and their different compartments, interspersing its description of the heavens with numerous magic formulas. In the following heavenly scene, which has some clear affinities with the *Testament of Abraham*, the angelic figures found in the second firmament are depicted.

---

116. One difference between Abel and Jesus is the location of their judging activities. Abel is a judge in heaven (*T. Abr.* 12.4-18) while Jesus appears to judge on earth (Mt. 25.31).

Sep. Raz. 2.92-95: These are they who stand on the sixth step. They behave with humility, but their faces are full of glory. Their garments are garments white as light. They stand like giants, awesome as the scholars of a court, seated on thrones of glory, trusted to give true (judgments), and in charge of healing.[117]

Like Abel these angels are enthroned and act as judges. And the reference to several enthronements provides a parallel to that dual enthronement of Adam and Abel. Attention should also be given to the association with glory these angels have. Along with Adam they have the distinct appearance of 'glory', since their 'faces are full of glory' and they sit on 'thrones of glory', like Adam does in recension B (*T. Abr.* B 8.5).

There are other parts of *Sepher Ha-Razim* which reflect the same interests as the judgment scene of *Testament of Abraham*. In 3.2, the second firmament is said to be ruled by three enthroned princes. In 5.4, 12 enthroned 'princes of glory' are said to rule the fifth firmament. In 6.6 there are two angels who rule the sixth firmament and who are presumably enthroned, though this is not stipulated in the text. In the seventh and final firmament, God alone is enthroned on a 'throne of glory' and judges (7.5-6) as the 'Ancient of Days' (7.30). All in all, *Sepher Ha-Razim* presents a picture of the heavens outfitted with a hierarchy of enthroned judges, much like the *Testament of Abraham* and its presentation of Adam, Abel, the 12 tribes of Israel and the Master God of all.

In *3 Enoch* the exalted angel Metatron, who was formerly the patriarch Enoch, is also given a role quite similar to that of Abel in the *Testament of Abraham*.

3 En. 16.1-5: At first I sat upon a great throne at the door of the seventh palace, and I judged all the denizens of the heights on the authority of the Holy One, blessed be he. I assigned greatness, royalty, rank, sovereignty, glory, praise, diadem, crown, and honor to all the princes of kingdoms, when I sat in the heavenly court. The princes of kingdoms stood beside me, to my right and to my left, by authority of the Holy One, blessed be he. But when Aher came to behold the vision of the chariot and set eyes upon me, he was afraid and trembled before me. His soul was alarmed to the point of leaving him because of his fear, dread, and terror of me, when he saw me seated upon a throne like a king, with ministering angels standing beside me as servants and all the princes of kingdoms crowned with crowns surrounding me.[118]

117. Translation taken from Morgan, *Sepher Ha-Razim*.
118. See also *3 En.* 10.1-5.

3 En. 48 c. 8 appears to summarize *3 En.* 16.1-5: 'I have fixed his throne at the door of my palace, on the outside, so that he might sit and execute judgment over all my household in the height.' Both these passages teach that Metatron, like Abel, was placed on a throne, positioned at an entrance, given the duties of judgment, and assisted by angelic beings in his duties.

In *Gedullat Mosheh* Metatron sits at the door of the palace of God judging and is then followed by God who in turn pronounces judgment. This is similar to Abel, who, in the *Testament of Abraham*, sits between the gates judging and is then followed by the judging activities of (the '12 tribes of Israel' and then) the 'Master God of all' (*T. Abr.* 12.4; 13.5-7).

> *Gedullat Mosheh*: I (Moses) saw further Michael, the great prince, standing at the right side of the throne, and Gabriel at the left; and Lefefiyah, the guardian of the law, standing before it; and Metatron, the angel of the presence, standing at the door of the palace of God. And he sits and judges all the heavenly hosts before his master. And God pronounces judgment and he executes it.[119]

Abel's position as a enthroned judge in the *Testament of Abraham* can thus be set alongside other Jewish figures like Melchizedek, Jesus, Enoch and Metatron. His characteristics were not peculiar but similar to other candidates for the 'Son of Man'.

In addition to his enthronement, Abel's appearance in the *Testament of Abraham* can also be seen in light of other exalted figures and thus placed in a broader setting. In *T. Abr.* 12.5 Abel is described as being 'bright as the sun (ἡλιόρατος). The word 'bright as the sun' does not appear anywhere else except in the *Testament of Abraham*, where it is also used to describe the angel Michael (2.4) and the angel Death (16.10). This is important because it shows that a supernatural being can appear with divine attributes.

But other figures do have similar descriptions. Ps. 84.11 says 'the Lord God is a sun (Hebrew: שֶׁמֶשׁ) and shield'. In Rev. 1.16 Jesus' 'face was like the sun (ἥλιος) shining with full force'. Rev. 10.1 uses a similar description when describing a mighty angel: 'I saw another mighty angel coming down from heaven, with a rainbow over his head; his face was like the sun (ἥλιος).' Another angel, in Rev. 19.17, is seen 'standing in the sun' (ἥλιος), assisting God in the apocalyptic

119. Translation taken from Gaster (ed. and trans.), *Studies and Texts: In Folklore*.

judgment. In *Sepher Ha-Razim* there is a prayer to an angel who ascends into heaven and appears to have authority over men: 'I beseech thee O great angel who art called "sun", who ascend the steps of the firmament, who watch the children of men, that you will perform my request...' (2.148).

Abel's likeness to the 'sun' appears to be a traditional way of describing figures associated with mediatorial activities and righteousness. In a prophesy of the savior king from Book 3 of the *Sibylline Oracles*, which is Egyptian in origin and dates to the first century BCE, it is said that God 'will send a king from the sun who will stop the entire earth from evil war'.

According to Mt. 13.43, 'the righteous will shine like the sun in the kingdom of their Father'. These texts may help explain Abel's exaltation which includes his likeness to the 'sun'. Abel, the righteous 'son of man' candidate ascended and became a heavenly being. He was even entrusted with judgment, as is often the case with the elect and righteous. Like Jesus the 'Son of Man', whose face shone like the 'sun' at his transfiguration and his later appearance to John in Revelation (Mt. 17.2; cf. Rev. 1.16), Abel the 'son of Adam' has been fashioned after other mediator figures.[120]

Conclusion

There can be little doubt that Middle Jewish literature contains references which depict Adam and Abel as exalted figures. Adam is variously depicted as enthroned, stationed at the gates of heaven and hell, as having a divine appearance, and as overseeing the world. Abel too is described as enthroned, residing in heaven, even as an intermediary. In addition, these interests should be understood as a persistent strain of Jewish thought that was able to penetrate both the Christian and rabbinic traditions. The interpretive choice of the author of the *Testament of Abraham* was not made in a vacuum. The position granted to Adam and Abel is in keeping with the types of traditions associated with them and other patriarchal figures.

---

120. In Rev. 7.2 an angel ascends from the 'rising of the sun'. Paradise was placed in the east (Gen. 2.8; cf. *1 En.* 32.2-3) and this may explain the association of looking like the sun and heavenly exaltation.

Chapter 5

THE PLACE OF THE *TESTAMENT OF ABRAHAM*
IN MIDDLE JUDAISM

The *Testament of Abraham* stands within a diverse history of traditions
taking shape during the period of Middle Judaism (300 BCE–200 CE).
There are elements from the apocalyptic judgment scene (chs. 11–13)
which can be used to identify both the traditions and the possible location of the writing of the *Testament of Abraham*. A careful examination
of this section reveals an author who incorporated Jewish, Egyptian and
Greek literary materials; interacted with Jewish ideas; was drawn to
ambiguous biblical texts; contributed to the developing interest in Hellenistic Jewish mysticism;[1] and polemicized against certain types of
throne mysticism, commonly called Merkavah mysticism.

Jewish, Egyptian and Greek Sources

The judgment scene of the *Testament of Abraham* has incorporated
materials from Daniel and other texts, both Jewish and non-Jewish.[2]
James's early work on the *Testament of Abraham* argued for the use of
'existing Jewish legends' and Egyptian judgment motifs by a second-
century 'Jewish Christian' who also added relevant Christian texts to
his account.[3] James was convinced of an Egyptian provenance for the

1. By Hellenistic Jewish mysticism, reference is being made to interest in the
divine throne as described by Ezekiel the prophet (1.26-29) and the celestial throne
world which is called Merkavah or 'throne' mysticism. This type of mysticism
ultimately led to a literature called Hekhalot or 'heavenly palaces' literature.
Scholem was the first to attempt to present a study of Jewish mysticism in its
entirety (*Major Trends in Jewish Mysticism* [New York: Schocken Books, 3rd edn,
1954]). For a full bibliography of this subject see Schafer, *The Hidden and Manifest God*, pp. 1-2 n. 2.
2. Dan. 7 was often drawn upon in combination with other biblical texts
(cf. Mk 14.62; Dan. 7.13; Ps. 110.1).
3. James (ed.), *The Testament of Abraham*, pp. 52-55, 76, 123-26. James's

Testament of Abraham. He carefully outlined a series of parallels with Egyptian religious materials, such as the recording angels (*T. Abr.* 12.12-13), which has a parallel in the Egyptian *Book of the Dead*, and the weighing of souls (*T. Abr.* 12.14), which is a prominent feature of Egyptian mythology.[4]

Box developed James's identification that Jewish traditions were being relied upon by the author by tying in a broader base of allusions to apocryphal literature. He concluded by denying any Christian influence on the original text.[5] Macurdy, writing in 1942 and developing the insight of Kohler, was the first to question seriously James's (and implicitly also Box's) omission of Hellenistic Greek texts as a source for the apocalyptic section of the *Testament of Abraham* 11–13.

> I wish to add to Dr. James's discussion of the apocalyptic chapters of re-cension A of the Greek text, the point that this 'christianized' part of the work, so akin in its eschatology to that of the Apocalypse of St. John, has *traits* derived from the Orphic doctrines of Plato's great eschatologi-cal myths, especially the Myth of Er in the *Republic*.[6]

According to Macurdy the apocalyptic judgment scene represents a mixture of 'Jewish, Christian, and Greek literature'—with the stress being on Plato as a contributor. An example will demonstrate how Pla-tonic literary themes have found their way into the *Testament of Abra-ham*. In the *T. Abr.* 12.4-5 Abraham notes how between the narrow gate and the broad gate, outside of which Adam was enthroned in 11.4, sat

insistence on a 'christianizing' of the *Testament of Abraham* is strange because after this suggested redaction Jesus is still missing from the text, even from the judgment vision where Abel is the judge. According to Christian teaching, Jesus is the judge. Bousset and H. Gressmann favored James's view that a Christian author used already existing Jewish materials (*Die Religion des Judentums im späthellenistischen Zeitalter* (Tübingen: J.C.B. Mohr, 3rd edn, 1926), p. 45.

4. James (ed.), *The Testament of Abraham*, p. 76.

5. Box (ed. and trans.), *The Testament of Abraham*, pp. xix, 17-22. Box also illustrated how many of the interests of the *T. Abr.* 11–14 became prominent in later rabbinic literature (*The Testament of Abraham*, p. 17 n. 2).

6. Macurdy, 'Platonic Orphism', p. 213 (emphasis his). Macurdy is not argu-ing for direct derivation from Plato, but that the 'philosophical and religious ideas of Plato sifted down through the hellenistic centuries and altered religious concep-tions, producing new literary forms' ('Platonic Orphism', pp. 225-26). Apparently Macurdy wrote in complete ignorance of Kohler's work in which he paralleled the judgment scene in Plato's Myth of Er with the judgment scene of the *Testament of Abraham* (Kohler, 'The Apocalypse of Abraham', p. 601).

the enthroned Abel who served as the first judge.

> *T. Abr.* 12.4-5: and between the two gates there stood a terrifying throne
> with the appearance of terrifying crystal, flashing like fire. And upon it
> sat a wonderous man [Abel], bright as the sun, like unto a son of God.[7]

Macurdy agrees with James that the idea of two gates is drawn from
the Gospel of Matthew (7.13-14), yet he adds that placing judges
between 'openings' is Greek in origin.[8] Plato's *Republic*, in its description of Er's vision of the judgment, places the judges of the afterlife
between the two openings of heaven.

> *Rep.* 10.614: He said that when his [Er] soul went forth from his body he
> journeyed with a great company and that they came to a mysterious
> region where there were two openings side by side in the earth, and
> above and over them in the heaven two others, and that judges were
> sitting between these, and that after every judgment they bade the righ-
> teous journey to the right...[9]

In fact, immediately prior to Abraham's sighting of Abel on his
throne, he encounters two angels 'with fiery aspect and merciless
intention and relentless look' who mercilessly drive and beat the
deceased souls (*T. Abr.* 12.1). This depiction of fearsome assistants
appears to be drawn directly from a later portion of Plato's description
of the judgment according to Er: 'And there they could see standing by,
he said, savage men and all fiery to look at, who understood the sound,
and seized some and carried them away' (*Rep.* 10.614).[10]

---

7.   Translations from the *Testament of Abraham* are mine.

8.   Dean-Otting points out how the heavenly gates through which the dead pass
is traceable to both Greek and Egyptian literature (*Heavenly Journeys*, p. 118).
Dean-Otting also presents a good survey of the Jewish, Egyptian and Greek allu-
sions in the *T. Abr.* 11–14, but unfortunately says nothing about the use of Dan. 7
(*Heavenly Journeys*, pp. 196-209). Ginzberg was convinced that by the first century
CE the idea of the 'two ways' and the 'two gates' was thoroughly assimilated by
Judaism ('Abraham', *JewEnc*, I, p. 95). Delcor connects the reference to the two
gates with the theme of the two ways found in the Hebrew Bible (Jer. 21.8 and
Deut. 30.15) and traces its development to the *Manual of Discipline* with its
description of the way of life and the way of darkness, which are associated with
specific angels—the Prince of Light and the Angel of Darkness (1QS 3.18-21), and
Mt. 7.13-14 (*Le Testament*, pp. 133-34).

9.   Translations from Plato are taken from *The Loeb Classical Library: Plato's
Republic* (2 vols.; ed. T. Page; Cambridge, MA: Harvard University Press, 1935).

10.   Macurdy, *Platonic Orphism*, p. 217. P. Kobelski identifies the parallels to
the two angelic scribes who operate as assistants in the judgment scene

The *Testament of Abraham*'s blending of judgment texts from both Jewish and non-Jewish literatures, from both religious and philosophical literatures, into a Greek text, reminiscent in both style and vocabulary of Jewish texts originating in Egypt, implies an Egyptian origin.[11] Macurdy looks to Egypt and specifies Alexandria as the most likely provenance.

> Dr. James notes that the book is chiefly Jewish, slightly christianized. It may have been composed or at least redacted by a Jewish Christian of Alexandria. This provenance would account satisfactorily for its Egyptian and its Greek Orphic traits.

Alexandrian 'Judaisms'[12]

When commenting on the apocalyptic portion of the *Testament of Abraham*, James observes,

> And this section is doubtless the kernel of the whole book. The chief object of the original author of it was to give publicity to his views on the judgment of souls. They are peculiar views, and so the redactors of the book have felt: the author of the B-text has revised them so much that he has left little of what we find in A. That the author of the A-text must have removed some glaring heterodoxies we feel almost certain, but cannot so clearly show.[13]

(*Melchizedek and Melchiresa* [Washington: CBQ Press, 1980], pp. 75-84).

11. See Chapter 1. For a rehearsal of the Egyptian features see Schmidt, 'Le Testament d'Abraham', I, pp. 71-76, 101-10.

12. There was no 'normative' rabbinic Judaism before 70 CE, but a variety of 'Judaisms'. What orthodoxy that existed had to do broadly with the temple and its cult and a few fundamental characteristics which were common to most Jews. Sanders has identified the beliefs common to Jews from the first century BCE through the first century CE (*Judaism: Practice and Belief*). A good example of the different Judaisms would be the varying conceptions of the Messiah(s) during this period. See J. Neusner and E. Frerichs (eds.), *Judaisms and their Messiahs at the Turn of the Christian Era* (Cambridge: Cambridge University Press, 1987). Neusner has criticized Sanders for his description of a 'single common-denominator Judaism' and argues that what results is a 'banal' form of Judaism which is of no scholarly value (B. Chilton and J. Neusner, *Judaism in the New Testament: Practice and Beliefs* [New York: Routledge, 1995], pp. 9-18).

13. James (ed.), *The Testament of Abraham*, p. 52. See also the marginal note of M. Blastares, dated to the fifteenth century CE, which James identifies as highlighting the unorthodox theology of the *Testament of Abraham* (*The Testament of Abraham*, p. 28).

James is not clear on what he terms the 'peculiar' nature of the apocalyptic section which was later redacted, but it probably had to do with at least two interests: the non-Jewish elements, such as the Egyptian materials like the recording angels and the weighing of souls; and especially the provocative image of Abel as 'Judge of souls', a theme which James does 'not find recurring in Jewish mythology'.[14]

Of most significance, however, is James's identification of a 'heterodox'[15] setting for this testament, a characteristic which Macurdy also highlighted.[16] Given the probability of the *Testament of Abraham*'s origin in first-century CE Alexandria, the issue of diversity of Alexandrian 'Judaisms' needs to be explored. What was the nature of Jewish thought in Alexandria at this period and can the apocalyptic section of the *Testament of Abraham* be related to it?

In a study entitled, *Der vorchristliche jüdische Gnosticismus*, M. Friedlander presented the thesis that Gnosticism was a pre-Christian phenomenon and originated in the Jewish antinomian communities of Alexandria.[17] He argued that later Christian 'heresies' such as the Ophites, Cainites and Sethians are the theological descendants of the radical antinomian groups against which Philo had polemicized. Friedlander believed that the origin of these groups could be traced to the situation in Alexandria where allegorical exposition of the biblical text flourished and where, as a result, antinomian practices could be defended. These antinomian Jews were taken to be the proto-gnostic

---

14. James (ed.), *The Testament of Abraham*, pp. 76, 125.

15. By heterodox James is making reference to those beliefs at variance with the accepted doctrines of what has come to be known as rabbinic or normative Judaism. The term itself is now seen to be anachronistic. There was great diversity among the Jewish communities of Middle Judaism.

16. Macurdy agrees with James that the author's views on the judgment of souls are peculiar, but appears to argue that any peculiar nature is really do to the Platonic element found in the *Testament of Abraham* (*Platonic Orphism*, pp. 213, 226). Strangely, the heterodox element has gone largely unnoticed by later interpreters such as Sanders (*OTP*, I, pp. 877-78).

17. M. Friedlander, *Der vorchristliche jüdische Gnosticismus* (Göttingen: Vandenhoeck & Ruprecht, 1898). H. Graetz anticipated Friedlander by tracing the reports of Gnosticism in the church fathers back to reports of sectarianism and heresy in rabbinic texts and argued that Gnosticism represented hellenistic speculative metaphysics which had penetrated Judaism (*Gnosticismus und Judentum* [Krotoschin: Monasd & Sohn, 1846]).

nucleus from which Gnosticism developed.[18]

Friedlander's thesis is important for the *Testament of Abraham* for two reasons. First, it provides a possible setting for the 'peculiar' views of the apocalyptic section of the *Testament of Abraham* by arguing for the existence of diverse Jewish communities in Alexandria. Secondly, and more significant, this thesis of antinomian Jewish communities can be modified to provide a better fit for the distinctive interests of the *Testament of Abraham*'s judgment scene.

B. Pearson has already modified Friedlander's proposal, but without specific reference to the text in question. In his article, 'Friedlander Revisited: Alexandrian Judaism and Gnostic Origins', Pearson sought to illustrate how Friedlander's idea of a pre-Christian, Jewish origin of Gnosticism deserved a second hearing.[19] In his effort to update and improve the thesis Pearson observed:

> Indeed, Friedlander's case could have been strengthened considerably had he referred to yet another class of antinomians in Alexandria, who apparently not only rejected the ritual laws, but did not even bother to resort to allegory in their denunciation of the 'objectionable' portions of Scripture. Such a class of 'antinomian' Jews are clearly referred to by Philo in *Conf.* 2f. ...[20]

Philo describes Jews who denounce and deny the Laws in *De confusione linguarum*.[21]

> *Conf. Ling.* 2.2: Persons who cherish a dislike of the institutions of our fathers and make it their constant study to denounce and deny the Laws find in these and similar passages openings for their godlessness. 'Can you still', say these impious scoffers, 'speak gravely of the ordinances as containing the canons of absolute truth?'[22]

18. Friedlander, *Der vorchristliche jüdische Gnosticismus*, pp. 17, 25-27.

19. B. Pearson, 'Friedlander Revisited: Alexandrian Judaism and Gnostic Origins', *StudPhilo* 2 (1973), pp. 23-39. See also Pearson's chapter, 'Jewish Sources in Gnostic Literature', in Stone (ed.), *Jewish Writings of the Second Temple Period*, pp. 443-81. L. Grabbe, in his historical survey of Judaism, has also argued for a pre-Christian Jewish Gnosticism (*Judaism from Cyrus to Hadrian* [2 vols.; Minneapolis: Fortress Press, 1992], II, pp. 514-19).

20. Pearson, 'Friedlander Revisited', p. 30.

21. P. Borden, in his survey of the writings of Philo of Alexandria, agrees with Pearson that Philo is refering to apostates of the Jewish community when defending the laws of Moses and the Jewish community in *De confusione linguarum* ('Philo of Alexandria', in Stone [ed.], *Jewish Writings of the Second Temple Period*, p. 244).

22. All translations of Philo are taken from Colson and Whitaker (eds.), *The*

Pearson's contribution to Friedlander's thesis allows it to be seen in a broader light, and thus in connection with 'examples of Gnostic literature wherein the literal sense of the Biblical text is taken at face value'.[23] While the argument here is not that the *Testament of Abraham* is gnostic, the existence of antinomian Jewish communities in Alexandria who interpreted biblical texts in a non-allegorical fashion is directly relevant for the study of the *Testament of Abraham* 11–13. The relevance lies in the literal fashion in which the figures of Dan. 7.9-25 are interpreted[24] and in the complete absence of the law as a factor in the final judgment, where the law is replaced by what Sanders calls 'the lowest common denominator universalism'.[25]

Another relevant insight offered by Pearson has to do with the interest paid to Cain and Abel by Philo. Pearson has demonstrated the symbolic nature of Cain and Abel for Philo, showing how Cain served as a type of heresy while Abel represented just the opposite, a 'God-loving creed'.[26] Continuing Philo's contrast between Cain as a prototype of heresy and Abel as a representative of the truth is the haggadic expansion on Gen. 4.8 in the Palestinian targum, *Targum Neofiti*, which Delcor referred to his commentary on the *Testament of Abraham* when commenting on Abel's role in *T. Abr.* 13.2.[27]

Loeb Classical Library: Philo.

23. Pearson, 'Freidlander Revisited', p. 31.

24. James writes that 'It is interesting to notice the tendency to literal interpretation, which is the parent of so many legends...' and goes on to identify a 'too literal' interpretation of Abel's blood crying out in Gen. 4.10 as the influencing factor in the author's selection of Abel as the first judge (*The Testament of Abraham*, p. 125 n. 1). However, it should be noted that a literal interpretation of Dan. 7.13 and its phrase 'one like a son of man' results in an interpretation akin to *T. Abr.* 12.2: 'This is the son of Adam, the first formed, who is called Abel.' This is similar to what Schmidt suggests: namely, that the Greek translator of the Semitic original of the *T. Abr.* misunderstood *ben adam* to mean 'son of Adam'; thus Abel as son of Adam equals Daniel's son of man (Schmidt, 'Le Testament d'Abraham', I, p. 64).

25. Sanders, *OTP*, I, p. 877. Concerning the theme of universalism without the law in the judgment scene of the *Testament of Abraham*, Boccaccini writes: 'The unit of measure is not the law, but rather a universally applied morality for which not even idolatry is a sin' (*Middle Judaism*, p. 259).

26. See *Det. Pot. Ins.* 1-2, 32-48, 178; *Poster. C.* 35, 52-53; *Sacr.* 2-5, 71 (Pearson, 'Friedlander Revisited', pp. 32-34).

27. Delcor, *Le Testament*, p. 143. The comparison of Philo with a Palestinian text should not be viewed as an anomaly. Both are Hellenistic Jewish texts that

Targ. Neof. 4.8: And Cain said to Abel his brother: Come! let the two of us go out into the open field. And when the two of them had both gone out into the open field, Cain answered and said to Abel: I perceive that the world was not created by mercy and that it is not being conducted according to the fruits of good words, and that there is favoritism in Judgment. Why was your offering received favorably and my offering was not received favorably from me? Abel answered and said to Cain: I perceive that the world was created by mercy and that it is being conducted according to the fruits of good words. And because my works were better than yours, my offering was received from me favorably and yours was not received favorably from you. Cain answered and said to Abel: There is no judgment, and there is no judge, there is no other world. There is no giving of good reward to the just nor is vengeance exacted of the wicked. Abel answered and said to Cain: There is a judgment, and there is a judge, and there is another world. And there is giving of good reward to the just and vengeance is exacted of the wicked in the world to come.[28]

This significance of Abel in Philo and *Targum Neofiti*, a second-century CE document,[29] parallels the importance Abel has in the *Testament of Abraham* where he is glorified and, more interestingly, contrasted with 'Cain the wicked' (*T. Abr.* 13.2). Segal points out that many heretical groups during this period and later came to be identified with Cain.[30] Strousma has argued that some second-century rabbis labeled Jews as heretics for exalting certain antediluvian figures.[31] Even

share a common interest in identical antediluvian figures. It is no simple matter to distinguish Hellenistic Judaism from Palestinian Judaism. See Grabbe, 'Hellenistic Judaism', in J. Neusner (ed.), *Judaism in Late Antiquity*. II. *Historical Syntheses* (Leiden: E.J. Brill, 1995), pp. 53, 72-73.

28. Translations from *Neofiti* are taken from McNamara (ed. and trans.), *The Aramaic Bible*.

29. For a second-century CE date of *Targ. Neof.* 15.17 see Alexander, 'Targum/Targumim', *ABD*, VI, p. 323; McNamara, 'Targums', *IDBSup*, pp. 856-61. See Boccaccini and his forthcoming book on *Targum Neofiti* for a detailed argument dating this tradition to the second century CE. P. Flesher dates *Targum Neofiti* to the second or third century ('The Targumim', in J. Neusner (ed.), *Judaism in Late Antiquity*. I. *The Literary and Archaeological Sources* [Leiden: E.J. Brill, 1995], p. 44). S. Isenberg argues that this exchange in *Targum Neofiti* was originally directed against the Sadducees, which, if true, may imply a date earlier than the second century ('An Anti-Sadducee Polemic in the Palestinian Targum Traditions', *HTR* 63 [1970], pp. 433-44 [437]).

30. Segal, *Two Powers in Heaven*, pp. 81-82.

31. Strousma, 'Aher: A Gnostic', II, pp. 808-18.

more compelling are the themes found in *Targum Neofiti* concerning
the merciful governance of the 'world', 'favoritism in judgment', the
final 'judgment', the presence of a 'judge', the existence of a 'world' to
come, and the issue of 'reward' and 'vengeance' described in *Targ.
Neof.* 4.8. J. Bassler notes how *Targ. Neof.* 4.8 is touching upon an
eschatological heresy in light of Cain's denial of basic eschatological
beliefs and represents a polemic attack against such ideology.[32] All of
these interests are specifically dealt with in the apocalyptic section of
the *Testament of Abraham*. Philo and *Targum Neofiti* testify to Jewish
speculative interests, both in Egypt and Palestine, surrounding an antediluvian figure like Abel during the time of the *Testament of Abraham's*
composition.

Quispel, who was among the first to adopt the position of what he
called a pre-Christian Jewish 'heterodoxy' at Alexandria,[33] has
extended Friedlander's thesis by adding the issue of the 'heavenly man'
to the controversies which Philo and Alexandrian Jewery debated. He
notes how Philo writes of a heavenly man whom he identifies with the
Logos, sometimes calling him the 'Man according to God's image'
(*Conf. Ling.* 28) or 'immortal, the Man of God' (*Conf. Ling.* 11).[34] This
notion of a heavenly man is a development from Ezek. 1.26-28 where
the appearance of God in a human form is described as 'the likeness of
the glory of the Lord'. According to Quispel, Philo's idea of a divine
Adam who is an 'idea, incorporeal, neither male nor nor female, by
nature incorruptible' is testimony to a pre-Philonic, Alexandrian
blending of Ezekiel's human figure of glory with the Platonic idea of
man.[35] Quispel quotes Philo to make his case that the Jewish philoso-
pher was familiar with Alexandrian speculations about a heavenly
Adam who was male and female.

---

32. J. Bassler, 'Cain and Abel in the Palestinian Targums: A Brief Note on the
Old Controversy', *JSJ* 17 (1986), pp. 56-64 (62-64). Bassler connects the Cain and
Abel controversy passages of the targums with the 'two powers' debate and sees
the insertion of this debate at Gen. 4.8 as an attempt to fill in the Masoretic Text
since it fails to record what Cain said nor to specify why Abel's offering was more
acceptable than Cain's ('Cain and Abel', pp. 56-62). The explanation of Dan. 7.9-
25 was an interest of the *Testament of Abraham*.

33. See 'Der gnostische Anthropos und die jüdische Tradition', *ErJb* 12 (1954),
pp. 195-234; 'Gnosis', in Vermaseren (ed.), *Die orientalischen Religionen im
Römerreich* (EPRO, 93; Leiden: E.J. Brill, 1981), pp. 413-35.

34. Quispel, 'Ezekiel 1:26', p. 4.

35. Quispel, 'Ezekiel 1:26', p. 4.

> *Rev. Div. Her.* 33: For, says Moses, God made man; in the image of God created he him; male and female created he them. He no longer says him, but them in the plural number, adapting the species to the genus, which have, as I have already said, been divided with perfect equality.

Philo's polemical attack on an Adam tradition in Alexandria, wherein Adam is portrayed as having the same androgynous nature as God, serves to enlarge the historical setting for the *Testament of Abraham*'s portrayal of Adam as an enthroned figure of such glory that he has an appearance like 'the Master's' (*T. Abr.* 11.5). Jews in Egypt and Palestine were taken with the significance of ancient figures. Of even more importance than the exalted status of Adam is the focal point of Philo's attention—an ambiguous biblical text like Gen. 1.26 which was the subject of differing interpretations and ensuing beliefs about Adam.

Ambiguous Texts

Hurtado, at the close of his chapter 'Exalted Patriarchs as Divine Agents', suggests this theme was prompted by two concerns.[36] First, the exaltation of such figures helped to elevate Jewish religious traditions above all others.

> In the eyes of earthly rulers, Judaism might be only one peculiar religion among others, but for God, the heavenly king over all, to appoint Moses, Jacob, or Esau as his honored viceroy or vizier surely meant that the religious tradition they represented was in fact the divinely endorsed truth, above all other claims to the truth.

Secondly, the exalted figures served as an assurance of eschatological reward.

> In similar fashion it seems likely that the installation of Moses or other patriarchs was seen as prefiguring, and giving assurance of, the ultimate vindication of the Jewish faithful.

These are worthwhile insights. The exaltation of Adam and Abel in the *Testament of Abraham* is compatible with the concerns identified by Hurtado. Still, the contents of Dan. 7.9-27 are such that an additional motivation can be offered. Daniel 7 deals with a series of figures who are taking part in an admittedly baffling (by Daniel's account) scene.

---

36. Hurtado, *One God, One Lord*, pp. 65-69.

It is mysterious. Segal may hold the key to *Testament of Abraham*'s use of Dan. 7.9-27. His comments on the development of Christology brings to light the motivation behind the interpretation of Adam, Abel and Israel as the entities of Daniel 7.

> It does not seem necessary to believe that early Christians merely associated Jesus with some pre-existent savior model who came equipped with a fixed title and job description. Rather, it appears the debate between Christianity and Judaism proceeded partially on midrashic or exegetical lines. Ambiguous passages in scripture were clarified by each side of the debate through the use of other scriptural passages which mentioned the same vocabulary or concept.[37]

'Ambiguous passages' which needed clarification contributed to Christological speculation.[38] W. Meeks argues that the Moses speculation of *Ezekiel the Tragedian* was probably drawn from an early exegetical tradition based on Deut. 33.5.[39] In line with this thought, I. Gruenwald proposes that the traditions of apocalyptic literature 'were invented mainly for exegetical purposes, that is, to clear up the vague references made in scripture'.[40] Gruenwald may not be correct in arguing that apocalyptic literature is *mainly exegetical* in origin, but there can be no doubt that Dan. 7.9-27 is a passage exegeted by different communities of Middle Judaism, messianic and non-messianic—often in apocalyptic texts.[41] Stone has argued for real visions behind the apocalyptic texts, and has been supported by Rowland.[42] J. VanderKam

37. Segal, *Two Powers in Heaven*, pp. xi-xii.

38. Juel also takes this approach and argues persuasively that 'The beginnings of Christian reflection can be traced to interpretations of Israel's Scriptures, and the major focus of that scriptural interpretation was Jesus' (*Messianic Exegesis*, p. 1).

39. W. Meeks, *The Prophet King: Moses Traditions and the Johannine Christology* (NTSup, 14; Leiden: E.J. Brill, 1967), p. 94.

40. I. Gruenwald, *From Apocalypticism to Gnosticism: Studies in Apocalypticism, Merkavah Mysticism and Gnosticism* (BEATAJ, 14; Frankfurt: Peter Lang, 1988), p. 58.

41. Besides the New Testament texts referred to earlier which allude to Dan. 7.9-27, 4.4 of the Revelation of John has a heavenly court scene with enthroned 'elders' (aged human beings) dressed in white, and 2.6 of Ephesians says believers are enthroned with Christ in heaven. Eph. 1.17–2.6 describes a heavenly court with three entities: God, Christ, and believers. Like Adam and Abel of the *Testament of Abraham*, the elders of Rev. 4.4 and God, Christ, and the believers of Eph. 2.6 are all enthroned before the end.

42. See M. Stone, 'Apocalyptic-Vision or Hallucination?', *Milla wa-Milla* 14

has introduced a mediating position which sees in the visions of
1 Enoch a reliance on 'mantic wisdom' and 'scriptural texts'.[43] Most
recently, M. Himmelfarb has presented a strong case for understanding
apocalyptic texts as written works based upon exegetical work and
asserts that 'the adaptation of earlier traditions (often written), the per-
vasive allusions to the Bible and to other apocalyptic works, and the
centrality of interpretation are possible only in writing'.[44] Daniel served
as exegetical 'fodder' for centuries[45] and it is the foundational text for
the *Testament of Abraham*'s judgment scene, which can best be
explained as an exegetical reworking of Daniel 7.

Even Josephus, a first-century non-apocalyptic writer, elaborated
upon Daniel and departed from the biblical account in order to clear up
inconsistencies in the text. According to Vermes, the result of Josephus's minor alterations was a more detailed and coherent Daniel
'which at the same time is smoother and more logical'.[46] L. Feldman
identified one of Josephus's aims in paraphrasing his Bible was to
'clear up or explain apparent contradictions in his Biblical text'.[47] And
there are apocalyptic writings such as the Parables of *Enoch* which
demonstrate how this ambiguous passage of Daniel was exegeted non-
Christologically.

> *1 En.* 46.1-3: At that place, I saw the One to whom belongs the time
> before time. And his head was white like wool, and there was with him
> another individual, whose face was like that of a human being. His coun-
> tenance was full of grace like that of one among the holy angels... Who
> is this, and from whence is he who is going as the prototype of the
> Before Time? And he answered me and said to me, This is the Son of
> Man to whom belongs righteousness, and with whom righteousness
> dwells.[48]

> *1 En.* 71.13-14: Then the Antecedent of Time came with Michael,
> Gabriel, Raphael, Phanuel, and a hundred thousand and ten million times

(1974), pp. 47-56, and Rowland's comments in *The Open Heaven*, pp. 214-28.

43. J. VanderKam, *Enoch and the Growth of the Apocalyptic Tradition*
(CBQMS, 6; Washington: Catholic Biblical Association, 1984), p. 190.

44. M. Himmelfarb, *Ascent to Heaven in Jewish and Christian Apocalypses*
(New York: Oxford University Press, 1993), p. 99.

45. See Collins's survey of the interpretation of Daniel (*Daniel*, pp. 72-126).

46. Vermes, 'Josephus' Treatment of the Book of Daniel', *NTS* 92 (1991),
pp. 151-68 [162].

47. L. Feldman, 'Josephus' Portrait of Daniel', *Hen* 14 (1992), pp. 80-97 (89).

48. All translations from the Pseudepigrapha are taken from the *OTP*.

a hundred thousand angels that are countless. Then the angel came to me and greeted me and said to me, You, son of man, who art born in right-eousness and upon whom righteousness has dwelt, the righteousness of the Antecedent of Time will not forsake you.

This text is well known for its interpretation of Enoch as the 'Son of Man'. Jesus and Enoch are not the only candidates for the 'Son of Man'. The Qumran War Scroll probably retold Daniel 7 with the angel Michael as the 'Son of Man'.

> 1QM 17.6-8: He will send eternal succour to the company of His redeemed by the might of the princely Angel of the kingdom of Michael. With everlasting light he will enlighten with joy (the children) of Israel; peace and blessing shall be with the company of God. He will raise up the kingdom of Michael in the midst of the gods, and the realm of Israel in the midst of all flesh. Righteousness shall rejoice on high, and all the children of His truth shall jubilate in eternal knowledge.[49]

In 1QM 17.6-8 Michael is empowered in a manner analogous to the 'one like a son of man' in Dan. 7.13-14, who is given dominion by the Ancient of Days. The Qumran author's angelic interpretation of the 'one like a son of man' has been argued by a growing number of inter-preters as in keeping with the original intention of Dan. 7.13.[50]

Scholars have noted how Dan. 7.13 in the LXX says the 'Son of Man' came as (ὡς) the 'Ancient of Days'.[51] Segal argues that such an identification of the 'Son of Man' could be taken as defending against a 'two powers' doctrine, though this seems unlikely,[52] or as an early speculative attempt in identifying 'who' the 'Ancient of Days' may be. This type of 'blurring' between two exalted beings can be seen in *Gedullat Mosheh* where the 'Almighty sits and judges the ministering angels' (5) and 'Metatron, the angel of the presence...sits and judges

49. Rowland suggests the dependence of 1QM 17 on Dan. 7 ('Apocalyptic Lit-erature', p. 178). All quotations of the Dead Sea scrolls are taken from Vermes, *The Dead Sea Scrolls in English*.

50. M. Black, 'The Throne Theophany Prophetic Commission', pp. 57-73; Rowland, 'The Vision of the Risen Christ in Rev. 1:13ff.: The Debt of an Early Christology to an Aspect of Jewish Angelology', *JTS* 31 (1980), pp. 1-11; Fossum, 'Jewish Christian Christology', pp. 260-87.

51. See Fossum, *The Name of God*, p. 319; and Rowland, *The Open Heaven*, p. 98.

52. Segal, *Two Powers in Heaven*, pp. 201-202. See Fossum, *The Name of God*, pp. 163-64.

all the heavenly hosts' (8).[53] Since the author quotes Dan. 7.10 when describing the setting for the judgment scene in v. 5, it is clear that the 'Almighty' is taken to be the 'Ancient of Days' of Dan. 7.9.[54]

In the second century CE Justin came into contact with Jews who puzzled over Daniel 7. Afterwards Justin quotes Daniel 7:

> *Dial.* 31-32: Trypho says, Sir, these and such like passages of scripture compel us to await One who is great and glorious, and takes over the everlasting kingdom from the Ancient of Days as Son of man. But this your so-called Christ is without honour and glory, so that He has even fallen into the uttermost curse that is in the Law of God, for he was crucified.[55]

Evidence even exists which illustrates how the Rabbis debated the 'two powers' doctrine with the 'minim' (heretics). These contentions involved, among other verses, Dan. 7.9.

> *b. Sanh.* 38b: R. Yohanan said: in all the passages which the minim have taken (as grounds) for their heresy, their refutation is found near at hand. Thus: let us make man in our image (Gen. 1.26)—and God created (singular) man in His own image (1.27)... Til thrones were placed and (one that was) the ancient of days did sit (Dan. 7.9).[56]

Concerning these rabbinic controversies over 'heretical' interpretations of enigmatic biblical passages like Daniel 7, I. Culianu writes:

> Different rabbinic sources, the earliest of which is the Mekhilta, a II cent. midras in Shemot, record a 'heretical' doctrine, viz. that of STY RSWYWT BSMYM, 'Two Heavenly Powers.' The rabbinic evidence comes from Palestine and precedes the religious contact with Zoroastrianism in Amoraic Babylonia. The accursed doctrine, i.e. ditheism or binitarianism, derives from the interpretation of 'dangerous' biblical passages, e.g. the (formal?) plural Elohim in Bereshith, the angel in Shemot 20f. or the Son of Man in Dan 7,9.[57]

---

53. Quotes from *Gedullat Mosheh* are taken from Gaster's *Studies and Texts: In Folklore*. Like Iaoel, in the *Apocalypse of Abraham*, Metatron shares divine attributes with the Almighty.

54. '...a fiery stream issued and came forth before him; thousand thousands ministered unto him, and ten thousand times ten thousand stood before him; the judgment was set and the books opened' (Dan. 7.10).

55. Translations from the Church Fathers are taken from Roberts and Donaldson (eds.), *The Ante-Nicene Fathers*.

56. Translations of the *Babylonian Talmud* are taken from Epstein (ed.), *The Babylonian Talmud*.

57. I. Culianu, 'The Angels of the Nations and the Origins of Gnostic Dualism',

Segal takes note of the centrality of Daniel 7 in Jewish mystical speculations which bordered on the 'dangerous' according to rabbinic Judaism, and states,

> The now familiar reference to Dan. 7:9f. further substantiates that other groups were making 'dangerous' interpretations of that verse, and that Daniel's vision substantiated the mystical doctrine [which drew parallels between Metatron and God]. The mystics of the third century and fourth century inherited these esoteric traditions about the night vision of Daniel and used them in an exegesis central to their position.[58]

It is not hard to imagine why the author of the *Testament of Abraham*, a book which deals with the controversial topic of judgment, would use a text like Daniel 7. Besides being a passage of great interest susceptible to various interpretations, it has one of the few scenes of judgment in the scriptures and apparently was the textual starting point for competing eschatological speculations because of its elusive nature. The homiletic midrash *Tanhuma*, which existed in substance no later than 400 CE, bears witness to the exegetical problem which Dan. 7.9 generated when rabbinic Judaism sought to explain the judgment. In this text the problem of a plural 'thrones' and the 'white' hair of God needs to be resolved. The 'thrones' are ultimately designated for God and the 'great men of Israel' and the anthropomorphic 'white' hair of God is interpreted symbolically.

> *Tanh Qid.* 1: The Lord of Hosts will be exalted in judgment (Is. v. 16). When will the Holy One, blessed be He, be raised on high in His universe? When He executes judgment on the gentile nations; as it is said, The Lord standeth up to plead, and standeth to judge the the peoples (ibid. iii. 13); and also, I beheld till thrones were placed (Dan. vii. 9). Are there, then, many celestial thrones? Is it not written, I saw the Lord sitting upon a throne high and lifted up (Is. vi. 1), and also, A king that sitteth on the throne of judgment (Prov. xx. 8)? What, then means thrones? R. Jose of Galilee declared, The term implies the Throne and its footstool. R. Akiba declared, It refers to the thrones of the gentile nations which He will overturn; as it is said, I will overthrow the thrones of kingdoms (Hag. ii. 22). The Rabbis declared, In the Hereafter the Holy One, blessed be He, will sit, and the angels will set thrones for the great men of Israel who will be seated upon them; the Holy One, blessed be He, will sit with the Elders of Israel like a President of a Beth Din and

in R. van der Broek and M. Vermaseren (eds.), *Studies in Gnosticism and Hellenistic Religions* (EPRO, 91; Leiden: E.J. Brill, 1981), p. 85.

58. Segal, *Two Powers in Heaven*, pp. 66-67.

judge the gentile nations; as it is said, The Lord will enter into judgment
with the elders of His people (Is. iii. 14). It is not written against the
elders but with the elders, which indicates that the Holy One, blessed be
He, will sit with them and judge the gentile nations. What means, The
hair of His head like pure wool (Dan vii. 9)? The Holy One, blessed be
He, clears Himself with respect to the gentile nations by giving them
their reward for the minor precepts which they observed in this world so
as to judge and sentence them in the World to Come, that they may have
no plea to make and no merit can be found on their behalf.[59]

Regarding the lack of clarity in Daniel 7's vision, Goldingay writes,
'its allusiveness makes it at least likely that an element of mystery is
built into the vision'.[60] And given the figures of Daniel 7, it is no mystery why the author would want to interpret them—his purpose is to
inform his reader about the judgments to come and those persons who
participate in them. It can even be surmised that the author interpreted
the figures in the reverse order of their appearance in Daniel, working
from the most obvious, God as the 'Most High', to the least obvious,
Adam as the 'Ancient of Days', who could legitimately be understood
as the 'Ancient of Days' because of the existing Jewish traditions about
Adam's likeness to God, enthronement, and presence in the heaven.

Incipient Mystical Interests

Kohler, in an early response to James in which he contested the thesis
of a Christian origin for the *Testament of Abraham*, was the first to
detect mystical interests in the apocalyptic section.[61] His opinion was
based upon Abraham's chariot ride through heaven in *T. Abr.* 10.1–
11.1, which leads to his vision of the judgment. Kohler goes on to cite
the parallels in the *Gedullat Mosheh* and the Parables of *Enoch*, where
prominent biblical figures ascend into heaven under the guidance of a
heavenly being just as Abraham does. He states:

> We have here the 'mystery of the מעשה מרכבה,' 'the practical use of the
> divine chariot,' about which the oldest Rabbinical traditions...speak so
> characteristically as of an actual miracle-working power.[62]

---

59. Translation taken from A. Cohen (ed.), *Everyman's Talmud* (New York:
E.P. Dutton, 1949).
   60. Goldingay, *Daniel*, p. 169.
   61. Kohler, 'The Apocalypse of Abraham', pp. 579-606.
   62. Kohler, 'The Apocalypse of Abraham', pp. 592-93.

Turner, in his unpublished doctoral dissertation, added to Kohler's detection of mysticism in Abraham's chariot ride and traced this interest to Babylonian sources.

> It goes back to Babylonian antiquity as the mythology which later developed mysticism. A chariot ride through the heavens was often the method by which a certain mystical experience was described of the experience of the initiate into sacred mysteries, who then proceeded to learn the secrets of the universe.[63]

Turner was also drawn to a second mystical element of the text, that of Abraham's vision of the exalted Adam in *T. Abr.* 11.4-12, and refers to parallels with mystical midrashim legends about the creation of Adam and his tremendous size.[64] The strength of the mystical interests in the apocalyptic section moves Turner to conclude:

> The evidence given above does nothing to resist the conclusion, and in fact supports it, that the *Testament of Abraham* either emerged from an esoteric environment, or else was afterwards used and adapted by that kind of theosophical circle.[65]

The studies of Jewish mystical literature by G. Scholem and Gruenwald confirm Turner's conclusion about the *Testament of Abraham*'s association with esoteric Jewish interests.[66] By comparing chs. 11–13 of the *Testament of Abraham* with the characteristics of later Merkabah mysticism that Scholem and Gruenwald identify, such as ascents to heaven, terrified human visionaries, revelations about the divine and

---

63. Turner, 'The Testament of Abraham: A Study', pp. 12-122. The knowledge given to Abraham is a central motif of the testament (*T. Abr.* 9.8; 19.7-16).

64. Turner, 'The Testament of Abraham: A Study', p. 122. According to R. Eliezer, 'He [God] so created him [Adam] as to fill the entire world from the east to the west... north to south... through the entire world' (*Gen. R.* 8.1; translation taken from *Genesis Rabbah: The Judaic Commentary on the Book of Genesis: A New Translation* [ed. J. Neusner; Atlanta: Scholars Press, 1982]).

65. Turner, 'The Testament of Abraham: A Study', p. 120. Turner argues that Abraham's words to death in *T. Abr.* 17.11—'Yes, I shall be able to behold all your ferocity, on account of the name of the living God, because the power of my heavenly God is with me'—reflects the mystical theme concerning the power of the divine name and finds its use in theosophy with the claims of mystical devotees that they knew the pronunciation of the four sacred letters and could, by means of the divine name, visit paradise ('The Testament of Abraham: A Study', p. 136).

66. Scholem, *Major Trends*; Gruenwald, *Apocalyptic and Merkavah Mysticism* (AGJU, 14; Leiden: E.J. Brill, 1978) and *From Apocalypticism to Gnosticism*.

throne visions, the status of the *Testament of Abraham* as a mystically oriented text can be demonstrated.[67]

However, as Dean-Otting proposes, it is best to situate the *Testament of Abraham* at a juncture between the scriptures of ancient Judaism and that vast body of esoteric literature known as Hekaloth.[68] Unlike the ancient Jewish scriptures in general, it is not silent on the motif of ascent into heaven. Yet, this document does not include that type of experience typical of Hekaloth writings—the 'descent' to the Merkabah and a vision of the enthroned deity. Instead, like other Hellenistic Jewish literature sharing the same theme of a heavenly ascension,[69] the *Testament of Abraham* represents a literature in transition between apocalypticism and mysticism which shares characteristics of both. Delcor recognizes the embryonic mystical elements of the text and builds a case for an Essene provenance because of the Essene interest in these types of speculations.[70]

67. Scholem argues that in *1 Enoch* the 'main subjects of the later Merkavah mysticism already occupy a central position' and lists them as celestial hosts, heaven with angels, new revelations, throne visions, palace visions, the celestial spheres, paradise, hell, and the containers of souls (*Major Trends*, p. 43). Gruenwald also works with *1 Enoch* and identifies it as possessing the elements 'which became typical of later Merkavah mysticism'. He singles out four elements that he considers to be common in the literature of Merkavah mysticism: an ascent to heaven, the idea of a house within a house, the terror felt by the visionary, and the vision of God seated on a throne (*Apocalyptic and Merkavah Mysticism*, pp. 36-37). See also Gruenwald, *From Apocalypticism to Gnosticism*, pp. 20-23.

68. Dean-Otting, *Heavenly Journeys*, p. 262.

69. Dean-Otting summarizes the features common to all Jewish heavenly journey descriptions of the Hellenistic period, a category which includes *1 En.* 14, the *Testament of Levi*, *3 Baruch*, the *Testament of Abraham*, *2 Enoch*, *4 Ezra* and the *Apocalypse of Abraham* (*Heavenly Journeys*, pp. 265-89).

70. Delcor, *Le Testament*, pp. 71-73. The mystical interests of the *Testament of Abraham* makes an Essene authorship more attractive given the mystical interests of the Essene-Qumran community. Kohler first argued for this position ('The Apocalypse of Abraham', p. 591), but was usually dismissed because his characteristics for Essenism were too general (*OTP*, I, p. 876). J. Kaufmann proposed an origin in Jewish mystical circles, 'perhaps even Essene' for the origin of the hypothetical Adam book ('Adambuch', *EncJud*, I, p. 792). Stone, while admitting that Kaufmann's idea of Essenism was dated, is reluctant to dismiss an Essene connection for the Adam literature (*A History of the Literature of Adam and Eve*, pp. 60-61).

Throne Polemics?

The *Testament of Abraham*'s major difference with regard to Hekaloth mysticism, the absence of a vision of the enthroned deity, is also an indication of a polemical setting. The distinguishing characteristic of the *Testament of Abraham*, in contrast to other Jewish Hellenistic texts which deal with heavenly ascensions, is the complete absence of a vision of God by a human being, in this instance, Abraham. Rowland says nothing about the *Testament of Abraham* and instead looks to *3 Baruch* as an apocalypse which lacks the typically explicit description of God once the seer completes an ascent to heaven.[71] But even this text does not fully support the theme of an absent deity, since, as Dean-Otting illustrates, God twice reveals himself in a 'physical manner: in 6:14 and 11:5 an anonymous voice is heard' which 'is certainly the voice of Deity'.[72] This testament is the *only* Jewish Hellenistic ascension text which so avoids a physical description of God and in God's place substitutes *divine* looking enthroned figures. Abraham never hears the voice of God while alive in the *Testament of Abraham*, but appears to after his death, and, according to the text, this is not even certain (*T. Abr.* 20.13-14). There is even an emphasis given to the *invisibility* of God in the *Testament of Abraham* with a repeated emphasis on his unseen (ἀόρατος) nature.

> *T. Abr.* 16.3-4: When Death heard, he shuddered and trembled, overcome by great cowardice; and he came with great fear and stood before the *unseen* Father, shuddering, moaning and trembling, awaiting the Master's command. Then the *unseen* God said to Death... [emphasis mine].

Schmidt lists only two occurrences of ἀόρατος in recension A.[73] James argued that the phrase 'unseen Father' had its origin in Christian circles and used this as evidence for a Christian redaction of the *Testament of Abraham*.[74] However, ἀόρατος is found as a designation for God in the literature of Middle Judaism and was used by both Christian authors (Col. 1.15; 1 Tim. 1.17; Heb. 11.27) and Philo when speaking of God (*Op. Mund.* 68; *Vit. Mos.* 2.65; *Spec. Leg.* 1.18). Delcor, who

---

71. Rowland, *The Open Heaven*, pp. 85-86.
72. Dean-Otting, *Heavenly Journeys*, pp. 155-56.
73. Schmidt (ed.), *Le Testament grec d'Abraham*, p. 179.
74. James (ed.), *The Testament of Abraham*, p. 50.

resists James's explanation for the significance of 'unseen' in *T. Abr.* 16.3-4, illustrates how 'Father' (πατήρ) was a common name of God in Jewish writings of this period.[75] Given the mystical elements of the *Testament of Abraham*, it is important to add that Philo of Alexandria had a program, for the benefit of mystic initiates, geared towards teaching men how to gain an apprehension of the invisible (ἀόρατος) God through reason (*Op. Mund.* 69).[76] Moses is even portrayed by Philo as a model of one who 'entered... into the darkness where God was, that is into the unseen, invisible (ἀόρατον), incorporeal and archetypal essence of existing things. Thus he beheld what is hidden...' (*Vit. Mos.* 1.158).

In God's absence, the *Testament of Abraham* transfers two divine features to human beings: God's appearance and enthronement. Adam has an appearance like the 'Master's', in essence becoming the seen Father, and is enthroned (*T. Abr.* 11.4). Abel is also enthroned and has an appearance 'like unto a son of God' (*T. Abr.* 12.6), which obviously calls to mind angelic status, but in view of the fact that Abel is the 'son of Adam', an association between Adam and God is probably also indicated.[77]

And in distinction to Adam, Abel is given an additional divine prerogative, judgment. Dean-Otting highlights this characteristic and sees the transfer of some features of the deity to other figures as an innovation of the pseudepigraphical literature, an observation first made by Rowland about apocalyptic literature.[78] In fact, since God is 'unseen' according to the *Testament of Abraham*, the author's interpretation of Dan. 7.9 and its unnamed figure, the Ancient of Days as Adam, is better

75. Delcor, *Le Testament*, p. 155.

76. Goodenough, *By Light, Light*, p. 339. Goodenough places ἀόρατος within the context of Orphism, the Greek theosophical school connected with the cult of Dionysus (*By Light, Light*, p. 339). One of the fragment of the *Apostolic Constitutions*, which is thought to be part of a Jewish liturgy, coincidentally refers to both the invisible (ἀόρατος) God and Abel as the first of the priests (*By Light, Light*, p. 330).

77. The description of Abel as 'bright as the sun' in *T. Abr.* 12.5 (see also 2.4; 7.4; 16.6) matches the description of God in *1 En.* 14.20. There are also descriptions of angels looking like the sun in apocalyptic literature (Rev. 10.1). See also the section on Abel in Chapter 4. Both thrones of Adam and Abel also closely parallel the divine throne described in *1 En.* 14.18-19.

78. Dean-Otting, *Heavenly Journeys*, p. 282. Rowland, *The Open Heaven*, pp. 106-107.

understood as an attempt to avoid a physical representation of God by substituting a character who best approximates the setting of Daniel 7. This is all the more striking given what Rowland calls Daniel's 'daring' physical description of the the Ancient of Days, an aspect of Dan. 7.9 which goes beyond Ezek. 1.26-28, the text it is based on.

2 *Enoch*, which was part of this trajectory of Jewish authors interested in a physical description of God, provides the most detailed description of God found among the Jewish Hellenistic ascension texts of the first century CE.

> 2 *En.* 39.3-5 (short recension): I have heard the words from the fiery lips of the Lord. For the lips of the Lord are a furnace of fire, and his words are fiery flames which come out. You, my children, you see my face, a human being created just like yourselves; I, I am one who has seen the face of the Lord, like iron made burning hot by a fire, emitting sparks. For you gaze into (my) eyes, a human being created just like yourselves; but I have gazed into the eyes of the Lord, like the rays of the shining sun and terrifying the eyes of a human being. You, [my] children, you see my right hand beckoning you, a human being created identical to [y]ourselves; but I, I have seen the right hand of the Lord, beckoning me, who fills the heaven.

The studied avoidance of a physical description of God in the *Testament of Abraham* implies that one of the author's aims was to counter the belief in a throne vision of God by means of a heavenly ascension. Collins notes how the *Testament of Abraham*, in comparison to other Hellenistic apocalypses, shows little interest in the heavenly world.[79] Rowland was the first to detect a growing reluctance among apocalyptic texts, like *4 Ezra* and *2 Baruch*, to speak of God's form.[80] However, the *Testament of Abraham* stands apart from these texts on two accounts: unlike *4 Ezra* and *2 Baruch*, the *Testament of Abraham* has a narrative describing a heavenly ascent and emphatic statements about God's invisibleness.

This seeming non-Merkavah document at the same time explicitly presents the glorification and enthronement of human beings, Adam and Abel. Collins believes that the *Testament of Abraham* shows no evidence of being 'tied to a particular ideology', nor does it show evidence of being 'produced by a sect or conventicle'.[81] However, the

---

79. Collins, 'The Genre Apocalypse', p. 543.
80. Rowland, *The Open Heaven*, pp. 86-87.
81. Collins, *The Apocalyptic Imagination*, p. 204.

Testament of Abraham's perspective on enthroned human figures suggests some ideological convictions. While there were Jewish communities who accepted enthroned figures, there are texts, and presumably communities behind those texts, which rejected such depictions, especially when referring to a human being. One such text is the ancient tradition recorded in *b. Ḥag.* 14a II; *b. Sanh.* 38b, where Rabbi Akiba, who is presented as being enmeshed in the 'two powers controversy', is rebuked for suggesting that the Davidic messiah is to be enthroned next to God.[82] If Akiba's enthronement of David next to God aroused criticism, might not Adam's enthronement and divine likeness in the *Testament of Abraham*? At the least, this puts the author of the *Testament of Abraham* at odds with those Jewish communities which were opposed to the sharing of the divine throne and prerogatives.

D. Frankfurter has recently argued that there were two types of Jewish apocalypticism in Egypt. One could be described as 'millennialist prophecy' and was organized around holy men, prophets and literati. The other can be described as 'speculative apocalypticism' and was generated out of conventicles.[83] This second category would fit the *Testament of Abraham*. Reflecting upon Egyptian Jewish apocalyptic literature, Frankfurter writes:

> Egyptian Jewish apocalypses like 2 Enoch, 'apocalyptic' works like the Third Sibylline Oracle and Wisdom of Solomon, and the writings of Philo offer various reflections of the gnosis typical of Jewish apocalypticism in general. But whether these works represent solitary authors, 'schools', or religious sects is quite hard to judge. L.W. Barnard once argued that the Epistle of Barnabas could be used as evidence for at least one constituency of Alexandrian Jews (a member of which, christianized, wrote the document); and interestingly, Barnabas stresses the

82. Another ancient tradition, *b. Ḥag.* 15a, illustrates how strongly rabbinic tradition felt about any creature being seated in the presence of God and even suggests how being seated in heaven might be taken as deification. Metatron, the exalted Merkabah angel who is identified as Enoch in *3 Enoch*, is punished for his part in confusing Aher about the number of divinities by *sitting* in the heavenly court. This controversy over the status of enthronement is continued in *b. Sanh.* 38b, where Rabbi Yohanan refutes the 'minim' (heretics) who apparently interpreted the plural 'thrones' of Dan. 7.9 as indicative of 'many powers in heaven'.

83. D. Frankfurter, 'The Legacy of Jewish Apocalypses in Early Christianity: Regional Trajectories', in J. VanderKam and W. Adler (eds.), *The Jewish Apocalyptic Heritage in Early Christianity* (CRINT, 3; Minneapolis: Fortress Press, 1996), p. 196.

gaining of a *gnosis* or esoteric wisdom similar to that of the apocalypses... Birger Pearson has gone further, noting Philo's own subtle
polemics against radical inversions of the biblical ideas and arguing that
the author of such 'out-of-control' exegeses must have been circles of
proto-Gnostic Jews. In both cases we see the silhouettes of the kind of
sects or conventicles that studied and wrote apocalypses [emphasis
his].[84]

The potential for ideological conflict in the *Testament of Abraham*
suggests that the author may have made use of pseudepigraphy, not just
in order to conceal his identity, but because his ideas were not in line
with the teachings of other contemporary Judaisms and a respected
biblical figure, like Abraham, would lend authority to his views. As
Gruenwald states: 'when dissident sectarian ideas are preached, the
authority of a revelation is eagerly sought', and in this instance Abraham is the mouthpiece.[85] With regard to the choice of Abraham in the
apocalyptic work, the *Apocalypse of Abraham*, Rowland observes:

> This example from the Abraham cycle of apocalypses shows that the
> choice of figure from Israel's past was no arbitrary matter. It was not just
> a case of picking any figure as a peg upon which to hang any speculative
> revelations may have.[86]

It may even be the case that rival communities were represented by
different biblical figures as the Enoch literature may indicate. In contrast with *1 Enoch*, another Hellenistic Jewish text making use of
Daniel 7, recension A of the *Testament of Abraham* gives prominence
to Abel as the enthroned judge without making any reference to Enoch.
Recension B does refer to Enoch, but he is in a subservient role to Abel
(11.3-10). These two apocalyptic books may be witnesses to the competing interpretations of different Jewish communities—each champi-
oning their mediators. These differing viewpoints do not necessarily
imply that the authors of these texts were locked in polemical dis-
agreements, but at the least, differing ideological schema are being presented and defended. Some of these texts did reach the status of

84. Frankfurter, 'The Legacy of Jewish Apocalypses', pp. 144-45.

85. Gruenwald, *From Apocalypticism to Gnosticism*, p. 24. Gruenwald observes
how people like Enoch, Abraham and Moses 'were considered the great savants of
antiquity' and that 'pieces of knowledge that looked for an author' could be brought
together under their renown (*From Apocalypticism to Gnosticism*, pp. 34-35, 56).
See also B. Wacholder, *Eupolemus: A Study of Judaeo-Greek Literature*
(Cincinnati: Hebrew Union College Press, 1974), pp. 71-72.

86. Rowland, *The Open Heaven*, p. 62.

'inspired literature' among certain Jewish groups.[87] Heresiologists like
Irenaeus and Epiphanius were familar with groups that named them-
selves after biblical figures, like the Cainites, some of whom were anti-
Christian and Jewish in background.[88] Gruenwald adds:

> ...there seems to be a tension between the assumption that Enoch was
> the great savant of antiquity and the rival assumption that the role was in
> reality assigned to Abraham, as testified, for instance, in Josephus and in
> the rabbinic midrashic writings. But logic is not always the major factor
> in the history of ideas. Several Jewish, and later, Christian writers had it
> that Abraham and Moses, and no other heroes in the ancient world, were
> the first and most profound scholars of antiquity.[89]

The closest parallel to this first-century CE phenomenon of enthroned
figures with human forms who are in the company of an unseen deity
would be the Pauline tradition. Jesus, like Adam, is portrayed as the
enthroned 'image of the invisible God' in the epistle to the Colossians.

> Col. 1.15; 3.1: He is the image of the invisible God, the firstborn of all
> creation...

> Col. 3.1: So if you have been raised with Christ, seek the things that are
> above, where Christ is seated at the right hand of God.[90]

---

87. VanderKam identifies how *1 Enoch* was regarded as a sacred text by the
Qumran community (*Enoch: A Man for All Seasons* [Columbia: University of
South Carolina Press, 1995], pp. 183-85).

88. See Irenaeus, *Ag. Heresies* 1.31; Epiphanius, *The Panarion of St. Epiphanius, Bishop of Salamis* 133-35. Pearson has argued that the 'Cainites', as an
alleged group, 'is a figment of the heresiologists' imaginations' (*Gnosticism,
Judaism, and Egyptian Christianity* [Minneapolis: Fortress Press, 1990], pp. 106-
107). Pearson's argument that 'Cainite' was another way of saying heretic is sound.
It may also be true that the heresiologists used 'Cainites' to refer to particular
groups of gnostics. But to infer that no references to 'Cainites' denote a specific
gnostic community devoted to Cain appears extreme. As he admits, there is at least
one gnostic text which views Cain in a positive light (*On the Origin of the World;
Gnosticism, Judaism, and Egyptian Christianity*, pp. 101-103).

89. *From Apocalypticism to Gnosticism*, p. 35. Rowland is of the mind that
traditional views about the chosen figures led to their selection, 'So we find that a
vision of the heavens and a heavenly journey are linked with those figures to whom
such experiences were attributed either by Scripture or tradition' (*The Open
Heaven*, p. 64). See also D. Russell whom is credited by Rowland for his ideas
about pseudonymity (*The Method and Message of Jewish Apocalyptic* [London:
SPCK, 1964], p. 133).

90. F. Francis was the first to detect a mystical interest in Colossians which had

The Johannine tradition is also relevant. Jesus, like Abel, is portrayed as the 'son of God' sent by the unseen God as the 'seen' Father,[91] and who, as the 'son of man' (Adam), is given the mediatorial function of judgment.

Jn 1.18: No one has ever seen God. It is God the only Son, who is close to the Father's heart, who has made him known...

Jn 5.27: and he has given him authority to execute judgment, because he is the Son of Man...

Jn 14.9: Whoever has seen [the son] has seen the Father.

The *Testament of Abraham* represents an incipient tradition of exalted human mediators, akin to the binitarian traditions of early Christianity.[92] C. Caragounis is persuaded that the judgment scene of the *Testament of Abraham*, with its teaching that Abel and the 12 tribes of Israel serve as judges, is part of a 'conscious polemic against the NT tenet of the Son of Man (= Jesus)', which he sees as 'clumsily executed'.[93] If Caragounis is correct, then later Christian copyists, who felt moved to add several terms and concepts from the New Testament to the *Testament of Abraham*, completely overlooked its polemical stance against Jesus as the Son of Man and left the place of Abel intact. In fact, the role of Abel as the heavenly judge prompted Turner to ask, 'Why should a Christian redactor have omitted all references to a personal messiah when dealing with the judgment scene?'[94] Perhaps this is

to do with heavenly visions concerning angels and the ascetic practices which Paul's Jewish opponents taught as mystical devices ('Humility and Angel Worship in Col. 2:18', *ST* 16 ([1962–63], pp. 109-34). See also Rowland, 'Apocalyptic Visions and the Exaltation of Christ in the Letter to the Colossians', *JSNT* 19 (1983), pp. 73-83. There is perhaps a similarity, though not duplication, in the attitudes of Paul and the author of the *Testament of Abraham* towards visions of God and heavenly ascensions.

91. Macurdy identified Abel as the 'deputy' who could be looked upon in place of the unseen God (*Platonic Orphism*, p. 224).

92. For a description of the binitarian interests of early Christianity see Hurtado, 'The Binitarian Shape of Early Christian Devotion and Ancient Jewish Monotheism', in K. Richards (ed.), *Society of Biblical Literature 1985 Seminar Papers* (Atlanta: Scholars Press, 1985), pp. 377-91.

93. Caragounis, *The Son of Man*, p. 92.

94. Turner also adds that, 'Another chance which a Christian redactor missed would be that of placing Adam in need of redemption... hardly possible in the

why Caragounis says the polemical effort is 'clumsily' done—it is not obvious to later readers of the text! Why must every text which touches upon an idea shared with Christian documents be directly related to them?

It is better to understand the judgment scene of *T. Abr.* 11.1–13.7 as one of several attempts, in Middle Judaism, to make exegetical sense out of Dan. 7.9-27. It stands alongside some documents in the New Testament (and texts like the Parables of *Enoch*[95]), implicitly criticizing the interpretations of of other Judaisms by virtue of its alternative exegesis of Daniel 7. However, the interpretation of the judgment scene involves broader interests than simply the identity of the 'one like a son of man' (Dan. 7.13). The *Testament of Abraham*'s agenda adds the ideas of heavenly ascensions, throne visions, exalted patriarchs, and the (non) appearance of God to its doctrine of the judgment.

Conclusion

What early Christianity and the *Testament of Abraham* bear witness to is an ongoing exegetical interest in apocalyptic materials. Just as the Jesus community of the first century studied apocalyptic passages, so too, other Jewish communities worked to interpret the same enigmatic passages, like Dan. 7.9-27. The author of the *Testament of Abraham* shared in this interest and produced his own speculative revision of Daniel's judgment scene. This was an intra-Jewish development, rooted in pre-Christian speculations about exalted biblical figures, and fueled by dependence on the same scriptures. The diverse interpretations reflect the traditions held dear by each community. Their writings illustrate how they associated their revered figures, whether they be Jesus, Adam, Abel or some other exalted person, with ambiguous biblical texts.

Christian church in view of Romans' ('The Testament of Abraham: A Study', pp. 44-45).

95. Mearns understands the *Testament of Abraham* to be polemicizing against the Parables of *Enoch* and its exaltation of *Enoch* ('Dating the Similitudes', pp. 360-69).

BIBLIOGRAPHY

Primary Sources

Amidon, P. (ed. and trans.), *The Panarion of St. Epiphanius, Bishop of Salamis: Selected Passages* (New York: Oxford University Press, 1990).

Archer, G. (trans.), *Jerome's Commentary on Daniel* (Grand Rapids: Baker Book House, 1958).

Bialik, H., and Y. Ravnitsky (eds. and trans.), *The Book of Legends: Sepher Ha-Aggadah* (New York: Schocken Books, 1992).

Box, G.H. (ed. and trans.), *The Testament of Abraham: Translated from the Greek Text with Introduction and Notes* (London: SPCK, 1927).

Colson, F., and G. Whitaker (eds. and trans.), *The Loeb Classical Library: Philo* (10 vols.; 2 suppls.; Cambridge, MA: Harvard University Press, 1929).

Copenhauer, B. (ed. and trans.), *Hermetica: The Greek Corpus Hermeticum and the Latin Asclepius in a New English Translation, with Notes and Introduction* (Cambridge: Cambridge University Press, 1992).

Epstein, I. (ed.), *The Babylonian Talmud* (35 vols.; London: Soncino Press, 1961).

Gaster, M. (ed. and trans.), 'The Apocalypse of Abraham', in *Transactions of the Society of Biblical Archaeology* 9 (1887), pp. 1-32.

—*Studies and Texts: In Folklore, Magic, Medieval Romance, Hebrew Apocrypha and Samaritan Archaeology* (3 vols.; London: Maggs Brothers, 1925–28).

Ginzberg, L. (ed.), *The Legends of the Jews* (7 vols.; Philadelphia: Jewish Publication Society of America, 1925).

Husik, E. (ed. and trans.), *Joseph Albo: Sepher ha-Ikkarim: Book of Principles* (4 vols.; New York: Jewish Publication Society of America, 1929).

Issaverdens, D., *The Uncanonical Writings of the Old Testament* (Venice: Armenia Monastery of St Lazarus, 1907).

James, M. (ed.), *The Testament of Abraham: The Greek Text Now First Edited with an Introduction and Notes* (T & S, 2.2; Cambridge: Cambridge University Press, 1892).

Lipscomb, W., *The Armenian Apocryphal Adam Literature* (ATS, 8; Philadelphia: University of Pennsylvania, 1990).

MacDonald, J. (ed. and trans.), *Memar Marqah: The Teachings of Marqah* (2 vols.; Berlin: Alfred Töpelmann, 1963).

MacRae, G. (ed. and trans.), 'The Coptic Testament of Abraham', in G. Nickelsburg (ed.), *Studies in the Testament of Abraham* (SBLSCS, 6; Missoula, MT: Scholars Press, 1976), pp. 327-39.

—'The Judgment Scene in the Coptic Apocalypse of Paul', in Nickelsburg (ed.), *Studies in the Testament of Abraham*, pp. 285-88.

Mahé, J. (ed. and trans.), 'Le Livre d'Adam georgien', in M. Vermaseren (ed.), *Studies in Gnosticism and Hellenistic Religions: Presented to Gilles Quispel on the Occasion of his 65th Birthday* (EPRO, 91; Leiden: E.J. Brill, 1981), pp. 227-60.

Marcovich, M. (ed.), *Hippolytus: Refutatio Omnium Haeresium* (PTS, 25; New York: Walter de Gruyter, 1986).

McNamara, M. (ed. and trans.), *The Aramaic Bible: Targum Neofiti I: Genesis* (18 vols.; Collegeville: The Liturgical Press, 1992).

Morgan, M. (ed. and trans.), *Sepher Ha-Razim: The Book of the Mysteries* (T & T, 25; Chico, CA: Scholars Press, 1983).

Nautin, P. (ed. and trans.), *Hippolyte: Contre les Hérésies* (Paris: Cerf, 1949).

Neusner, J. (ed. and trans.), *Genesis Rabbah: The Judaic Commentary on the Book of Genesis: A New Translation* (3 vols.; Atlanta: Scholars Press, 1982).

—*Pesiqta de Rab Kahana* (2 vols.; Atlanta: Scholars Press, 1987).

—(ed.), *The Talmud of the Law of Israel* (35 vols.; Chicago: University of Chicago Press, 1990).

Page, T., and W. Rouse (eds. and trans.), *The Loeb Classical Library: The Shepherd of Hermas* (2 vols.; New York: Macmillan, 1913).

—(eds.), *The Loeb Classical Library: Plato's Republic* (2 vols.; Cambridge, MA: Harvard University Press, 1935).

Parrot, D. (ed.), *Nag Hammadi Codices V.2-5 and VI with Papyrus Berolinensis to 502, 1 and 4* (NHS, 11; Leiden: E.J Brill, 1979).

Pearson, B. (ed.), *Nag Hammadi Codices IX and X* (NHS, 15; Leiden: E.J. Brill, 1981).

Preuschen, E. (ed. and trans.), 'Die apockryphen gnostischen Adamschriften', in W. Diehl (ed.), *Festgruss Bernhard Stade* (Giessen: Ricker's, 1900), pp. 163-252.

Roberts, A., and J. Donaldson (eds.), *The Ante-Nicene Fathers* (repr.; 12 vols.; Grand Rapids: Eerdmans, 1989).

Robinson, J. (ed.), *The Nag Hammadi Library* (San Francisco: Harper & Row, rev. edn, 1988).

Schmidt, F. (ed.), 'Le Testament d'Abraham: Introduction, edition de la recension courte, traduction et notes' (2 vols.; PhD Dissertation, University of Strasbourg, 1971).

—*Le Testament grec d'Abraham* (TSAJ, 11; Tübingen: J.C.B. Mohr, 1986).

Schneemelcher, W. (ed.), *New Testament Apocrypha* (2 vols.; Philadelphia: Westminster Press, 1963).

Scott, W., and A. Ferguson (eds. and trans.), *Hermetica: The Ancient Greek and Latin Writings which Contain Religious or Philosophic Teachings Ascribed to Hermes Trisegistus* (4 vols.; Oxford: Clarendon Press, 1924–36).

Sieber, J. (ed.), *Nag Hammadi Codex VIII* (NHS, 31; Leiden: E.J. Brill, 1991).

Snell, B. (ed.), *Tragicorum Graecorum Fragmenta* (4 vols.; Göttingen: Vandenhoeck & Ruprecht, 1971).

Sparks, H. (ed.), *The Apocryphal Old Testament* (Oxford: Clarendon Press, 1984).

Stone, M. (ed. and trans.), 'The Death of Adam—An Armenian Adam Book', *HTR* 59 (1966), pp. 283-91.

—(ed.), *The Armenian Apocryphal Adam Literature* (Atlanta: Scholars Press, 1990).

Tardieu, M. (ed. and trans.), 'Les Trois steles de Seth-Un écrit gnostique retrouvé à Nag Hammadi, introduit et traduit', *RSPT* 57 (1973), pp. 545-75.

Vermes, G. (ed. and trans.), *The Dead Sea Scrolls in English* (Harmondsworth: Penguin Books, 4th edn, 1995).

Secondary Sources

Alexander, P., 'Targum/Targumim', *ABD*, VI, pp. 320-31.
Altmann, A., 'The Gnostic Background of the Rabbinic Adam Legends', *JQR* 35 (1944–45), pp. 371-91.
Aptowitzer, V., *Kain und Abel in der Agada, den Apokryphen, der hellenistischen, christlichen, und muhammedanischer Literatur* (Vienna: R. Lowit, 1922).
Aune, D., *Prophecy in Early Christianity* (Grand Rapids: Eerdmans, 1983).
Barrett, C., *The First Epistle to the Corinthians* (HNTC, New York: Harper & Row, 1968).
Bassler, J., 'Cain and Abel in the Palestinian Targums: A Brief Note on the Old Controversy', *JSJ* 17 (1986), pp. 56-64.
Beale, G., *The Use of Daniel in Jewish Apocalyptic Literature and in the Revelation of St. John* (Lanham, MD: University Press of America, 1984).
—'The Influence of Daniel Upon the Structure and Theology of John's Apocalypse', *JETS* 27 (1984), pp. 413-23.
Beasley-Murray, G.R., 'The Interpretation of Daniel 7', *CBQ* 45 (1983), pp. 44-58.
—*Jesus and the Kingdom* (Grand Rapids: Eerdmans, 1986).
Bentzen, A., *Daniel* (HAT, 19; Tübingen: J.C.B. Mohr, 1952).
Bianchi, U., 'Gnostizismus und Anthropologie', *Kairos* 11 (1969), pp. 6-13.
Black, M. (ed.), *An Aramaic Approach to the Gospels and Acts* (Oxford: Clarendon Press, 3rd edn, 1967).
—'The Throne-Theophany Prophetic Commission and the "Son of Man"', in R. Hammerton-Kelly and R. Scroggs (eds.), *Jews, Greeks and Christians: Religious Cultures in Late Antiquity* (Festschrift W.D. Davies; trans. J. Smith; SJLA, 21; Leiden: E.J. Brill, 2nd edn, 1976), pp. 56-73.
—*The Book of Enoch or 1 Enoch* (SVTP, 7; Leiden: E.J. Brill, 1985).
Bockmuehl, M., *Revelation and Mystery* (WUNT, 36; Tübingen: J.C.B. Mohr, 1990).
Boccaccini, G., *Middle Judaism: Jewish Thought 300 BCE to 200 CE* (Minneapolis: Fortress Press, 1991).
Bohlig, A., 'Zum "Pluralismus" in den Schriften von Nag Hammadi', in M. Krause (ed.), *Essays on the Nag Hammadi Texts in Honour of Pahor Labib* (NHS, 6; Leiden: E.J. Brill, 1975), pp. 19-34.
Borden, P., 'Philo of Alexandria', in M. Stone (ed.), *Jewish Writings of the Second Temple Period* (CRINT, 2; Philadelphia: Fortress Press, 1984), pp. 233-82.
Borsch, F., *The Son of Man in Myth and History* (NTL; Philadelphia: Westminster Press, 1967).
Bousset, W., 'Eine jüdische Gebetssammlung im siebenten Buch der apostolischen Konstitutionen', in *Nachrichten von der königlichen Gesellschaft der Wissenschaften zu Göttingen: Philologische-Historische Klasse*, 1913–16, pp. 435-85.
Bouset, W., and H. Gressmann, *Die Religion des Judentums im späthellenistischen Zeitalter* (Tübingen: J.C.B. Mohr, 3rd edn, 1926).
Brock, S., 'Jewish Traditions in Syriac Sources', *JJS* 30 (1979), pp. 212-32.
—*Studies in Syrian Christianity: History, Literature and Theology* (Norfolk: Ashgate, 1992).
Bruce, F., 'The Oldest Greek Version of Daniel', *OTS* 20 (1977), pp. 25-26.
Burkett, D., *The Son of the Man in the Gospel of John* (JSNTSup, 56; Sheffield: JSOT Press, 1991).

Canivet, M.-T., and P. Canivet, 'La mosaïque d'Adam dans l'église syrienne de Huarte (Ve S)', *CahArch* 34 (1975), pp. 49-69.

Caragounis, C.C., *The Son of Man: Vision and Interpretation* (WUNT, 38; Tübingen: Mohr-Siebeck, 1986).

Casey, M., *Son of Man: The Interpretation and Influence of Daniel 7* (London: SPCK, 1979).

—*From Jewish Prophet to Gentile God: The Origins and Development of New Testament Christology* (Louisville, KY: Westminster/John Knox Press, 1991).

Charles, R.H., *The Book of Daniel* (Edinburgh: T.C. & E.C. Jack, 1913).

Charlesworth, J., *The Pseudepigrapha and Modern Research* (SCS, 7; Missoula, MT: Scholars Press, 1976).

—(ed.), *Graphic Concordance to the Dead Sea Scrolls* (Tübingen: J.C.B. Mohr, 1991).

Chazon, E., 'Moses' Struggle: *Testament of Abraham*, the Greek Apocalypse of Ezra, and the Apocalypse of Sedrach', *SecCent* 5 (1986), pp. 151-64.

Chilton, B., and J. Neusner, *Judaism in the New Testament: Practice and Beliefs* (New York: Routledge, 1995).

A. Cohen (ed.), *Everyman's Talmud* (New York: E.P. Dutton, 1949).

Collins, J.J., *The Apocalyptic Vision of the Book of Daniel* (HSM, 16; Missoula, MT: Scholars Press, 1977).

—'The Genre Apocalypse in Hellenistic Literature', in D. Hellholm (ed.), *Apocalypticism in the Mediterranean World and the Near East* (Tübingen: J.C.B. Mohr, 1983), pp. 531-48.

—'Testaments', in M. Stone (ed.), *Jewish Writings of the Second Temple Period* (CRINT, 2; Philadelphia: Fortress Press, 1984), pp. 325-55.

—*The Apocalyptic Imagination* (New York: Crossroad, 1989).

—*Daniel: A Commentary on the Book of Daniel* (Minneapolis: Fortress Press, 1993).

—*The Scepter and the Star: The Messiah of the Dead Sea Scrolls and Other Ancient Literature* (New York: Doubleday, 1995).

Colpe, C., 'ὁ υἱός τοῦ ἀνθρώπου', *TDNT*, VIII, pp. 400-77.

Cooke, G., *Old Testament Essays* (London: Charles Griffin and Co., 1927).

Conzelmann, H., *1 Corinthians* (Hermenia; Philadelphia: Fortress Press, 1975).

Cope, O., *Matthew: A Scribe Trained for the Kingdom* (CBQMS, 5; Washington: Catholic Biblical Association, 1976).

Cross, F., *Canaanite Myth and Hebrew Epic: Essays in the History of the Religion of Israel* (Cambridge, MA: Harvard University Press, 1973).

Culianu, I., 'The Angels of the Nations and the Origins of Greek Dualism', in R. van den Broek and M. Vermaseren (eds.), *Studies in Gnosticism and Hellenistic Religion* (EPRO, 91; Leiden: E.J. Brill, 1981), pp. 78-91.

Dalman, G., *Die Worte Jesu* (Leipzig: Darmstadt, 1930).

Danielou, J., *The Theology of Jewish Christianity* (London: Darton, Longman & Todd, 1964).

Davies, W.D., *Paul and Rabbinic Judaism* (Philadelphia: Fortress Press, 4th edn, 1980).

Day J., 'The Old Testament Utilization of Language and Imagery Having Parallels in the Baal Mythology of the Ugaritic Texts' (PhD Dissertation, Cambridge University, 1977).

—*God's Conflict with the Dragon and the Sea* (Cambridge: Cambridge University Press, 1985).

Dean-Otting, M., *Heavenly Journeys: A Study of the Motif in Hellenistic Jewish Literature* (JU, 8; Frankfurt: Peter Lang, 1984).

Delcor, M., *Le Testament d'Abraham* (SVTP, 2; Leiden: E.J. Brill, 1973).

Denis, A.-M., *Introduction aux pseudépigraphes grecs d'Ancien Testament* (SVTP, 1; Leiden: E.J. Brill, 1970).

Dillman, A., 'Das christliche Adambuch des Morgenlandes aus dem Äthiopischen mit Bemerkungen übersetzt', *Jahrbücher der biblischen Wissenschaft* 5 (Göttingen: Vandenhoeck & Ruprecht, 1853), pp. 1-44.

Drower, E. (ed. and trans.), *The Haran-Gawaita and the Baptism of Hibil-Ziwa* (Studi e Testi, 176; Citta del Vaticano: Biblioteca Apostolica Vaticana, 1953).

—*The Secret Adam: A Study of Nasoraean Gnosis* (Oxford: Clarendon Press, 1960).

Dunn, J., *Romans 1–8* (WBC, 38a; Dallas: Word Books, 1988).

—*The Parting of the Ways: Between Christianity and Judaism and their Significance for the Character of Christianity* (Philadelphia: Trinity Press International, 1991).

Eccles, R., 'The Purpose of the Hellenistic Patterns in the Epistle to the Hebrews', in J. Neusner (ed.), *Religions in Antiquity: Essays in Memory of Erwin Ramsdell Goodenough* (SHR, 14; Leiden: E.J. Brill, 1968), pp. 207-26.

Eichrodt, W., *Ezekiel: A Commentary* (OTL; Philadelphia: Westminster Press, 1970).

Emerton, J.A., 'The Origin of the Son of Man Imagery', *JTS* 9 (1958), pp. 225-34.

Fabricius, J., *Codex Pseudepigraphus Veteris Testamenti* (Hamburg and Leipzig: Liebezeit, 1713).

—*Codicis Pseudepigraphi Veteris Testamenti volumen alterum accedit Josephi veteris christiani auctoria hypomnesticon* (Hamburg: Felginer, 1723).

Fallon, F., *The Enthronement of Sabaoth: Jewish Elements in Gnostic Creation Myths* (NHS, 10; Leiden: E.J. Brill, 1978).

Farrar, A., *The Revelation of St John the Divine* (Oxford: Clarendon Press, 1964).

Fee, G., *The First Epistle to the Corinthians* (NICNT; Grand Rapids: Eerdmans, 1987).

Feldman, L., 'Josephus' Portrait of Daniel', *Hen* 14 (1992), pp. 80-97.

Feuillet, A., 'Le fils de l'homme de Daniel et le tradition biblique', *RB* 60 (1953), pp. 170-202.

Fishbane, M., *Biblical Interpretation in Ancient Israel* (Oxford: Clarendon Press, 1985).

Fishburne, C., 'I Cor. III 10-15 and the *Testament of Abraham*', *NTS* 17 (1970), pp. 109-15.

Flesher, P., 'The Targumim', in J. Neusner (ed.), *Judaism in Late Antiquity. I. The Literary and Archaeological Sources* (Leiden: E.J. Brill, 1995), pp. 40-63.

Fossum, J., 'Jewish-Christian Christology and Jewish Mysticism', *VC* 37 (1983), pp. 260-87.

—*The Name of God and the Angel of the Lord* (WUNT, 36; Tübingen: J.C.B. Mohr, 1985).

—'The Magharians: A Pre-Christian Jewish Sect and Its Significance for the Study of Gnosticism and Christianity', *Hen* 9 (1987), pp. 303-44.

—'Colossians 1.15-18a in the Light of Jewish Mysticism and Gnosticism', *NTS* 35 (1989), pp. 183-201.

—'Partes posteriores dei: The "Transformation" of Jesus in the *Acts of John*', in *The Image of the Invisible God: Essays on the Influence of Jewish Mysticism on Early Christology* (NTOA, 30; Freiburg: Universitätsverlag; Göttingen: Vandenhoeck & Ruprecht, 1995), pp. 95-108.

Francis, F., 'Humility and Angel Worship in Col. 2:18', *ST* 16 (1962–63), pp. 109-34.

Frankfurter, D., 'The Legacy of Jewish Apocalypses in Early Christianity: Regional Trajectories', in J. VanderKam and W. Adler (eds.), *The Jewish Apocalyptic Heritage in Early Christianity* (CRINT, 3; Minneapolis: Fortress Press, 1996), pp. 129-200.

Friedlander, M., *Der vorchristliche jüdische Gnosticismus* (Göttingen: Vandenhoeck & Ruprecht, 1898).

Garcia Martinez, F., *Qumran and Apocalyptic: Studies on the Aramaic Texts from Qumran* (STDJ, 9; Leiden: E.J. Brill, 1992).

Ginzberg, L., 'Abraham, (Testament of)', *JewEnc*, I, pp. 93-96.

Goldingay, J., *Daniel* (WBC, 30; Dallas: Word Books, 1989).

Goodenough, E., *By Light, Light: The Mystic Gospel of Hellenistic Judaism* (Amsterdam: Philo Press, 1969).

Grabbe, L., *Judaism from Cyrus to Hadrian* (2 vols.; Minneapolis: Fortress Press, 1992).

—'Hellenistic Judaism', in J. Neusner (ed.), *Judaism in Late Antiquity. II. Historical Syntheses* (Leiden: E.J. Brill, 1995).

Graetz, H., *Gnosticism und Judentum* (Krotoschin: Monasd & Sohn, 1846).

Gray, J., *The Legacy of Canaan* (VTSup, 5; Leiden: E.J. Brill, 2nd edn, 1965).

Green, A., 'The Children in Egypt and the Theophany at the Sea', *Jud* 24 (1975), pp. 446-56.

Gruenwald, I., *Apocalyptic and Merkavah Mysticism* (AGJU, 14; Leiden: E.J. Brill, 1980).

—*From Apocalypticism to Gnosticism: Studies in Apocalypticism, Merkavah Mysticism and Gnosticism* (BEATAJ, 14; Frankfurt: Peter Lang, 1988).

Gunkel, H., *Genesis übersetzt und erklärt* (Göttingen: Vandenhoeck & Ruprecht, 1922).

Hare, D., *The Son of Man Tradition* (Minneapolis: Fortress Press, 1990).

Harris, W., *Dictionary of Concepts in Literary Criticism and Theory* (New York: Greenwood Press, 1992).

Hartman, L., *Prophecy Interpreted: The Formulation of Some Jewish Apocalyptic Texts and of the Eschatological Discourse Mark 13 and Parallels* (ConBNT, 1; Lund: C.W.K. Gleerup, 1966).

Hayward, C., 'The Figure of Adam in Pseudo-Philo's Biblical Antiquities', *JSJ* 23 (1992), pp. 1-20.

Hengel, M., *The Son of God* (Minneapolis: Fortress Press, 1976).

—*The Cross and the Son of God* (London: SCM Press, 1986).

Hill, D., *The Gospel of Matthew* (NCBC; Grand Rapids: Eerdmans, 1982).

Himmelfarb, M., *Ascent to Heaven in Jewish and Christian Apocalypses* (New York: Oxford University Press, 1993).

Holman, C., and W. Harmon (eds.), *A Handbook to Literature* (New York: Macmillan, 5th edn, 1986).

Hollander, J., *The Figure of an Echo: A Mode of Allusion in Milton and After* (Berkeley: University of California Press, 1981).

—*The Gospel According to St Mark* (BNTC; London: A. & C. Black, 1991).

Hooker, M., *The Son of Man in Mark* (Montreal: McGill University Press, 1967).

Hurtado, L., 'The Binitarian Shape of Early Christian Devotion and Ancient Jewish Monotheism', in K. Richards (ed.), *Society of Biblical Literature 1985 Seminar Papers* (Atlanta: Scholars Press, 1985), pp. 377-91.

—*One God, One Lord* (Philadelphia: Fortress Press, 1988).

Isenberg, S., 'An Anti-Sadducee Polemic in the Palestinian Targum Traditions', *HTR* 63 (1970), pp. 433-44.

Janssen, E., 'Testament Abrahams', *JSHRZ* 3 (1975), pp. 193-256.

Juel, D., *Messianic Exegesis: Christological Interpretation of the Old Testament in Early Christianity* (Philadelphia: Fortress Press, 1988).

Kaiser, O., *Isaiah 13–39: A Commentary* (TOTL; Philadelphia: Westminster Press, 1974).

Kaufmann, J., 'Adambuch', *EncJud*, I, pp. 788-92.

Kim, S., 'An Exposition of Paul's Gospel in the Light of the Damascus Theophany' (PhD Dissertation, University of Manchester, 1977).

—*The Origin of Paul's Gospel* (Grand Rapids: Eerdmans, 1981).

—*The 'Son of Man' as the Son of God* (WUNT, 30; Tübingen: J.C.B. Mohr, 1983).

Klijn, A.F.J., *Seth in Jewish, Christian, and Gnostic Literature* (NovTSup, 46; Leiden: E.J. Brill, 1977).

Kobelski, P., *Melchizedek and Melchiresa* (Washington: CBQ Press, 1980).

Kohler, K., 'The Pre-Talmudic Haggada II: The Apocalypse of Abraham and its Kindred', *JQR* 7 (1895), pp. 581-606.

—'Abraham, (Apocalypse of)', *JewEnc*, I, pp. 91-93.

—*Heaven and Hell in Comparative Religion* (New York: Scribners, 1923).

Kolenkow, A., 'What is the Role of Testament in the Testament of Abraham?', *HTR* 67 (1974), pp. 182-84.

—'The Genre Testament in the Hellenistic Jewish Milieu', *JSJ* 6 (1975), pp. 57-77.

—'The Genre Testament and the Testament of Abraham', in Nickelsburg (ed.), *Studies in the Testament of Abraham*, pp. 139-52.

Korpel, M., *A Rift in the Clouds: Ugaritic and Hebrew Descriptions of the Divine* (Münster: Ugaritic-Verlag, 1990).

Kraft, R.A., 'Reassessing the "Recessional Problem" in the *Testament of Abraham*', in Nickelsburg (ed.), *Studies in the Testament of Abraham*, pp. 121-37.

Kronholm, T., *Motifs From Genesis 1–11 in the Genuine Hymns of Ephrem the Syrian* (ConBOT, 2; Lund: C.W.K. Gleerup, 1978).

Lacocque, A., *The Book of Daniel* (Atlanta: John Knox Press, 1979).

Layton, B. (ed. and trans.), *The Gnostic Scriptures* (New York: Doubleday, 1987).

—*The Rediscovery of Gnosticism* (2 vols.; NumenSup, 41; Leiden: E.J. Brill, 1978–81).

Levison, J.R., *Portraits of Adam in Early Judaism: From Sirach to 2nd Baruch* (JSPSup, 1; Sheffield: JSOT Press, 1988).

Lindars, B., *The Gospel of John* (NCBC; London: Marshall, Morgan & Scott, 1972).

—*Jesus Son of Man* (Grand Rapids: Eerdmans, 1983).

Loewenstamm, S., 'The Death of Moses', in Nickelsburg (ed.), *Studies in the Testament of Abraham*, pp. 185-217.

—'The Testament of Abraham and the Texts concerning the Death of Moses', in Nickelsburg (ed.), *Studies in the Testament of Abraham*, pp. 219-25.

Lust, J., 'Daniel 7.13 and the Septuagint', *ETL* 54 (1978), pp. 62-69.

Macurdy, G.H., 'Platonic Orphism in the *Testament of Abraham*', *JBL* 61 (1942), pp. 213-26.

Marmorstein, A., *The Old Rabbinic Doctrine of God* (2 vols.; London: KTAV, 1927).

Martin, R.A., 'Syntax Criticism of the *Testament of Abraham*', in Nickelsburg (ed.), *Studies in the Testament of Abraham*, pp. 95-102.

McNamara, M., 'Targums', *IDBSup*, pp. 856-61.

Mearns, C., 'Dating the Similitudes of Enoch', *NTS* 25 (1979), pp. 360-69.

Meeks, W., *The Prophet King: Moses Traditions and the Johannine Christology* (NTSup, 14; Leiden: E.J. Brill, 1967).

Merling Alomia, B., 'Los angeles en el contexto extrabiblico vesterotestamentario: Un estudio exegetico y comparativo', *Theo* 3 (1988), pp. 166-83.

—'Los angeles en el contexto extrabiblico vesterotestamentario: Un estudio exegetico y comparativo', *Theo* 4 (1989), pp. 44-99.

—'Los angeles en el contexto extrabiblico vesterotestamentario: Un estudio exegetico y comparativo', *Theo* 4 (1989), pp. 118-205.

Migne, J.-M., *Dictionnaire des Apocryphes ou collection de tous les livres apocryphes relatifs à l'ancien et au nouveau testament* (Troisième et dernière encyclopédie théologique, 23–24; Paris: Migne-Ateliers catholiques, 1856–58).

Miller, P., 'Targum, Midrash and the Use of the Old Testament in the New Testament', *JSJ* 2 (1971), pp. 29-82.

Morray-Jones, C., 'Transformational Mysticism in the Apocalyptic-Merkabah Tradition', *JJS* 43 (1992), pp. 1-31.

Mosca, P., 'Ugarit and Daniel 7: A Missing Link', *Bib* 67.4 (1986), pp. 496-517.

Newman, C., '"Lord of Glory", "Glory of the Lord": Tradition and Rhetoric in Paul's Doxa-Christology', Paper read to the International SBL (August, 1990).

Neusner, J., *Midrash in Context: Exegesis in Formative Judaism* (Philadelphia: Fortress Press, 1983).

Neusner, J., and E. Frerichs (eds.), *Judaisms and their Messiahs at the Turn of the Christian Era* (Cambridge: Cambridge University Press, 1987).

Newlyn, L., *Coleridge, Wordsworth, and the Language of Allusion* (Oxford: Clarendon Press, 1986).

Nickelsburg, G.W.E. (ed.), *Studies in the Testament of Abraham* (SBLSCS, 6; Missoula, MT: Scholars Press, 1976).

—*Jewish Literature between the Bible and the Mishnah* (Philadelphia: Fortress Press, 1981).

—'*Testament of Abraham*', in M. Stone (ed.), *Jewish Writings of the Second Temple Period* (CRINT, 2; Philadelphia: Fortress Press, 1984), pp. 60-64.

Pearson, B., 'Friedlander Revisited: Alexandrian Judaism and Gnostic Origins', *StudPhilo* 2 (1973), pp. 23-39.

—'Jewish Elements in Corpus Hermeticum I (Poimandres)', in M. Vermaseren (ed.), *Studies in Gnosticism and Hellenistic Religions: Presented to Gilles Quispel on the Occasion of his 65th Birthday* (EPRO, 91; Leiden: E.J. Brill, 1981).

—'Jewish Sources in Gnostic Literature', in Stone (ed.), *Jewish Writings of the Second Temple Period*.

—*Gnosticism, Judaism, and Egyptian Christianity* (Minneapolis: Fortress Press, 1990).

Perkins, P., 'Apocalypse of Adam: The Genre and Function of a Gnostic Apocalypse', *CBQ* 39 (1977), pp. 382-95.

Perrin, N., *Rediscovering the Teaching of Jesus* (New York: Harper & Row, 1967).

Peterson, E. *Frühkirche, Judentum und Gnosis* (Freiburg: Herder, 1959).

Pétrement. S., *A Separate God: The Christian Origin of Gnosticism* (San Francisco: Harper & Row, 1990).

Procksch, O., 'Die Berufungsvision Hesekiels', *in Beiträge zur alttestamentlichen Wissenschaft: Karl Budde zum siebzigsten Geburtstag* (BZAW, 34; Giessen: Lund, 1920), pp. 122-80.

Quispel, G., 'Der gnostische Anthropos und die jüdische Tradition', *ErJb* 12 (1954), pp. 195-234.

—'Ezekiel 1:26 in Jewish Mysticism and Gnosis', *VC* 34 (1980), pp. 1-8.

—'Gnosis', in M. Vermaseren (ed.), *Die orientalischen Religionen im Römerreich* (EPRO, 93; Leiden: E.J. Brill, 1981).

—'Hermetism and the New Testament, especially Paul', in W. Haase (ed.), *ANRW*, 2.22; Berlin, New York, forthcoming.

Renan, E., 'Fragments du livre gnostique intitulé Apocalypse d'Adam, ou Penitence d'Adam ou Testament d'Adam', *JA* 5 (2) (1853), pp. 427-71.

Robinson, S., *The Testament of Adam: An Examination of the Syriac and Greek Traditions* (SBLDS, 52; Chico, CA: Scholars Press, 1982).

Roth, W., 'Jesus as the Son of Man: The Scriptural Identity of a Johannine Image', in D. Groh and R. Jewett (eds.), *The Living Text: Essays in Honor of Ernest W. Saunders* (Lanham, MD: University Press of America, 1985), pp. 11-26.

Rowland, C., 'The Influence of the First Chapter of Ezekiel on Jewish and Early Christian Literature' (Doctoral Dissertation, Cambridge University, 1974).

—'The Vision of the Risen Christ in Revelation 1:13ff.: The Debt of an Early Christology to an Aspect of Jewish Angelology', *JTS* 31 (1980), pp. 1-11.

—*The Open Heaven* (New York: Crossroad, 1982).

—'Apocalyptic Vision and the Exaltation of Christ in the Letter to the Colossians', *JSNT* 19 (1983), pp. 73-83.

—*Christian Origins* (Minneapolis: Fortress Press, 1985).

—'Apocalyptic Literature', in D. Carson and H. Williamson (eds.), *It is Written: Scripture Citing Scripture. Essays in Honour of Barnabas Lindars SSF* (Cambridge: Cambridge University Press, 1988), pp. 170-89.

Rudolph, K., *Die Mandäer* (2 vols.; FRLANT, 75; Göttingen: Vandenhoeck & Ruprecht, 1961).

—*Gnosis: The Nature and History of Gnosticism* (San Francisco: Harper & Row, 1987).

Russell, D., *The Method and Message of Jewish Apocalyptic* (London: SPCK, 1964).

Sanders, E., *The Tendencies of the Synoptic Tradition* (Cambridge: Cambridge University Press, 1969).

—'The Testament of Abraham', *OTP*, I, pp. 871-902.

—*Judaism: Practice and Belief 63 BCE–66 CE* (Philadelphia: Trinity Press International, 1992).

Sandmel, S., 'Parallelomania', *JBL* 81 (1962), pp. 1-13.

Schaberg, J., *The Father, Son, and the Holy Spirit: The Triadic Phrase in Matthew 28:19b* (SBLDS, 61; Chico, CA: Scholars Press, 1982).

Schafer, P., 'Adam in der jüdischen Überlieferung', in W. Strolz (ed.), *Vom alten zum neuen Adam* (Freiburg: Herder, 1986), pp. 69-93.

—*Übersetzung der Hekhalot-Literatur* (2 vols.; Tübingen: J.C.B. Mohr [Paul Siebeck], 1987).

—*The Hidden and Manifest God: Some Major Themes in Early Jewish Mysticism* (Albany: State University of New York Press, 1992).

Schenke, H.-M., 'The Phenomenon and Significance of Seth', in B. Layton (ed.), *The Rediscovery of Gnosticism* (2 vols.; NumenSup, 41; Leiden: E.J. Brill, 1978–81), pp. 588-616.

Schmidt, F.,'The Two Recensions of the *Testament of Abraham*: In Which Way Did the Transformation Take Place?', in Nickelsburg (ed.), *Studies in the Testament of Abraham*, pp. 65-83.

Scholem, G.G., *Major Trends in Jewish Mysticism* (New York: Schocken Books, 3rd edn, 1954).

—*Jewish Gnosticism, Merkabah Mysticism, and Talmudic Tradition* (New York: Jewish Theological Seminary of America, 2nd edn, 1965).

—'Merkabah Mysticism or Ma'aseh Merkavah', *EncJud*, XI, pp. 1386-89.

Schürer, E., *The History of the Jewish People in the Age of Jesus Christ* (3 vols.; ed. G. Vermes, F. Millar and M. Goodman; Edinburgh: T. & T. Clark, 1987).

Scroggs, R., *The Last Adam* (Philadelphia: Fortress Press, 1966).

Seemuth, D., 'Adam the Sinner and Christ the Righteous: The Theological and Exegetical Substructure of Romans 5:12-21' (PhD Dissertation, Marquette University, 1989).

Seesemann, H., 'παλαιός', *TDNT*, V, pp. 717-20.

Segal, A., *Two Powers in Heaven: Early Rabbinic Reports about Christianity and Gnosticism* (SJLA, 25; Leiden: E.J. Brill, 1977).

—'The Risen Christ and the Angelic Mediator Figures of the Dead Sea Scrolls', in J. Charlesworth (ed.), *Jesus and the Dead Sea Scrolls* (New York: Doubleday, 1992), pp. 302-28.

Sharpe, S., *History of Egypt* (2 vols.; London: Edward Moxon and Co., 1859).

Smith, M., 'On the Shape of God and the Humanity of the Gentiles', in J. Neusner (ed.), *Religions in Antiquity: Essays in Memory of Erwin Ramsdell Goodenough* (SHR, 14; Leiden: E.J. Brill, 1968), pp. 315-26.

Stockhausen, C., *Moses' Veil and the Glory of the New Covenant* (Rome: Editrice Pontificio Istituto Biblico, 1989).

Stone, M., 'Features of the Eschatology of IV Ezra' (Doctoral Dissertation, Harvard University, 1965).

—'Apocalyptic-Vision or Hallucination?', *Milla wa-Milla* 14 (1974), pp. 47-56.

—*A History of the Literature of Adam and Eve* (SBLEJL, 3; Atlanta: Scholars Press, 1992).

—(ed.), *Jewish Writings of the Second Temple Period* (CRINT, 2; Philadelphia: Fortress Press, 1984).

Strousma, G., 'Polymorphie divine et transformations d'un mythologène l'Apocryphon de Jean et ses sources', *VC* 35 (1981), pp. 412-34.

—'Aher: A Gnostic', in B. Layton (ed.) *The Rediscovery of Gnosticism* (2 vols.; NumenSup, 41; Leiden: E.J. Brill, 1981), II, pp. 808-818.

Taylor, V., *The Gospel According to Mark* (London: Macmillan, 2nd edn, 1966).

Tcherikover, V., *Hellenistic Civilization and the Jews* (Philadelphia: Fortress Press, 1959).

Tenant, F., *The Source of the Doctrine of the Fall and Original Sin* (Cambridge: Cambridge University Press, 1903).

Theisohn, J., *Der auserwählte Richter: Untersuchungen zum traditionsgeschichtlichen Ort der Menschensohngestalt der Bilderreden des Aethiopischen Henoch* (SUNT, 12; Göttingen: Vandenhoeck & Ruprecht, 1975).

Trumbower, J., 'Hermes Trismegistos', *ABD*, III, pp. 156-57.

Turdeanu, E., 'Notes sur la tradition littéraire du Testament d'Abraham', in *Silloge bizantina in onore di Silvio Giuseppe Mercati* (Studi bizantini e neo ellenici, IX; Rome: Pontifical Institute, 1957), pp. 405-10.

Turner, J.D., 'Sethian Gnosticism: A Literary History', in C. Hedrick and R. Hodson (eds.), *Nag Hammadi, Gnosticism, and Early Christianity* (Peabody, MA: Hendrickson, 1986), pp. 55-86.

Turner, N., 'The Testament of Abraham: A Study of the Original Language, Place of Origin, Authorship, and Relevance' (PhD Dissertation, University of London, 1953).

—'The *Testament of Abraham*: Problems in Biblical Greek', *NTS* 1 (1954–55), pp. 219-23.

—*A Grammar of New Testament Greek*. IV. *Style* (Edinburgh: T. & T. Clark, 1976).

Ulrich, E., 'Daniel Manuscripts from Qumran. Part 1: A Preliminary Edition of 4QDan a', *BASOR* 268 (1987), pp. 17-37.

—'Daniel Manuscripts from Qumran. Part 2: Preliminary Edition of 4QDan b and 4QDan c', *BASOR* 274 (1989), pp. 3-26.

VanderKam, J., *Enoch and the Growth of the Apocalyptic Tradition* (CBQMS, 6; Washington: Catholic Biblical Association, 1984).

—*Enoch: A Man for All Seasons* (Columbia: University of South Carolina Press, 1995).

Vaux, R. de, *Ancient Israel* (2 vols.; New York: McGraw-Hill, 1965).

Vermes, G., *Jesus the Jew* (New York: Harper & Row, 1973).

—'The "Son of Man" Debate', *JSNT* 1 (1978), pp. 19-32.

—'The Present State of the "Son of Man" Debate', *JJS* 29 (1978), pp. 123-34.

—'Josephus' Treatment of the Book of Daniel', *NTS* 92 (1991), pp. 151-68.

—'The Use of bar nash/bar nasha in Jewish Aramaic', in M. Black (ed.), *An Aramaic Approach to the Gospels and Acts* (Oxford: Clarendon Press, 3rd edn, 1967), pp. 310-28.

Wacholder, B., *Eupolemus: A Study of Judaeo-Greek Literature* (Cincinnati: Hebrew Union College Press, 1974).

Widengren, G., *The Ascension of the Apostle and the Heavenly Book* (UUÅ, 7; Uppsala: A.-B. Lundequistska Bokhandeln, 1950).

—*The King and the Tree of Life* (UUÅ, 4; Uppsala: A.-B. Lundequistska Bokhandeln, 1951).

—'Early Hebrew Myths and their Interpretation', in S. Hooke (ed.), *Myth, Ritual, and Kingship: Essays on the Theory and Practice of Kingship in the Ancient Near East and in Israel* (Oxford: Clarendon Press, 1958), pp. 165-69.

—'Heavenly Enthronement and Baptism: Studies in Mandean Baptism', in J. Neusner (ed.), *Religions in Antiquity: Essays in Memory of Erwin Ramsdell Goodenough* (SHR, 14; Leiden: E.J. Brill, 1968).

Wright, A., *The Literary Genre Midrash* (Staten Island: Alba, 1967).

Zimmerli, W., *Ezekiel* (2 vols.; Hermenia; Philadelphia: Fortress Press, 1983).

INDEXES

INDEX OF REFERENCES

OLD TESTAMENT

NEW TESTAMENT

PSEUDEPIGRAPHA

CHRISTIAN AUTHORS

INDEX OF AUTHORS

JOURNAL FOR THE STUDY OF THE PSEUDEPIGRAPHA
SUPPLEMENT SERIES